D1267161

Mexican American War

Mexican American War

Kelly King Howes

Julie L. Carnagie, Project Editor

Detroit • New York • San Diego • San Francisco • Cleveland • New Haven, Conn. • Waterville, Maine • London • Munich

Mexican American War

Kelly King Howes

Project Editors
Julie L. Carnagie

Permissions
Shalice Shah-Caldwell

Imaging and Multimedia
Kelly A. Quin

Product Design
Pamela A.E. Galbreath

Composition
Evi Seoud

Manufacturing
Rita Wimberley

LIBRARY OF CONGRESS CATALOG CARD NUMBER

Mexican-American War / Kelly King Howes, editor.
    p. cm.
Summary: A comprehensive overview of the Mexican-American War, including biographies and full or excerpted memoirs, speeches, and other source documents.
Includes bibliographical references and index.
    ISBN 0-7876-6537-1
  1. Mexican War, 1846-1848–Juvenile literature. 2. Mexican War, 1846-1848–Biography–Juvenile literature. [1. Mexican War, 1846-1848.]
I. Howes, Kelly King.
    E404 .M47 2003
    973.6′2–dc21

                    2002155416

Contents

Almanac

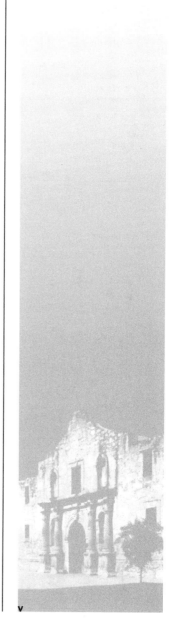

Biographies

Reader's Guide

It would be difficult for most U.S. citizens to imagine the United States without the area known as the Southwest, which includes the states of Texas, New Mexico, Arizona, and California. However, this territory might have remained in Mexican hands had it not been for the Mexican American War (1846–48). Although the Mexican American War is sometimes viewed as a war of aggression on the part of the United States, the results of the conflict allowed increased U.S. settlement in the West during a period in which the young nation was undergoing rapid population growth.

Mexican American War provides students with a clear understanding of the issues that caused the United States to declare war against Mexico, the important battles of the war, and how the United States's victory in the conflict eventually contributed to the American Civil War (1861–65). Also looks at the motivations of the people involved in the conflict—both American and Mexican—and their attitudes toward the war itself.

Format

Mexican American War is divided into two sections: Almanac and Biographies. The Almanac contains six chapters that chronicle the war from its origins with Spanish settlement during the sixteenth century to its end with the signing of the Treaty of Guadalupe Hidalgo in 1848. The Biographies section details the lives of ten people who had a strong impact on the Mexican American War. Coverage includes political figures James K. Polk and U.S. diplomat Nicholas Trist, military leaders Antonio López de Santa Anna and Winfield Scott, as well as California Bear Flag Rebellion leader John Charles Frémont and Texas revolutionary Sam Houston. Placed throughout the chapters and biographies are primary source documents, such as diary entries, letters, and newspaper articles, that allow readers the opportunity to see how the war affected ordinary people as well as political and military leaders.

Mexican American War includes more than sixty photographs, illustrations, and maps, a timeline of key events of the war, a glossary, research and activity ideas, a general bibliography, and a subject index.

Acknowledgments

A note of appreciation is extended to the *Mexican American War* advisors, who provided invaluable suggestions when this work was in its formative stages:

Frances Bryant Bradburn
Director of Educational Technologies
North Carolina Public Schools
Raleigh, North Carolina

Ann West LaPrise
Junior High/Elementary Media Specialist
Huron School District
New Boston, Michigan

Comments and Suggestions

We welcome your comments on *Mexican American War.* Please write: Editors, *Mexican American War*, U•X•L, 27500 Drake Rd., Farmington Hills, Michigan, 48331-3535; call toll free: 1-800-877-4253; fax: 248-414-5043; or send e-mail via http://www.galegroup.com.

Words to Know

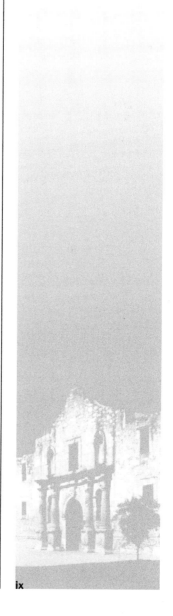

A

Abolitionist movement: A movement made up of people called abolitionists who worked to abolish or end slavery.

Alamo: An old Spanish mission (church building), located at San Antonio, Texas, that had been used as a fort by Mexico's Spanish colonizers but later abandoned. In March 1836, about two hundred U.S. settlers who were fighting to make Texas an independent state took refuge here; surrounded and then attacked by Mexican soldiers, all were killed.

All-Mexico movement: A movement made up of those who felt that, following the U.S. victory in the Mexican American War, the United States should seize the opportunity to take control of the entire country of Mexico, and not just the territory fought over in the war.

Alta California: Upper California; the area that is the now the state of California.

Amphibious assault: An attack conducted by both army (land) and navy (sea) forces.

Annexation: The process by which a territory becomes a state.

Armistice: A cease-fire, or halt, in fighting.

B

Baja California: Lower California; still part of Mexico, this area is adjacent to the southern border of what is now the state of California.

Bear Flag Rebellion: A movement of U.S. settlers in California's Sacramento Valley who declared their independence from Mexico and established their own short-lived nation; their flag featured a single star, a grizzly bear, and the words "California Republic." Renamed the California Battalion, the Bear Flaggers took part in the U.S. conquest of California.

C

California Gold Rush: The hurried scramble of fortune-seekers into California after the January 1849 discovery of gold at Sutter's Mill.

Californios: California residents of Mexican descent.

Casualties: Those killed, wounded, or missing in battle.

Cavalry: Soldiers mounted on horseback

Chapparal: A kind of dense, thorny brush common in north-eastern Mexico and part of what made this a difficult terrain for warfare.

Chapultepec Hill: A famous landmark located just outside the gates of Mexico City. Once occupied by the Aztec emperor Montezuma, it was the site of the National Military Academy and of a bloody battle that led to the U.S. conquest of Mexico City.

Civil War: The conflict fought from 1861 to 1865 between the United States and the Confederate States of America (made up of eleven southern states that had seceded from the union) over the issues of slavery and states' rights.

Compromise of 1850: An agreement by which California would be admitted to the United States as a free state, while both slaveholders and those who opposed slavery would be allowed to settle in the new territories of New Mexico and Utah; slavery would be abolished in the District of Columbia (Washington, D.C.); and the Fugitive Slave Law would be more strictly enforced.

Court martial: A trial held in a military court and involving a military officer or officers accused of war- or military-related crimes.

Criollos: Residents of colonial Mexico, or New Spain, who were of Spanish heritage but had been born in Mexico. They had less social status and power than the *gachupines,* who were those born in Spain.

E

Expansionism: The westward movement of white U.S. citizens across the borders of the United States and into the wide expanses of land between the Appalachian mountain chain in the East and the Pacific Ocean.

F

Flying artillery: A very effective weapon used by the U.S. Army in the Mexican American War, that was a kind of light cannon mounted between two big wheels that could be moved quickly and easily. It was developed by Major Sam Ringgold, who was killed in an early battle during the war.

G

Gachupines: Residents of colonial Mexico, or New Spain, who were of Spanish heritage and had been born in Spain. They had the highest social status and most of the power.

Guerrillas: Small groups of soldiers or individual fighters who operate outside of the regular army, often launching surprise attacks.

L

Lone Star Republic: The independent state established by U.S. citizens who had settled in the Mexican state of Tejas y Coahuila and who achieved independence from Mexico in the 1836 Texas Revolution.

Los Ninos Heroes: The boy heroes; a group of teenaged boys who were among the fifty cadets from Mexico's National Military Academy who fought and died in the Battle of Chapultepec Hill.

Louisiana Purchase: The agreement by which the United States bought 800,000 square miles of land from France. This area included the present-day states of Arkansas, Missouri, Iowa, part of Minnesota, North Dakota, South Dakota, Nebraska, Oklahoma, most of Kansas, parts of Montana, Wyoming, Colorado, and Louisiana.

M

Manifest destiny: A phrase coined by journalist John O'Sullivan in 1845 that referred to the deeply racist idea that it was the god-given right and duty of white U.S. citizens to settle in and "civilize" the entire continent of North America.

Mestizos: Residents of colonial Mexico, or New Spain, who were of mixed Spanish and Native American heritage. They occupied a low rung in their society, in which social status and power resided with the *gachupines* and *criollos*.

Mexican Revolution: The conflict fought from 1910 to 1911 that brought the harsh thirty-five-year reign of dictator Porfirio Díaz to an end.

Militia: An army made up of volunteers who have offered to serve in a war or other emergency in which military forces beyond the regular, professional army are needed.

Missouri Compromise: The 1820 agreement by which Missouri was admitted to the United States as a slave state and Maine as a free state, thus maintaining the delicate balance between states that allowed slavery and those that made it illegal. This agreement also prohibited slavery in any of the lands of the Louisiana Purchase that were north of the Missouri border.

Musket: The old-fashioned kind of gun used by the Mexicans, which did not shoot very far or accurately and thus gave the Mexicans a disadvantage when faced with the better equipped U.S. troops.

N

National Highway: A well-paved, evenly graded road, originally built by the Spanish, that allowed the U.S. Army a relatively smooth passage from the coastal city of Vera Cruz to the Mexican capital, Mexico City.

Nueces River: The traditional border between Texas and Mexico. After the annexation of Texas as a U.S. state, the United States began to claim the Rio Grande, located about 100 miles south of the Nueces, as the border.

O

"Old Fuss and Feathers": The nickname of General Winfield Scott, which he earned because of his formal dress and manners and belief in strict discipline.

"Old Rough and Ready": The nickname of General Zachary Taylor, given to him by soldiers in honor of his informal, rugged appearance and manners and his battlefield courage.

P

Panic of 1819: An economic depression, or a period of economic hardship, that hit hardest in the most western part of the United States (especially in Missouri, Kentucky, and Illinois) and that caused residents there to look toward Texas for a new start.

Pedragal: A 15-square-mile expanse of jagged lava rock, just south of Mexico City, over which the U.S. Army made an unexpectedly successful crossing.

R

Regular army: An army made up of officers and soldiers who have chosen the military as their permanent job or profession.

Rio Grande: The river that, after the 1845 annexation of Texas, the United States claimed as the border between Texas and Mexico (even though the border had traditionally been the Nueces River, located about 100 miles north of the Rio Grande).

S

Soldaderas: Mothers, sisters, wives, and girlfriends of Mexican soldiers who followed the Mexican army, providing a great service by feeding, clothing, and nursing the soldiers and even sometimes fighting in battles.

T

Tejas y Coahuila: The Mexican name for the area of northeastern Mexico that, in 1845, became the state of Texas.

Texas Revolution: The 1836 struggle through which U.S. citizens who had settled in the Mexican state of Tejas y Coahuila achieved independence from Mexico, establishing the Lone Star Republic.

Treaty of Guadalupe Hidalgo: The peace agreement that ended the Mexican American War. It resulted in Mexico acknowledging the Rio Grande as the border of Texas and agreeing to cede the territories of California and New Mexico, an area of 525,000 square miles and more than half of Mexico's total territory. In exchange, the United States agreed to pay Mexico $15 million and forgive debts owed by Mexico to the United States.

V

Valley of Mexico: The ancient volcanic crater (46 miles long and 32 miles wide) in which Mexico City is located;

during the mid-nineteenth century, it included swampy lakes as well as marshes and villages.

Volunteers: Citizens who are not members of the regular armed services but who offer to serve during a war or other emergency in which more military forces are needed.

Y

Yanquis: The Spanish-language version of Yankees, a nickname for Americans that was used scornfully by the Mexicans.

Yellow fever: A deadly disease that, during the mid-nineteenth century, was common along Mexico's swampy coast in the spring and summer. The disease was carried by mosquitoes, although this fact was not yet known.

Timeline of Events

1521 During the Spanish conquest of what is now Mexico, forces under the explorer and military leader Hernán Cortés crush the Aztec empire and kill its emperor, Montezuma. Thus the Spanish colony of New Spain is established.

1776 The United States declares its independence from Great Britain.

1783 The Treaty of Paris brings the Revolutionary War to an end and establishes the United States of America as an independent nation.

1803 Through the Louisiana Purchase, the United States acquires about 800,000 square miles west of the Appalachian Mountains, doubling the nation's size.

1810 Father Miguel Hidalgo y Costilla leads a revolt that pits a small army drawn from New Spain's poorest against the Spanish colonial army. Hidalgo is captured and executed, but the spirit of rebellion stays alive.

1819 An economic depression hits the western and southern parts of the United States, prompting people living there to look beyond U.S. borders for more opportunity.

1820 The U.S. Congress approved the famous Missouri Compromise. It outlawed slavery within the Louisiana Purchase territory north of 36°30' latitude. Missouri itself entered the Union as a slave state, while Maine entered as a free state.

1820–50 An estimated four million U.S. settlers move into the western parts of North America.

1821 Mexico gains independence from Spain. This allows the establishment of the Santa Fe Trail, enabling trade between the United States and Mexico. At the same time, the Mexican government grants Moses Austin 200,000 acres of land in Tejas y Coahuila (later called Texas), to which Austin plans to bring U.S. settlers; after Austin's unexpected death, his son Stephen carries on with his father's plan.

1824 Mexico's constitution establishes the nation as a republic.

1829 Mexico bans slavery, but most Texans ignore this law as well as others that restrict new immigration and gun registration.

1833 Dynamic military leader **Antonio López de Santa Anna** becomes president of Mexico as well as supreme commander of the country's army. He abolishes Mexico's constitution and sets up a centralized government, giving himself absolute power.

1833 Accused of urging Texans to revolt against Mexico, Stephen Austin is imprisoned.

1835 Santa Anna sends troops to Texas. Texans resist and take control of the towns of Gonzales, Goliad, and San Antonio.

March 2, 1836 Texans establish an independent nation, the Lone Star Republic. David Burnet is elected interim president, and **Sam Houston** is named commander of the Texan army. Mexico does not formally recognize Texas's independence.

March 6, 1836 A large Mexican force under Santa Anna attacks less than two hundred Texans holed up in the Alamo, an old Spanish mission at San Antonio. All of the Alamo's defenders are killed.

March 19, 1836 After losing a battle against the Mexican army at Goliad, three hundred Texan soldiers under the command of Colonel James Fannin are taken prisoner. On March 27, Santa Anna orders all of them executed. The massacres at Goliad and the Alamo enrage Texans, and the small Texan army expands.

April 21, 1836 In a surprise attack, Sam Houston leads 900 Texan soldiers against several thousand Mexican troops under Santa Anna's command. The Battle of San Jacinto is a victory for the Texans, who suffer only 40 casualties to the Mexicans' 600 killed and 730 captured. Santa Anna himself is among those captured and is forced to sign a treaty recognizing the independence of Texas. This treaty is later considered invalid by the Mexican government.

October 1836 Sam Houston becomes the first elected president of the Lone Star Republic.

1837 U.S. president Andrew Jackson recognizes the Lone Star Republic and wants to annex it, but these efforts to make it a part of the United States are for now unsuccessful.

1843 Mexico warns the United States that the annexation of Texas will mean war.

1844 Avid expansionist **James K. Polk** is elected president of the United States.

1845 In an article published in the *Democratic Review,* John O'Sullivan coins the term "manifest destiny," referring to the idea that white Americans have not only the right but the duty to impose their way of life and ideals across the continent.

March 1, 1845 Texas is annexed to the United States. In protest, Mexico immediately cuts off diplomatic relations with the United States.

Summer 1845 Polk orders General **Zachary Taylor** to take several thousand U.S. troops to Corpus Christi on the

Nueces River, the traditional border between Texas and Mexico.

November 1845 Polk sends Louisiana legislator John Slidell to Mexico to offer its government $5 million for New Mexico and $25 million for California. The offer is rejected.

March 28, 1846 Taylor's troops move several hundred miles south to the banks of the Rio Grande, which the United States is now claiming as its border with Mexico. On a site across from the Mexican city of Matamoros, Taylor begins construction on Fort Texas (later renamed Fort Brown).

April 11, 1846 Mexican general Mariano Arista arrives at Matamoros and takes charge of several thousand Mexican troops stationed there.

April 26, 1846 A small U.S. patrol unit of sixty-three soldiers is attacked by a much larger Mexican force. Eleven soldiers are killed, prompting Taylor to inform Polk that hostilities have begun.

May 8 and 9, 1846 Taylor's troops defeat the Mexican army in the battles of Palo Alto and Resaca de la Palma, causing the Mexicans heavy casualties and exposing the weakness of their artillery.

May 11, 1846 Polk sends a declaration of war to Congress, claiming that Mexico has started the war by shedding "American blood upon American soil."

May 13, 1846 Despite a few dissenting voices, the war declaration passes through both houses of Congress and is signed by the president.

June 1836 Led by Colonel **John Charles Frémont** of the U.S. Corps of Topographical Engineers, a group of U.S. settlers in California revolts against Mexico, establishing the short-lived Bear Flag Republic.

July 1846 New England philosopher and writer Henry David Thoreau, vowing that his money will not go to support the war in Mexico, is jailed for refusing to pay his taxes. The experience inspires him to write his famous essay "Civil Disobedience" about the duties of a good citizen.

August 13, 1846 Combined navy and army forces under the command of Commodore Robert Stockton take control of Los Angeles, capping a series of peaceful conquests of towns along the California coast.

August 18, 1846 General **Stephen Watts Kearny** arrives in Santa Fe at the head of the U.S. Army of the West. The town is captured bloodlessly, and Kearny soon sets off for California with several hundred troops.

September 1846 After tricking the U.S. government into allowing him past a naval blockade, Santa Anna returns to Mexico from Cuba, where he had been exiled. Ignoring his promise to work for peace with the United States, he begins building up his army to vanquish the U.S. invaders.

September 21–25, 1846 Taylor's troops take control of the town of Monterrey after a bloody battle that ends with hand-to-hand fighting. Polk is displeased when Taylor arranges an eight-week ceasefire.

September 29, 1846 General José María Flores leads a small Mexican force in recapturing Los Angeles.

November 1846 Polk offers General **Winfield Scott** command of the Army of Invasion. Scott begins to plan an amphibious (using both army and navy forces) attack to be launched from the coastal city of Vera Cruz. From there he will lead his army west toward the capital, Mexico City.

December 6, 1846 Exhausted by their journey from Santa Fe to California, Kearny's troops lose the Battle of San Pascual. They sustain thirty-six casualties, while no Mexicans are killed.

January 8, 1847 The combined forces of Stockton, Frémont, and Kearny reconquer Los Angeles. As a result, California comes firmly under U.S. control.

February 24, 1847 Taylor's force meets Santa Anna's army near the Buena Vista ranch, about 45 miles west of Monterrey. After a long day of fighting and an estimated three thousand casualties, the Mexicans flee. The United States casualty rate also is high, with about seven hundred men killed, wounded, or missing.

March 22, 1847 Having landed more than ten thousand troops near Vera Cruz, Scott begins bombarding the city. Almost two hundred Mexicans (half of them civilians) are killed in the attack, while the United States loses only nineteen. The city comes under U.S. control on March 28.

April 18, 1847 A short battle at a mountain pass called Cerro Gordo sends the Mexican army fleeing after a thousand of them are killed or wounded, and another three thousand are captured.

May 1847 Spanish-speaking diplomat **Nicholas Trist** joins Scott's army at Puebla, where it is resting before continuing on to Mexico City. Sent to negotiate a peace treaty with the Mexicans, Trist clashes with Scott at first but the two eventually become friends.

August 11, 1847 Scott's army enters the Valley of Mexico. Their assault on Mexico City will take place over the next month, with a series of battles culminating in a U.S. victory.

August 19 and 20, 1847 At the battles of Contreras and Churubusco on the outskirts of Mexico City, the Mexicans sustain about four thousand casualties, while the United States has nearly one thousand. The surviving seventy-five members of the **San Patricio Battalion**, a Mexican army unit made up of U.S. Army deserters and other foreigners, are captured; fifty are sentenced to death by hanging while the rest are to be severely punished.

August 21, 1847 An armistice takes effect as the two sides enter into peace talks. Each determines that the other is simply stalling for time, and the armistice is called off on September 7.

September 8, 1847 U.S. troops attack a fort called El Morino del Rey, where it is suspected that the Mexicans are manufacturing cannons. The United States sustains its highest casualties for a single battle of the war (23 percent of those participating) and no cannon factory is found.

September 12, 1847 The United States attacks Chapultepec Hill, site of Mexico's National Military Academy and the last obstacle before the capture of Mexico City. Most of the eight hundred Mexican defenders are killed, including fifty cadets from the Academy who will be long remembered as Los Ninos Heroes (the boy heroes).

September 14, 1847 After a bloody two-day assault, the United States takes control of Mexico City. Having resigned the presidency, Santa Anna flees. The city is chaotic, and the Mexican government is in disarray.

November 11, 1847 A new Mexican Congress is formed and an interim president, Manuel de la Pena y Pena, elected. The movement toward peace negotiations is agonizingly slow.

November 16, 1847 Trist receives a message from Polk ordering him to return to the United States. Convinced that the opportunity for peace will otherwise be lost, Trist decides to defy the order and enter into peace talks.

January 2, 1848 Trist begins secret negotiations at Guadalupe Hidalgo with three Mexican peace commissioners.

February 2, 1848 The Treaty of Guadalupe Hidalgo is signed. Mexico agrees to recognize the Rio Grande border and to cede California and New Mexico to the United States, while the United States agrees to pay Mexico $15 million and forgive all debts owed to American citizens.

March 16, 1848 Despite his anger at Trist's defiance, Polk signs the treaty, which has been ratified by the U.S. Congress.

May 30, 1848 The Mexican government ratifies the treaty, making it official.

July 4, 1848 The United States receives its copy of the signed treaty.

January 1849 Gold is discovered at Sutter's Mill, near the present-day city of Sacramento, California. Inspired by the prospect of instant wealth, many U.S. settlers take part in the Gold Rush.

1850   Tensions over the slavery issue that had been intensified by the addition of new territories to the United States after the Mexican American War are only temporarily eased by the Compromise of 1850. This agreement admits California as a free state, with both slaveholders and others allowed to settle in New Mexico and Utah. Slavery is abolished in the District of Columbia, but the Fugitive Slave Law is to be more strictly enforced.

1861–65 After eleven states secede from the Union to form the Confederate States of America, the country is embroiled in a bloody civil war over the issues of slavery and states rights. The war ends with the defeat of the Confederacy, but has long-lasting effects on the nation.

1910–11 The Mexican Revolution brings to an end the harsh reign of dictator Porfirio Díaz.

Research and Activity Ideas

The following list of research and activity ideas is intended to offer suggestions for complementing English, social studies, and history curricula; to trigger additional ideas for enhancing learning; and to suggest cross-disciplinary projects for library and classroom use.

- **A Woman's Thoughts:** Write several entries in the journal of a woman who moves with her family from Missouri to Texas in the early 1830s. Include entries that cover a span of years through the late 1840s, to show how the woman's life is affected by events such as the Texas Revolution, Texas statehood, and the Mexican American War.

- **The Many Sides of Manifest Destiny:** The concept of manifest destiny (the idea that white Americans had both the right and the duty to settle and dominate the entire North American continent) was viewed in different ways by different people. Think about how a white U.S. farmer, a Native American, and a Mexican citizen living in southern California might feel about westward expansion. In their voices, write narratives that either justify or object

to the movement of white U.S. citizens into the southwest.

- **Is This a Just War?**: With several classmates, write and perform a skit that dramatizes the congressional debate about whether the United States should declare war on Mexico. Find out which members of Congress were for and against the war, and what they said about it.

- **How Officers and Soldiers Dressed:** After researching the uniforms worn by those who fought on both sides of the Mexican American War, create a series of drawings or other illustrations that show how both officers and regular soldiers might have looked.

- **The Role of the *Soldaderas:*** Make a table display that illustrates the important role played by Mexican women in the Mexican American War (as well as other Mexican conflicts). Include both written text and illustrations to help describe the jobs—including nursing, cooking, washing clothes, and even fighting—these women performed.

- **Thoreau Goes to Jail:** Working with one or more classmates, use a tape recorder to record an interview with war protester Henry David Thoreau. Pretend you are visiting the famous author and philosopher in his cell on the evening of the night he spent in jail for refusing to pay his taxes. Ask him why he has chosen to take this action. You might also interview Thoreau's jailer, and the friend who comes to bail him out.

- **The Life of a Soldier:** There are many first-hand accounts of what U.S. soldiers experienced during the Mexican American War and how they lived in camp. Pretend you are one of these soldiers and either write letters home to your family or write and perform a monologue, describing what your life is like and what you have seen and done.

- **Chronicling the War:** The Mexican American War was the first in which journalists and photographers were able to document first-hand the people, places, and events that made up the war. Many hometown reporters joined the army or otherwise found their way to Mexico and sent back their accounts. Use photocopies of photographs and other images and write text to create a full-page feature article about the war.

- **A Training Ground for Officers:** Trace the careers of several of the young men who served in the Mexican American War (such as Ulysses S. Grant or Franklin Pierce) and later went on to achieve fame as military or political leaders. Present what you have learned in an essay, timeline, or chart format.

- **Before-and-After Dialogue:** With a classmate, write and perform a dialogue between two friends, both of them Mexican citizens living at the time of the Mexican American War in the territory that would become the state of New Mexico. One of them chooses to stay and become an American citizen while the other decides to move farther south and retain his or her Mexican citizenship and identity. You might wish to include a second dialogue that takes place in the twenty-first century between residents of New Mexico and Mexico.

Mexican American War

Almanac

The United States and Mexico: Close Neighbors with Different Goals

It would be hard for most U.S. citizens to imagine their country without the area known as the Southwest. The states of Texas, New Mexico, Arizona, and California (as well as the southern parts of Nevada and Utah) make up an important, colorful, and much treasured corner of the United States. In the Southwest exists a blend of traditions that can be found nowhere else and that grew out of the intermingling of the different peoples who have lived in the region.

During the sixteenth century, European explorers began arriving in the southern part of the North American continent. Native Americans were already in the area following their own traditions. Until the middle of the nineteenth century, the Southwest would be dominated by the Spanish, who conquered Mexico, which then included territory that later became part of the United States. When the Spanish arrived in the area in the early 1500s, they brought their own language, customs, and religion with them, adapting these things to this new environment. Later, people from the eastern and southern United States also settled in the Southwest. As far as most them were concerned, they had little in com-

mon with the Mexicans or Native Americans already inhabiting the region, yet they, too, had to adapt to the place, and they, too, were changed by it.

The unique southwestern tapestry

Over the years, these strands of different people came together in a tapestry as bold as the blankets woven by the southwestern Native Americans, as rugged as the worn hat of a *vaquero* (cowboy), and as delicate as the silver comb in the black hair of a woman on a Mexican *hacienda* (ranch). According to U.S. Census Bureau figures collected in 2000, close to twenty one million people in the United States (or 7.3 percent of the total population) claim Mexican heritage, and Spanish is the nation's second most widely spoken language. Mexican food is enjoyed by Americans from coast to coast, and teenagers dance to Latin-flavored music. Tourists from all fifty states (as well as other countries around the world) travel long distances to view the dramatic geography of the Southwest: from the towering redwood trees of California to the rolling ranch lands of Texas, and from the lonesome spread of Death Valley to the awesome depths of the Grand Canyon.

There are probably few U.S. citizens who have never tasted a tortilla or heard "La Bamba" (an old Mexican folk song made popular in the late twentieth century by several U.S. singers). But many more have never heard the story of how their nation acquired this unique part of its territory and culture. Although the story begins earlier and continues later, it centers on the Mexican American War, a relatively short, but very bloody conflict that took place between 1846 and 1848. When it was over, Mexico had given up two-fifths of its total territory to the United States, land that was gradually divided into the states of Texas, New Mexico, Arizona, and California (as well as the southern parts of Nevada and Utah).

A controversial conflict

In some ways, the Mexican American War brought positive results for the United States. Yet it was and continues to be a controversial conflict that highlights troubling issues.

On the U.S. side, the war was viewed by most as necessary if the young and growing nation was to push its boundaries westward. Most U.S. citizens believed it was the "manifest destiny" (the God-given right and duty) of white Americans to take over this vast, resource-rich land, even if it meant taking land from the Mexicans or Native Americans who had been living there for hundreds, and even thousands, of years.

Mexicans, on the other hand, had lived on and ruled over this area for centuries. They believed that it belonged to them, and that the United States was simply trying to steal their land. A notable minority of U.S. citizens agreed with the Mexicans, including a young Illinois congressman and future U.S. president named Abraham Lincoln (1809–1865); a passionate New England idealist named Henry David Thoreau (1817–1862); and an army lieutenant named Ulysses S. Grant (1822–1885), who fought in the war but later condemned it. (Grant later gained fame as one of the most important generals on the Union side in the American Civil War [1861–65].)

Despite this controversy, most U.S. citizens supported the Mexican American War. A little more than one hundred thousand of them fought for the United States, while an even larger number took up arms in defense of Mexico. As in all wars, there was bravery and sacrifice as well as death and brutality on both sides. But it seems that it is the Mexican people, perhaps because the outcome was tragic for them, who have most nurtured the bitter memory of this war, and best honored their fallen soldiers.

A variety of problems lead to war

The Mexican American War took place at an important moment in U.S. history, when a whole variety of problems were about to reach a boiling point. Immigrants were streaming into the United States (often to be greeted with resentment and even discrimination), and this resulted in a rapid growth of the U.S. population. This growth made economic pressures more intense and created a need for more space and new opportunities.

Another problem facing the United States was the issue of slavery. It was at this time that people were becoming more and more divided on the issue, with southerners set on defending their way of life, which was dependent on slave labor, and northerners just as set on ending a practice that many viewed as inhumane. The Mexican American War would take its place in a chain of events that finally led to the American Civil War (1861–65), when U.S. citizens fought each other over the issues of slavery and the rights of individual states.

In addition, when the Mexican American War was over, the United States acquired more than 50,000,000 square miles of land, which created a whole new set of issues. These included how to manage the region's plentiful mineral resources (including gold, silver, copper, and uranium), how to deal with hostile Native American populations, and how to integrate the Mexicans who were now living within the United States' borders into U.S. society. In Mexico, the political instability and widespread poverty that had plagued the country before, during, and after the Mexican American War would eventually erupt into the Mexican Revolution (1910–11). Existing side by side in an uneasy relationship, both the United States and Mexico would face struggle and hardship in the years to come. Certainly both had some inkling of this future as they began a war played out amidst the arid landscapes and graceful Spanish architecture of Mexico and Texas.

Americans are eager to settle the West

In 1776, the residents of Great Britain's thirteen North American colonies (New Hampshire, Massachusetts, Rhode Island, Connecticut, New Jersey, New York, Delaware, Pennsylvania, Maryland, Virginia, North Carolina, South Carolina, and Georgia) declared their independence and began the Revolutionary War, in which many lost their lives in pursuit of freedom. The 1783 signing of the Treaty of Paris ended the war, but brought a whole new set of difficult tasks to the new United States of America. The government of this young nation had not only to protect and govern the citizens of the first thirteen states, but it also had to shepherd the country into a period of rapid expansion.

Due to immigration and a high birth rate, which was nurtured by the belief that families needed many children to

A map of the land that was in dispute during the Mexican American War.
Photograph reproduced by permission of Getty Images.

keep their farms and businesses afloat, the U.S. population grew rapidly during the early nineteenth century. In fact, it expanded from five million in 1800 to more than twenty-three million by 1850. And all those people needed space! As a result of this growth, many people began moving past the country's original borders into the vast territory that lay west of the Appalachians (the mountain chain that runs north to south through the eastern United States). Between 1790 and 1803, Vermont, Kentucky, Tennessee, and Ohio became states, and settlers began pouring into them.

Another large chunk of western land opened up for settlement in 1803, when the United States signed the Louisiana Purchase. This area, totaling about 800,000 square miles, was to become the states of Arkansas, Missouri, Iowa, North Dakota, South Dakota, Nebraska, Oklahoma, Wyoming, and Colorado and included parts of western Minnesota, eastern Montana, and western Louisiana as well as most of Kansas and the city of New Orleans. Long held by Spain, this territory had been taken over by France at the end of the eighteenth century. Strapped for cash to support his war against his European neighbors, especially Great Britain, French emperor Napoleon I (1769–1821) offered to sell this land to the United States for $15 million. This was an incredibly good bargain, and President Thomas Jefferson jumped at the chance to double the size of the United States.

The Louisiana Purchase added fuel to an already burning expansionist fire. Things heated up even more nine years later when the United States went to war once again with Great Britain. Although the War of 1812 (1812–14) was supposedly fought over the issues of trade and sailors' rights, some who supported the conflict hoped it would allow the United States to acquire both Canada and Florida.

The war did not actually accomplish this, but it did secure the Northwest Territory (now the states of Ohio, Indiana, Illinois, and Michigan) for settlement by U.S. citizens. In fact, all of the West became safer for white settlers after the War of 1812, for the great Native American leader Tecumseh (c. 1768–1813), a Shawnee war chief who had tried to convince Indian tribes to join together to resist white settlement, had been killed in the war. After the War of 1812, Native Americans would continue to be pushed off their traditional lands, despite treaties made with the U.S. government, and forced to move farther and farther west. Eventually, most Native Americans would be required to live on reservations, blocks of land designated for their use and often located far from their original homes and in undesirable locations. It is estimated that between 1820 and 1850, almost four million white settlers moved west.

A newly divided society

The United States was becoming a much different place from that created by the first colonists. Once the nation's life had been concentrated on the East Coast, where farmers, artisans, and traders had all lived and worked together. As the nineteenth century progressed and people spread out across a rapidly expanding country, U.S. society split into three main regions. One was the West, with its frontier settlements and emphasis on hard work and self-reliance. Another

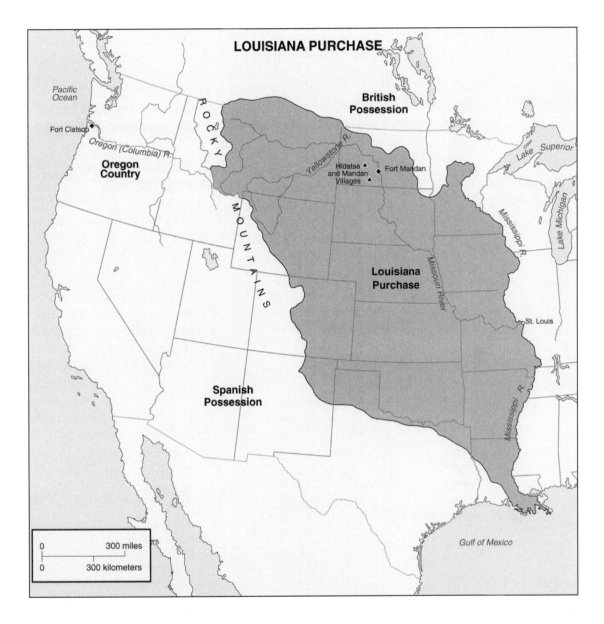

LOUISIANA PURCHASE

Pacific Ocean

Fort Clatsop

Oregon (Columbia) R.

Oregon Country

ROCKY MOUNTAINS

British Possession

Yellowstone R.

Hidatsa and Mandan Villages

Fort Mandan

Lake Superior

Lake Michigan

Mississippi R.

Louisiana Purchase

Missouri River

St. Louis

Spanish Possession

Mississippi R.

Gulf of Mexico

| 0 | 300 miles |
| 0 | 300 kilometers |

was the South, where the owners of large plantations used slave labor to maintain a lifestyle that imitated that of the British upper class. The third region was located in the northeastern states, where residents had turned from farming to fishing, shipbuilding, and trade to support themselves. These divisions in livelihood and outlook would become more pronounced in the decades just before and just after the Mexican American War.

A map showing the area encompassing the Louisiana Purchase. This land purchase doubled the size of the United States and added fuel to an already burning expansionist fire. *Photograph courtesy of the Gale Group.*

A group of white settlers moving west. Many people moved to the West hoping for a better life. *Photograph reproduced by permission of Getty Images.*

"Manifest destiny" is used to justify U.S. actions

Several important factors drove the expansionism of the early nineteenth century. One was the hardship suffered by many citizens during the economic depressions of 1818 and 1839. Western lands were cheap, and sometimes even free to those willing to settle and cultivate them, and to many Americans, land ownership signified wealth, self-sufficiency, and independence. It took a great deal of courage and optimism for U.S. citizens to pack up their families and belongings and head west toward a future in which the only certainty was a lot of back-breaking work and hardship. Yet these white settlers also were armed with their own arrogance. Most of them believed that people of European ancestry were superior to others. These settlers believed that this cultural superiority was simply a fact upon which everyone, even God, agreed. The idea that people of Native American, African, Mexican, or mixed heritage deserved equal rights or equal respect was alien to them.

In addition, most U.S. citizens believed that God had put the continent of North America in the possession of white people, and that it was not only their right to expand across its vast reaches, but their duty. They had come to "civilize," or in other words, to reshape according to their own ideas and customs, this land and the people already living in it. They believed that all countries and peoples should adopt the U.S. form of democratic government, in which power is held by the people and not by a supreme ruler. (It is important to remember, though, that they did not believe that people of non-European descent, including blacks and Native Americans, were capable or deserving of this kind of self-government.) Described as the "manifest destiny" of the United States in an article published at the time of the Mexican American War (see Chapter 3), this concept of superiority would be used to justify the nation's aggression toward its neighbor to the south.

Mexico's colonial background

While the nineteenth century found U.S. citizens feeling confident and eager to expand their borders, Mexicans of the period were struggling with poverty and political instability. These conditions had resulted from forces put in motion several centuries earlier.

European explorers who arrived in Mexico during the first quarter of the sixteenth century found not only an inviting landscape, but also a rich, thriving civilization of the Aztec people. The Aztec empire was crushed when, from 1519 to 1521, Spanish forces under Hernán Cortés (1485–1547) conquered those lands of the Aztec king Montezuma (c. 1480–1520). Spain's New World colony continued to grow during the seventeenth and eighteenth centuries, when the Spanish conquered the areas that are now New Mexico and California. In the early 1700s, they also took control of land occupied by the Tejas Indians, which became the Mexican state of Tejas y Coahuila. It was a dispute about the ownership of this area that would set off the Mexican American War in the mid-nineteenth century.

A rigidly stratified, Catholic society

In the Mexico (then called New Spain) that took shape during the 1700s, the Spanish culture and traditions were

Aztec king Montezuma greeting Spanish explorer Hernán Cortés as he and his party arrived in Mexico. Spanish forces under Cortés conquered Aztec land and began Spanish rule of the country. *Photograph reproduced by permission of the Corbis Corporation.*

dominant while those of the Native Americans, along with their rights, were oppressed. Mexican society was, in fact, rigidly stratified or divided into five layers. At the top were the *gachupines*, Spaniards who had been born in Spain and who now ran the colonial government of Mexico. Next came the *criollos*, people of unmixed Spanish heritage who had been born in Mexico and who were often frustrated by their lack of power. *Mestizos*, people of mixed Spanish and Native American blood, had even less status. Next came Native Americans, whose miserably paid labor supported those above them on the social and economic scale. On the bottom rung were black slaves and free blacks (who had never been slaves, had paid their way out of slavery, or had been released by their masters) as well as those called *zambos* (a mixture of Native American and African heritages). Even after Mexico gained its independence from Spain, this social hierarchy would remain in place, with a small number of wealthy people living in luxury while the vast majority of Mexicans worked for little or no pay, endured harsh living conditions, and received no education.

Another fact of life in colonial Mexico was the Roman Catholic Church. One of the most important aspects of their culture that the Spanish had brought with them from the Old World was their religion, which dominated life in Mexico as it did in Spain. The church was state-sponsored, which meant that it took an active part not just in people's private lives but in public matters, such as education and law. Mexicans were required to be members of the Catholic Church. (By contrast, the political system of the United States calls for a strict separation of church and state and upholds the value of freedom of religion.)

The seeds of rebellion

During the American Revolution, Mexicans supported the colonists' war for freedom and even lent them some assistance. In turn, the Mexican people were influenced by the independence ideals expressed not only in the United States but in France, where a revolution against the ruling monarchy took place from 1789 to 1799. All over the world, the concept of the republic—in which power is held by all of a nation's citizens who elect representatives to pursue their interests—as the most just form of government was being discussed and even put into practice. At the same time, Mexico's criollos were increasingly resentful of the power and status held by the gachupines and by Spain's tight control of the colony's politics and economy.

This rebellious mood was heightened in 1808, when Napoleon invaded Spain and replaced its ruling monarch, King Ferdinand VII (1784–1833), with his own brother, Joseph Bonaparte (1768–1844). Mexicans cheered when the Spanish revolted. Ferdinand would be returned to his throne six years later, but in the meantime, the spark of revolution had been lit in Mexico. Soon an on-again, off-again war for independence had begun there.

This rebellion started with an 1810 revolt led by a Catholic priest, Miguel Hidalgo y Costilla (1753–1811), who managed to gather an army of sixty thousand mestizos before he was captured and executed by the Spanish. Despite his fate, Hidalgo became a popular folk hero, and the first day of his revolt, September 16, is still celebrated as Mexico's independence

Catholic priest Miguel Hidalgo y Costilla began the Mexican rebellion against the Spanish. *Photograph courtesy of The Library of Congress.*

day, even though independence had not yet been achieved. From 1813 to 1815, another priest emerged to lead a rebellion against the Spanish. Like his predecessor, Father José María Morelos de Pavón (1765–1815) was eventually put to death by the Spanish.

Mexico achieves independence

Morelos's uprising had involved people from many different levels of Mexican society, including Native Americans and mestizos. The revolution that finally did liberate Mexico from the Spanish, however, was dominated by the criollos. Led by Agustín de Iturbide (1783–1824), a former officer in Spain's army, it took place in 1821. Weakened by its own troubles at home, Spain had no choice but to sign Mexico's declaration of independence. Iturbide became president but soon declared himself emperor of Mexico. In 1823, Gaudalupe Victoria (1785–1843) led a successful revolt against the very unpopular Iturbide, and by the next year Mexico had a constitution that established the country as a republic. This still did not mean that all Mexicans were better off, however, for only criollos (who made up 10 percent of the nation's population of seven million) could vote.

The new country's borders stretched from what is now the country of Panama in the south to the present-day state of Kansas in the north. The area contained 1,000,000 square miles of diverse landscapes and climates, including jungles, deserts, plains, and fertile farmland. The years of war had left Mexico drained both socially and economically, and its new leaders had little experience in running such a large, troubled nation. As a result, two groups formed and now vied for dominance. One group, known as the conservatives, believed that political power should reside in a strong, centralized government that worked side by side with the Catholic

Church. The other group, the liberals, thought that power should be spread across the separate Mexican states and that the church's influence should be limited. The liberals also advocated public education and social reforms that would benefit more ordinary people. It was these two very different outlooks that would lead to turmoil in the days to come.

A national hero emerges

In 1829, the liberal Vicente Guerrero (1783–1831) was elected president. He oversaw the abolishment of slavery in Mexico, but was soon killed by forces loyal to the conservative Anastasio Bustamente (1780–1853), who then became president. Meanwhile, Spain made one last attempt to recapture its lost colony by attacking Mexico at the coastal city of Vera Cruz in 1829. Mexico's successful resistance to this attack was led by Antonio Lopéz de Santa Anna (1794–1876; see biographical entry), a general who quickly became a national hero, and who would play an important role in the nation's later war with the United States.

Santa Anna was a criollo born in Vera Cruz in 1794. He had joined Spain's colonial army at the age of sixteen, and spent a decade as a cavalry officer. In Mexico's war for independence, he had first fought on the Spanish side but for unknown reasons joined the rebels in 1821. Two years later, he led the revolt that ousted the dictatorial Iturbide from power. Santa Anna's strong leadership during Spain's attempt to recapture Mexico was much appreciated by the Mexican people, and he made as much of their adoration as he could. For example, during the fighting, Santa Anna had received a severe leg wound and the leg had to be amputated, so he arranged to have his severed limb buried with full military honors! Dressed in fancy uniforms bedecked with shining metals and parading astride a powerful horse, Santa Anna established himself as a grand figure in the public eye.

After Bustamente became president, conditions in Mexico grew even worse than before. Santa Anna helped to overthrow Bustamente in 1832, and in the next year elections were held. Santa Anna was elected to the presidency and, backed by the conservative faction, spent the next few years stripping away any remaining traces of liberal reform. In

1835, Mexico's 1824 constitution was abolished and a strong centralist government was established. This meant that the individual Mexican states were now under the control of the federal government, which was based in Mexico City. It also meant trouble for the large, thriving colony of U.S. settlers who were living in the area called Tejas y Coahuila, (called Texas by U.S. citizens) some 800 miles north of Mexico City.

For More Information

Books

Frazier, Donald, ed. *The United States and Mexico at War*. New York: Simon and Schuster, 1997.

George, Isaac. *Heroes and Incidents of the Mexican War*. San Bernardino, CA: Borgo Press, 1982.

Meyer, Michael C., and William L. Sherman. *The Course of Mexican History*. New York: Oxford University Press, 1982.

Nardo, Don. *The Mexican-American War*. San Diego, CA: Lucent Books, 1991.

Nevin, David. *The Mexican War*. Alexandria, VA: Time-Life Books, 1978.

Web Sites

Descendants of the Mexican War Veterans. *The U.S.-Mexican War: 1846–1848*. [Online] Available http://www.dmwv.org/mexwar/mexwar1.htm (accessed on January 31, 2003).

PBS Online. *U.S.-Mexican War: 1846–1848*. [Online] Available http://www.pbs.org/kera/usmexicanwar/ (accessed on January 31, 2003).

The Fight for Texas Independence

Perhaps it was inevitable that as both the U.S. population grew and economic pressures increased, U.S. citizens looking for new horizons would turn their gaze south toward Mexico. There they saw miles and miles of unpopulated land well suited for growing cotton and grazing cattle. Tejas y Coahuila, called Texas by Americans, the part of Mexico that was closest to the U.S. border, was sparsely populated for several reasons. Located about 800 miles from the Mexican capital, Mexico City, it was difficult for either the government or the Roman Catholic Church (Mexico's state religion) to exert much control or influence over Texas. The military could not do much to protect settlers from attack by hostile Native Americans, communications were minimal, and most Mexicans were too poor to consider a move to the frontier.

Mexico attracts U.S. attention

Before Mexico gained its independence, the Spanish colonial authorities had forbidden all trade between the Mexican outpost of Santa Fe (now located in the state of New

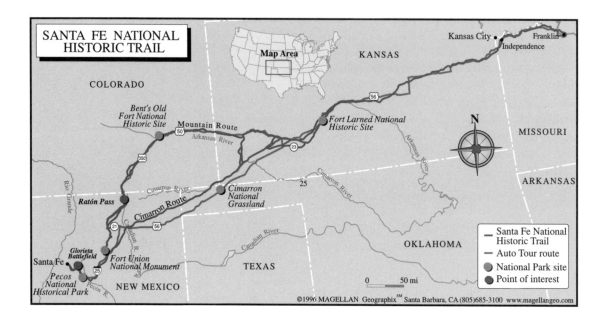

SANTA FE NATIONAL HISTORIC TRAIL

A map of the Santa Fe Trail. The route was established after the Mexican Revolution in order to extend trade between the United States and Mexico. *Photograph reproduced by permission of the Corbis Corporation.*

Mexico) and the United States. After the revolution, however, the new Mexican government began to encourage trade between the northern part of Mexico and the southern part of the United States. As a result, the Santa Fe Trail was established in August 1821, linking St. Louis, Missouri, to Santa Fe and extending trade as far south as Chihuahua in north-central Mexico. Mexicans in this region now began buying goods from U.S. traders.

At the same time, many in the United States realized that gaining ports on the western coast of the continent would allow access to trade with Asia and the rest of the Pacific region. The Mexican state of California, located even farther from the capital than Texas, offered several such ports. At this time there were about seven hundred Americans living in California.

An economic depression (a period of economic hardship, when many people are out of work) called the Panic of 1819 hit hardest in the most western part of the United States, especially in Missouri, Kentucky, and Illinois. Many people in these states as well as those bordering on Texas, such as Arkansas and Louisiana, were desperately looking for a place to make a new start. So it is no surprise that several hundred of them were willing to follow a man named Moses Austin into an unfamiliar land.

Moses Austin plans a colony

Moses Austin (1761–1821) was a land speculator (someone who buys and sells land in the hope of making a profit) who had lived in Connecticut, Virginia, Missouri, and Arkansas and who was now facing bankruptcy. Austin decided that Texas was the answer to his own and other people's problems. In early 1821, he convinced Mexico's colonial government to grant him 200,000 acres on which to establish a colony of U.S. settlers. In June of that year, however, Austin died unexpectedly. As result, the role of leading the U.S. settlers into Texas fell on the somewhat unenthusiastic shoulders of his twenty-seven-year-old son, Stephen.

Soft-spoken Stephen Austin (1793–1836) had been a Congressional delegate from the territory of Mississippi, but he was now studying law in New Orleans. Feeling a sense of familial duty, he agreed to take over for his father. Soon Stephen Austin was leading a group of three hundred families (including many whose farms, plantations, or businesses had failed in recent years) to an area of Texas that lies between the Colorado and Brazos rivers. The settlers worked hard to establish their colony, while Austin tried to convince the newly independent Mexican government to honor the land grants. Mexico's president, Agustin de Iturbide (1783–1824), was a self-styled emperor who did not like the idea of U.S. citizens settling in Mexico. But in 1823 Iturbide was ousted and a new president, Guadalupe Victoria (1785–1843), took power. He approved of the settlements, but with certain conditions.

At this early stage, the Mexican authorities could see the advantages of Austin's proposal. The newcomers would cultivate land that was currently uninhabited, and they could help to keep the local Native Americans under control. Even-

After his father's death, Stephen Austin took over as the leader of the colony that settled in Texas.
Photograph courtesy of The Library of Congress.

tually, it was thought, they would blend in with the Mexican people and culture around them, bringing more stability to the region. So the Mexican government agreed to let the U.S. settlers to stay, as long as they became Mexican citizens and Roman Catholics, giving up their U.S. citizenship and any other religion they may have previously followed. Austin's followers agreed to these conditions.

Trouble brewing between Mexicans and U.S. settlers

For the next few years, the colony flourished. Texas was viewed as a land of hope and opportunity, where a person who was down on his luck could buy as many as 600 acres at a very cheap price. According to Nathaniel W. Stephenson in his book *Texas and the Mexican War*, Texas was a powerful magnet:

> "From every section, from every class, pilgrims were drawn to Texas, the very seat of fortune in the American mind during the [eighteen] twenties. Young and old, rich and poor, wise and foolish, a great host of Americans poured into the colonies of Texas."

By 1827, there were twelve thousand U.S. citizens in Texas, while the area's Mexican population numbered only five thousand. Problems, however, were already developing. Austin had made his bargain in good faith, promising that the settlers would obey Mexican laws, follow the Catholic religion, and, in effect, attach themselves to the community and culture that had allowed them inside its borders. But that is not what happened.

One big issue of tension was slavery. Many of the U.S. settlers were slaveholders, and they insisted on bringing their slaves with them to Texas even though the practice was frowned upon in newly independent Mexico. In 1829, the Mexican government actually passed a law banning slavery, but the Texans ignored it. Many also broke the Mexican law that required them to register their guns; the settlers regarded such a law as a direct assault on their personal freedom. In addition, few of them bothered to learn Spanish or become Roman Catholics. Most kept themselves apart from the local people, whom they considered racially inferior to themselves.

Meanwhile, the local Mexicans resented their new neighbors for ignoring the government's laws. In addition, many of them believed that the U.S. settlers, and U.S. citizens in general, held religion in contempt and were especially hostile to the Roman Catholic Church.

Mexicans frustrated by yanqui arrogance

By the middle of the 1830s, the profile of the average Texas settler had changed somewhat. In the early days of the colony, most of the Texans had been poor farmers or bankrupt merchants with families, eager to make a new and honest start. Over the years a somewhat rougher, tougher, and extremely independent crowd had poured into Texas, and these people felt even less inclined to blend in with the local culture. The Mexican government was getting increasingly frustrated and concerned about these upstart *yanquis* (the Mexican version of "Yankees," a nickname for Americans that originated in the days of the American Revolution) and what their ultimate intentions might be. Some Mexicans suspected that the U.S. government might even be harboring a secret plan to take over all of Mexico. Still, there was not much the government could do. The region was too remote, separated from Mexico City by 800 miles of mountains, deserts, and more than a dozen rivers. And the Mexican government was plagued by instability, as presidents came and went every few years.

Hoping to stem the flow of U.S. immigrants, President Anastasio Bustamente (1780–1853) urged in 1830 that the government put in place strong restrictions on how many would be allowed into Texas. The resulting law, however, was hard to enforce and led to increased tensions as settlers were occasionally imprisoned. There were even a few shoot-outs between Mexican authorities and U.S. settlers. That led to another law custom-made to infuriate the Texans. Anyone caught with an unregistered gun would be considered a pirate, an unauthorized person who had obviously come to Texas only to make mischief and commit crimes, and would be immediately executed. However, the fiercely independent, gun-toting Texans refused to comply.

Hoping to propose a solution to this volatile situation, Austin went to Mexico City in 1833 to ask the govern-

Mexican president Anastasio Bustamente was unsuccessful in stemming the flow of U.S. immigrants into Texas. *Photograph reproduced by permission of The Granger Collection.*

ment to allow Texas to become a separate Mexican state. Then at least Texans would have a say in the making and enforcing of laws. The Mexican government turned down this suggestion, and Austin headed home. But then the Mexican authorities found a letter in which Austin recommended that the Texans revolt if they were not allowed to form a state. As a result, Austin was thrown in jail for eighteen months, during which period the anger of his followers neared the boiling point, despite his efforts to keep them from resorting to violence.

Santa Anna heats up the conflict

A big shift in the Mexican political scene spelled even more trouble for the Texans. In 1834, the celebrated war hero Antonio López de Santa Anna (1794–1876; see biographical entry) became president of Mexico. The conservative Santa Anna immediately put into place a centralist government that took power away from the individual Mexican states. Regarding the troublesome Texas colony, Santa Anna was adamant: no nonsense would be allowed! In 1835, Santa Anna made a major show of force by sending troops under General Martín Perfecto de Cos (1800–1854) to forts all along the Rio Grande, a river south of the Nueces River, which formed the border of the Texas colony. The borders were heavily patrolled, and troops kept up a very visible presence in Texas towns.

Instead of intimidating the Texans, however, this action just made them more angry. Settlers began firing on Mexican troops, who returned fire. Soon the Texans had formed an armed resistance group, or militia, that was small in number but big in spirit. In early October 1835, this militia took control of the towns of Gonzales and Goliad, and by the end of the month they had arrived at the fortified town of San Antonio, where there were 400 troops stationed under the command of Cos. The Texans, including about 100 from the original militia plus about 300 new volunteers, spent the next six weeks trading shots with the Mexicans, mounting a major seize on the fort in early December. On December 10, having lost 150 of his soldiers, while the Texans lost only 28, Cos surrendered San Antonio. He and his troops were stripped of their weapons but, after they promised not to fight the Texans again, they were allowed to march back into Mexico.

About a month earlier, the U.S. settlers had sent Austin to the United States to try to drum up some support for the Texan rebellion. U.S. president Andrew Jackson (1767–1845) sympathized with the Texans, but he did not feel he could offer more than moral support. Already there had been talk of statehood for Texas, but such a development would surely upset the delicate balance of states in which slavery was either legal or illegal. For now, the U.S. government could send no money or troops to help the Texans, but that restraint did not apply to individual U.S. citizens. Inspired by what they saw as a freedom struggle, and often hoping they would be rewarded with free land when the conflict was over, many people, especially those from border states like Georgia and Louisiana, began volunteering to help fight the Mexicans, while others sent guns, supplies, and money to Texas.

Santa Anna received the news of the Texans' rebellion with fury. In early 1836, convinced that he must teach the U.S. settlers a lesson—and also send a warning to the U.S. government, which he believed was involved—Santa Anna sent six thousand experienced troops on the long march to Texas. With his usual bravado, Santa Anna bragged to the British ambassador to Mexico that if the yanquis gave him any trouble he would plant the Mexican flag in Washington, D.C.

At San Antonio, the conquering Texans were under the command of Colonel J. C. Neill. As December drew to a close, 200 of the more restless volunteers had left San Antonio with the ambitious intention of taking Matamoros, a Mexican town located on the Rio Grande. Marching under the command of Colonel James Fannin (1804–1836), a Texas settler and slave trader who had graduated from the U.S. Military Academy at West Point, New York, these men stopped in the Texas town of Goliad. (Others would gradually join to bring their number to about 350.) That left only a little more than 100 men at San

Antonio, and these were short of food, medicine, horses, and adequate clothing for the surprisingly cold weather they faced. Still, most were in good spirits and fully convinced that the Mexicans would not return until spring. The Texans thought that the Mexicans would not make such a long, difficult journey over terrain made even rougher by winter.

Volunteers gather at San Antonio

Meanwhile, about 100 miles north of San Antonio, a big, friendly, feisty frontiersman named Sam Houston (1793–1863; see biographical entry) had taken charge of the effort to organize a real Texan army. But this force was not yet fully formed or trained, and Houston let the leaders of the resistance fighters at San Antonio and other small towns know that they would have to stand on their own for a while. At San Antonio, more volunteers were slowly trickling in, including such notable figures as Davy Crockett (1786–1836)—a legendary soldier, frontier scout, and former Congressman who carried a rifle named "Betsy"—and Jim Bowie (1796–1836), who was known for the big hunting knife he carried, and which would forever after bear his name. Crockett arrived with a dozen of his fellow Tennessee volunteers, wearing his usual buckskins (a rugged frontier outfit made from deerskin) and asking, according to Don Nardo in *The Mexican-American War*, "Where's the action?"

On February 2, command of San Antonio passed from Neale (who left to attend to family matters and also gather supplies for the town) to Colonel William Barrett Travis (1809–1836), who had just arrived with twenty-six volunteers. Tension between Travis and Bowie was resolved when the two agreed to a joint command. As the month progressed, the Texans received word that the Mexican army was on the march and moving fairly quickly. Sure enough, on February 23, a church bell alarm rang out when a sentry spotted a force of fifteen hundred cavalry (soldiers on horseback) approaching San Antonio. This was merely the advance guard of the six thousand troops Santa Anna was leading north.

Travis ordered the town of San Antonio abandoned, and he and Bowie, who was suffering from a bad case of pneumonia, led their 150 defenders across the San Antonio River to the Alamo, a deserted fort that had once been a Spanish mission (religious center). The Alamo consisted of a number of buildings set around a three-acre plaza (central, open area). The Texans mounted rifles as well as their fourteen cannons along the mission's high walls, and they also raised their new flag, which featured a single, large, white star mounted on a blue background.

"I shall never surrender or retreat."

That same day, the Mexicans took possession of the town of San Antonio and surrounded the Alamo. Santa Anna sent a messenger carrying a white flag (the universal signal for a pause in hostilities or aggression) and a message demanding that the Texans surrender. The Texans responded with a cannon shot that almost hit the messenger, an act that shocked and disgusted the Mexicans. The Mexicans now raised the red flag. This meant that they would take no mercy on their enemies, and their musicians began playing the ancient Spanish song "Deguello," which is a call for bloodshed. Then the Mexicans began what would turn out to be an almost two-week-long bombardment of the Alamo.

On the morning of February 24, Travis wrote a desperate plea for help that a messenger boy managed to carry past the Mexican line and north to Sam Houston. As quoted by Lon Tinkle in *The Alamo,* he addressed his message to "the people of Texas and all Americans in the world," reporting that he was surrounded by Santa Anna's troops but that, despite twenty-four hours of bombardment, he had not yet lost any men. "Our flag waves proudly from the walls—I shall never surrender or retreat," continued Travis, but he needed reinforcements. "I am determined to sustain myself as long as possible and die like a soldier who never forgets what is due his honor and that of his country—Victory or Death!"

The bombing continued, but it was becoming clear to both sides that the Mexicans would have to launch a direct assault on the Alamo if they wanted to break this stalemate. On the evening of March 1, thirty-two volunteers from the town of Gonzales managed to slip through the Mexican lines undetected, bringing the number of defenders inside the Alamo to a little more than 180. Although none of the Texans had even been injured so far, they were running out of am-

Davy Crockett: A legend meets his end

Raised in the backwoods of Tennessee, Davy Crockett enjoyed dual careers as both a politician and a frontier hero. Famous during his own lifetime and legendary ever since, Crocket died when the Mexican army attacked a small group of Texan fighters holed up at the Alamo, an old Spanish mission at San Antonio.

Crockett was born to debt-ridden, impoverished parents in Greene County, Tennessee. He attended school for only very brief periods and went to work herding cattle when he was twelve. After running away from this job, Crockett made his own way in the world for three years. He learned to read by trading his labor for lessons with a Quaker teacher. In 1806, he married Mary "Polly" Finley, only a few months after another young woman had spurned him.

In 1813, tensions that had been brewing between white settlers in southern Alabama and the Creek Indians who lived in that region finally erupted. About five hundred settlers were killed when a band of Creeks attacked them at Fort Mims. This incident inspired Crockett to join a militia (small army made up of volunteers) formed to fight the Creeks. He served for three months as a scout, later enlisting for another six months of service.

In 1816, he traveled to Alabama to investigate the territory taken from the Creeks. On his return trip he contracted malaria and, thought to be near death, was left along the road. Crockett survived and made it home. When told of the rumors about his death, Crocket quipped, "I know'd that was a whopper of a lie, as soon as I heard it."

Crockett became a justice of the peace and court official in 1816. The next year, he was elected lieutenant colonel in his local militia, followed by a job as town commissioner. In 1821, he ran for the Tennessee state legislature, using a campaign strategy that featured short, entertaining speeches followed by gatherings at nearby taverns. Crockett won the election, working during his term to help the poor, propertyless farmers and settlers of the West.

Crockett was re-elected to the state legislature in 1823. Defeated in an election for U.S. Congress in 1825, he ran again in

munition. The situation looked hopeless, for how could this tiny group possibly hold out against Santa Anna's massive, and still growing, force? On March 3, Travis told his men that this would be a fight to the death, and he offered each of them the chance to leave, with no honor lost. It is usually reported that none accepted Travis's offer, though some claim that one Texan did choose to leave.

Davy Crockett. *Photograph reproduced by permission of Archive Photos, Inc.*

1827 and won. Initially a supporter of Democratic president and fellow westerner Andrew Jackson, Crockett found himself increasingly disagreeing with Jackson's policies. Losing his re-election bid in 1831, Crocket again ran in 1833 and won. Upon losing re-election in 1835, Crocket ended his political career.

Crockett's next, and last, adventure took place in Texas, the Mexican territory to which many U.S. citizens were flocking in search of a fresh start. Planning to explore the area's possibilities, he traveled there with four friends. By early 1836, Texans had decided to launch a rebellion against Mexico and establish their own republic. Crocket joined the volunteers and, dressed in buckskins (clothing made from animal hides) and toting his beloved rifle he named "Betsy," showed up at the Alamo in February.

On March 6, all of the Alamo's 189 defenders, including Crockett, were killed by a large Mexican force under the merciless Mexican general, Antonio López de Santa Anna. Crockett's death at the Alamo cemented his reputation as an authentic American hero. To this day, he is remembered as the ideal westerner: rugged and rough-hewn, but also courageous, strong, and noble.

Sources: Davy Crockett Biographical Sketch, *[Online] Available http://www.infoporium.com/heritage/ crockbio.shtml (accessed on January 31, 2003); Frazier, Donald, ed.* The United States and Mexico at War. *New York: Simon and Schuster, 1997.*

A new battle cry: Remember the Alamo!

The end came on March 6. At about five o'clock in the morning, Santa Anna's cannons smashed two huge holes in the Alamo's walls, and somewhere between twenty-eight hundred and three thousand Mexican soldiers stormed the

The Texas defenders of the Alamo fighting Mexican soldiers within the walls of the fortress. Davy Crocket, center right, using his rifle "Betsy" as a club, died in the siege. *Photograph reproduced by permission of Getty Images.*

old mission. As they scrambled through the holes and over the walls, the Mexicans shouted, "Viva Santa Anna!" (Long live Santa Anna!). Travis is said to have turned to his men at this frightening point and urged them to "give 'em hell!" For a short time the Texans managed to keep up a steady and very damaging rain of bullets and cannon fire, but the struggle soon broke down into hand-to-hand fighting with bayonets and knives. Travis was shot as he was trying to load a cannon, and Crockett, after running out of bullets, was using his beloved "Betsy" as a club when he was finally surrounded and killed. Bowie died in the hospital bed he had been too sick to leave, but still managed to kill several of his attackers with his famous knife.

Within a half hour, the fight was over. One hundred eighty-two of the Alamo's defenders were killed in the battle, and five more who survived were shot soon after the battle. Their bodies were burned. The Mexicans allowed Susana Dickinson, the wife of a Texan soldier who had been nursing

The flag adopted by the
Lone Star Republic, after
Texas declared its
independence from Mexico.
*Photograph reproduced by
permission of Getty Images.*

Jim Bowie, and her baby to leave, as well as several Mexican women nurses and two slave boys. Meanwhile, the Mexicans had paid a high price for their assault on the Alamo. Although estimates of their losses vary, most historians agree that about six hundred Mexican soldiers lost their lives.

Even before the Mexicans' main assault on the Alamo had begun, an important meeting took place in a blacksmith's shop at Washington-on-Brazos, a town located about 150 miles northeast of San Antonio. There, on March 2, representatives from various parts of the colony had declared Texas independent from Mexico. This new nation was to be called the Lone Star Republic. Modeling their constitution closely after that of the United States, the Texans named David Burnet (1788–1870) their temporary president, and made Sam Houston commander of their army. That army would soon have a powerful rallying cry, for news of the massacre at the Alamo reached them several days after the battle took place. Now Texans would yell "Remember the Alamo!" as

they faced their enemy, and the old mission would become a symbol of sacrifice and the struggle for freedom for the Texans and their sympathizers.

The massacre at Goliad

After their victory at the Alamo, the Mexicans pressed on through Texas, intending to subdue the colony town by town. At Goliad, Fannin received orders from Houston to abandon the town, for his garrison of less than four hundred troops would soon be a target. On March 19, Fannin led his men out onto the nearby prairie. While they were taking an ill-advised rest in an open area (convinced that Mexican soldiers were no match for his own, Fannin had ignored advice to move the troops to a more sheltered spot), the Texans were attacked by about seven hundred Mexican cavalry led by General José Urrea (1797–1849). Another large force estimated to be between twelve hundred and fifteen hundred quickly surrounded them. Although the Texans managed to move their wagons into a protective circle and put up a surprisingly strong resistance, their situation was clearly hopeless.

The next day, Fannin agreed to surrender on the condition that his troops be treated as regular prisoners of war and not executed. The Texans were taken back to Goliad and imprisoned in a small chapel and yard. On March 27, the unwounded men were marched out of town, assuming that they were going to be sent home. But nothing could have been further from the truth. Even though Urrea and other Mexican officers believed the prisoners should be treated mercifully, Santa Anna had ordered that they all be shot as pirates who had baldly defied Mexico's law against unregistered weapons and who must now face the penalty. Reluctantly, Urrea directed his soldiers to carry out the order, and the guards who had led the Texans out of town turned and let loose a rain of bullets. In the largest single loss of lives during the Texas Revolution, 333 men died (about 20 managed to escape). About 80 Texans whose skills would be useful to the Mexicans, including medical personnel, carpenters, blacksmiths, and wheelwrights, were allowed to live.

The Battle of San Jacinto

Like the defeat at the Alamo, the Goliad massacre became a source of inspiration both for soldiers marching into battle and for those hoping to recruit volunteers to fight the Mexicans. Both of these events boosted Sam Houston's army-building efforts, and his tiny force of four hundred soldiers doubled in size within a few weeks. Now Houston began playing a game of cat and mouse with Santa Anna as the Mexican army moved around Texas, trying to catch up with the leaders of the newly formed Lone Star Republic and its army. Some of Houston's men were frustrated by their commander's cautious approach, but Houston was waiting for Santa Anna to make a mistake and give the much smaller Texan army an advantage. Finally the moment for action came. In late April, Houston learned that Santa Anna himself was in command of a small unit of the Mexican army near the town of New Washington, located on the San Jacinto River. Arriving on the scene with about nine hundred troops, Houston took up a position outside the town. The Mexicans began calling in re-inforcements, so the Texans decided to strike before their opponents could gather an even stronger force.

The Texan attack that came on April 21, was a surprise for two reasons. First, a hill blocked the Mexicans' view of the Texans' approach, and second, the Texans timed their assault for late afternoon, when the Mexicans were enjoying their traditional siesta (rest). Unprepared and panic-stricken, many of the Mexican soldiers fled. The Texans won the battle in about twenty minutes, but even when it was over, many of them continued to brutally slaughter every Mexican they could find until their officers urged them to stop. More than 600 Mexican soldiers were killed and another 730 captured, while the Texans had only 9 killed, and 30 wounded.

Santa Anna was able to escape the battle on horseback, riding into nearby marshes and later making his way on foot through tall grass. At some point he changed into the uniform of a low-ranking foot soldier to make himself less recognizable. He was picked up the next day by Texan army scouts and taken into the Texan camp, where the Mexican prisoners gave away his identity by rising to salute "El Presidente" (The President).

Now Houston had to decide what to do with Santa Anna. With the bitter memories of the massacres at Alamo and Goliad still fresh in their minds, many of his men favored executing the Mexican president and general. Houston, however, thought he was more valuable alive. In the end, Santa Anna was held until November, and during those months he was forced to sign a treaty that recognized Texas as an independent state. After Santa Anna's release, the Mexican congress rejected the treaty he had signed, proclaiming it completely invalid since Santa Anna had been a prisoner when he signed it. For a while Santa Anna was in disgrace, but it would not be long before he made another return to public life and widespread acclaim.

In what came to be known as the Texas Revolution, a hastily assembled army of U.S. settlers had succeeded in chasing the Mexican army away from Texas. The Lone Star Republic would exist for the next ten years, but during that period its claim of independence would never be accepted by Mexico. Despite the joy the news of the victory at San Jacinto brought to some, the battle signified not an end to the conflict, but a warning of more bloodshed to come. Mexico was merely waiting for a chance to reclaim its territory, while across the border, voices were calling for the United States to make Texas part of the Union.

For More Information

Books

Bredeson, Carmen. *The Battle of the Alamo*. Brookfield, CT: Millbrook Press, 1996.

Downey, Fairfax. *Texas and the War with Mexico*. New York: American Heritage, 1961.

Kalman, Bobbie. *Mexico: The Culture*. New York: Crabtree, 1993.

Nardo, Don. *The Mexican-American War*. San Diego, CA: Lucent Books, 1991.

Nevin, David. *The Mexican War*. Alexandria, VA: Time-Life Books, 1978.

Sanford, Charles L., ed. *Manifest Destiny and the Imperialism Question*. New York: John Wiley and Sons, 1974.

Stephenson, Nathaniel W. *Texas and the Mexican War*. New Haven, CT: Yale University Press, 1921.

Tinkle, Lon. *The Alamo*. New York: New American Library, 1958.

Web Sites

Descendants of Mexican War Veterans. *The U.S.-Mexican War: 1846–1848*. [Online] Available http://www.dmwv.org/mexwar.htm (accessed on January 31, 2003).

"The Mexican-American War." *Social Studies for Kids*. [Online] Available http://www.socialstudiesforkids.com/subjects/mexicanwar.htm (accessed on January 31, 2003).

PBS Online. *U.S.—Mexican War: 1846–1848*. [Online] Available http://www.pbs.org/kera/usmexicanwar/ (accessed on January 31, 2003).

Two Nations on the Brink of War

At the Battle of San Jacinto, a very young Texan army under the leadership of feisty frontiersman Sam Houston (1793–1863; see biographical entry) had defeated a section of the much more experienced Mexican army. They had captured the famous Mexican general, Antonio de Lopéz Santa Anna (1794–1876; see biographical entry), and made him sign a treaty that recognized Texas as an independent nation. Texans and other U.S. citizens were proud and elated, but that mood was short-lived. When the dust settled, most Texans realized that they faced an uncertain and risky future.

Calls for the annexation of Texas

Although the population of U.S.-born settlers in Texas was higher than the Mexican population in the region, the Texans were far outnumbered when Mexico's total population—more than eight million—was considered. Mexico could raise a much bigger army than could Texas. Most U.S. citizens admitted that the victory at San Jacinto had been a lucky break. It was not likely that the Texan army could win a real, full-scale war if Mexico chose to wage one.

Thus, more and more voices began to call for annexation, meaning that Texas would become part of the United States. The benefits of statehood had to do not just with defense (not only against Mexico but against the various Native American nations in the area, who also considered the Texans invaders) but with culture. In their hearts and in their habits, the vast majority of U.S. settlers in Texas were still Americans. They still spoke only English and practiced the Protestant religions of the U.S. majority. And they wanted all of the rights and privileges that belonged to U.S citizens.

The Lone Star Republic makes its way

For the time being, however, the Lone Star Republic made its way on its own. In October 1836, the revolutionary hero Sam Houston became the little nation's first elected president. Five months later, the United States set up diplomatic relations with Texas (a formal way of recognizing that another country has a right to exist), followed by similar steps taken by France, Great Britain, and other European nations. During the next decade, the government of the Lone Star Republic would be troubled by problems of defense and debt, but Texas itself would continue to grow in population.

There were two main reasons why Texas was attractive to certain people in the United States. Those who supported expansionism (the movement to expand the United States beyond its already established borders) welcomed this new territory as a likely place for more and more U.S. citizens to settle. And if Mexico wanted a war, so be it, for then perhaps the United States could gain even more land than just Texas. The other reason had to do with an issue that was already complex and troublesome, and that would continue to divide the people of the United States during the next few decades. That issue was slavery.

The issue of slavery divides the nation

By the mid-nineteenth century, slavery had been practiced in the United States for almost two hundred years.

During those centuries, Africans had been taken from their homes and transported under inhumane conditions across the ocean to North America (as well as to parts of South America, Central America, and the Caribbean islands). There they were made to work in the fields and in the homes of farms and plantations without wages and under harsh living conditions as well as the constant threat of punishment or death if they tried to escape. Supporters of slavery justified it as the only way to provide the vast numbers of agricultural workers needed to keep the U.S. economy going. Since Africans and other people of non-European heritage were viewed as racially inferior, it was not necessary to treat them equally, and it would be foolish and wrong to offer them the same rights as white people.

As the nineteenth century progressed, the United States began to change, however. A division between the northern and southern states began to develop, and this division would grow wider with the passing years. The North had become less dependent on agriculture and more dependent on trade and industry. These practices called for fewer workers, and as a consequence, there was no need to use slave labor. There had always been U.S. citizens in all parts of the country who disapproved of slavery, but now more northerners began to view the practice as being morally wrong. Eventually an abolitionist movement (whose members worked to end slavery) developed and grew in numbers and influence.

Meanwhile, the economy of the South was still based on agriculture. Southern farmers and plantation owners still depended on slaves to work their fields and harvest their cotton, rice, and other crops. Many southerners also were quite comfortable with and proud of their lifestyles and culture, and they did not want things to change. They felt that northerners understood neither the southern way of life nor the true nature of slaves and slavery. There were a few southern abolitionists, but most southerners viewed them with scorn and suspicion.

A delicate balance

During the first two decades of the nineteenth century, the number of states in which slavery was legal kept pace,

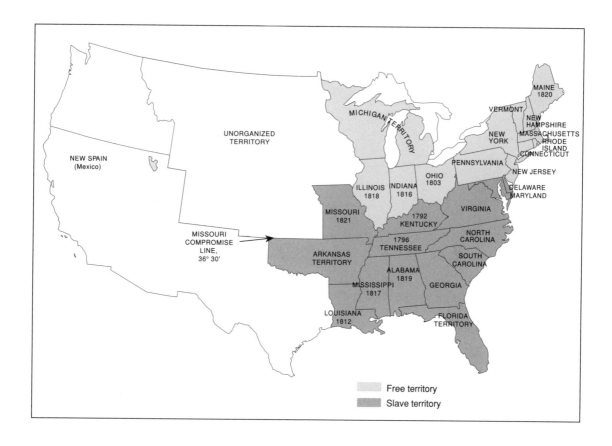

more or less, with the number of states in which it was illegal. This balance was important, because neither side wanted the other to have too much power in Congress. To northerners, that might mean that laws would be passed that would keep slavery strong and benefit the South too much, and to southerners, it might mean that slavery would be outlawed altogether, or that their region might otherwise be hurt. As the nineteenth century progressed, the distrust between North and South seemed to grow by leaps and bounds.

The issue reached a crisis point in 1820, when Missouri applied to be admitted to the union as a slave state. If this happened, the delicate balance between slave and free (nonslave) states would be upset. As a result, northerners strongly protested Missouri's admission. The issue was resolved with an agreement called the Missouri Compromise, through which Missouri was admitted as a slave state and Maine (which had previously formed the northern part of the

A map showing the line that made up the Missouri Compromise. The Compromise was put in place to keep the balance between free and slave states. *Photograph courtesy of the Gale Group.*

state of Massachusetts) was admitted as a free state, thus maintaining the balance. This agreement also prohibited slavery in any of the lands of the Louisiana Purchase (which included the present-day states of Arkansas, Missouri, Iowa, part of Minnesota, North Dakota, South Dakota, Nebraska, Oklahoma, most of Kansas, parts of Montana, Wyoming, Colorado, and Louisiana) that were north of the Missouri border.

Texas becomes a slavery battleground

After the admission of Missouri as a state, Texas was to become the next great slavery battleground. Those who wanted not only to uphold, but to extend the practice of slavery, and thus increase the power of the slaveholding states, saw Texas as the natural place to do it. In fact, many Texans already owned slaves and were as determined to keep owning them as they were to carry unregistered guns. It was thought that since Texas covered such a huge area of land (several hundred thousand square miles), it might eventually be divided into two or even three separate states, all of them allowing slavery. That would give slaveholders more influence in the Senate, where each state would have two votes.

These, of course, were the very reasons northerners opposed the annexation of Texas. They feared that southerners would take control of Congress and thus dominate national life and politics. In addition, many northerners believed that slavery was evil and must be stamped out, not extended. Abolitionists were sure that all this talk of annexation was generated by a proslavery conspiracy. Abolitionists foresaw dire consequences if Texas was allowed into the United States, including the possible breakup of the union. A few proponents of Texas annexation also objected to the way that Texans had gone back on their promise to obey Mexico's laws and had, in fact, simply taken land that really belonged to Mexico.

By the 1830s, the U.S. Congress was divided between those in favor of annexing Texas and those against it, with each group continually vying for power. Meanwhile, the man at the helm of the nation between 1828 and 1836, President Andrew Jackson (1767–1845), was in favor of Texas statehood but did not want to take a firm stand on the issue. He was afraid that annexing Texas at this time would look too much like the United States was trying to steal land from Mexico. Jackson's successor and fellow Democrat (one of two major political parties of the period), Martin Van Buren (1782–1862), also favored annexation, but he too avoided the issue during his term as president.

The 1840 presidential election

During the presidential election of 1840, the annexation of Texas was an important issue. Van Buren was running for re-election, and it was believed that if he was elected he would push for Texas statehood. Van Buren's opponent was General William Henry Harrison (1773–1841), a hero of the War of 1812 (1812–14). Like most other members of the Whig political party, which was dominated by northerners, Harrison was against the annexation of Texas. Fearing that his stand on this issue would hurt his popularity with voters in the South, party members chose southerner and well-known annexationist John Tyler (1790–1862) as Harrison's vice presidential candidate in order to balance the Whig ticket.

The Whig's plan was successful and Harrison and Tyler won the election. However, the plan to avoid the annexation issue collapsed when Harrison died only one month after taking office. Now a man who was in favor of Texas statehood was the president of the United States. As the annexationists' hope for eventual success rose, so too did the Mexican government's fear. They sent warnings to the United States that the annexation of Texas would mean war. Tyler ignored these threats and tried repeatedly to push annexation through Congress. Each of his attempts was defeated by a narrow margin, as the antislavery representatives and senators banded together to defeat them.

Whig party members chose well-known annexationist John Tyler as William Henry Harrison's running mate in order to balance the Whig ticket. *Photograph reproduced by permission of the Corbis Corporation.*

Texans turn up the heat

Meanwhile, back in Texas, Mirabeau B. Lamar (1798–1859) had been elected the second president of the Lone Star Republic. Lamar had much more extreme views than Houston, and he did not agree with those who wanted Texas to join the United States. He thought the Lone Star Republic should not only remain independent but also take New Mexico and California from Mexico. Lamar's aggressive stance led to an ill-fated excursion in 1841, when he sent twenty-two goods-laden wagons to Santa Fe, accompanied by 265 soldiers. The goal of the trek was not only to open up a trade route between Texas and New Mexico but to convince residents of Santa Fe to become citizens of the Lone Star Republic.

The Mexican army, however, had gotten wind of the plan and troops were waiting for the Texans when they arrived at Santa Fe. They were captured and forced to march about 2,000 miles to a fort near Mexico City. Several died along the way, stirring anger among annexationists and serving for them as proof of Mexican cruelty. Another big topic of conversation and a focus for contempt toward Mexico was the issue of U.S. claims from the Mexican war for independence from Spain. Some U.S. citizens whose property had been damaged or lost during the conflict wanted payment from Mexico. A two-year investigation begun in 1841 concluded that Mexico owed $2 million to the United States, but Mexico made only three of the twenty scheduled payments.

Despite these very real complaints against Mexico, most Texans did not share Lamar's extreme views, and in 1841 the more moderate Houston was again elected president of the Lone Star Republic. Although he was not in favor of a full-scale war with Mexico, Houston did want to show the Mexican government that Texans were willing and able to re-

A Texas Ranger.

Sam Houston, president of the Lone Star Republic, wanted to show Mexico that the Texas rangers, like the one pictured here, were willing and able to respond to that country's aggression. *Photograph courtesy of The Library of Congress.*

spond to aggression. To drive home this point, Houston sent 750 troops across the Rio Grande river (which Texans were now claiming as the border between Mexico and the Lone Star Republic, even though the more northern Nueces River had previously been the boundary) into Mexico.

This expedition was supposed to be a simple show of force, but it turned into something more violent. When Houston ordered the troops to return to Texas, about half of them defied him and went on their own to attack the Mexican town of Mier. After a three-day battle, the Texans surrendered. The Mexicans immediately shot forty Texan soldiers, sending the rest to a fort near Mexico City.

The Mexicans take a strong stance

News of this incident fueled anti-Mexican feelings in both Texas and the United States, and some U.S. politicians started calling for a war with Mexico. The Mexicans, however, felt that the fault for the conflicts lay squarely with the Texans. Mexico's Minister of Foreign Affairs, José María Bocanegra (1787–1862) sent a strongly worded message that accused the U.S. government of trying to stir up trouble by encouraging the Texans to rebel. Bocanegra's message stated that if the United States refused to stay out of Mexican affairs, especially in regard to Texas, Mexico would take action. But as the 1844 election drew nearer, Mexicans waited nervously to see which way the wind would blow in regard to annexation. Since they had already used forceful, threatening words that they could not take back, annexation would mean war.

In Mexico's capital, Mexico City, and all around the large nation, there were many people who did not want to go to war with the United States. Mexico's president, José Joaquín de Herrera (1792–1854), who had replaced Santa Anna in a coup (sudden action taken to obtain power), was one of those who did not think it was a good idea. Even though Mexico had a strong military tradition and a particularly fine cavalry, he knew that the general morale of the soldiers was very low, especially since the government lacked the money to pay them. That might make them unwilling or unable to put up a strong fight against the United States. While it was true that

José Joaquín Herrera

Considered one of the finest presidents to lead Mexico in the turbulent years following the nation's independence from Spain, José Joaquín Herrera tried in vain to avoid war with the United States.

Born in Jalapa in 1792, José Joaquín Herrera joined the Spanish colonial army at a young age, reaching the rank of captain by 1811. In 1821, Herrera retired as a lieutenant colonel from the military and opened a store in the town of Perote. The next year, Mexicans gained their independence from Spain, and Herrera joined the new Mexican army. He was soon promoted to the rank of brigadier general.

In 1824, Herrera helped to overthrow Mexico's president, Agustín Iturbide, who had become a harsh dictator. Herrera served as Minister of War from 1832 to 1834 and held other positions in the government, including member of congress, for the next ten years. When the dynamic, but dictatorial, general and president Antonio Lopéz de Santa Anna was removed from power and exiled to Cuba in 1844, Herrera was elected interim (temporary) president. He won the presidential election of 1845, taking charge of a nation that was in political chaos and economically troubled.

As a *moderado* (moderate), Herrera tried to maintain a balance between his country's liberals, who favored a more democratic form of government and society, and conservatives, who supported strong central control and limited freedom and rights for the states. It was even more difficult to keep that balance on the issue of Texas independence. In 1836, U.S. settlers living in the Mexican state of Texas had proclaimed themselves an independent republic. Mexico never officially accepted this action, and the two nations were now on the brink of war.

Herrera thought that Mexico should recognize Texas as long as the Texans would promise not to become part of the United States. But in March 1845, the United States did annex Texas (made it a state). Mexico had previously promised that annexation would mean war, and now it seemed that they would have to make good on their promise. However, Herrera did not believe that war was not the answer and thought that Mexico could not hope to win against the United States. Although he wanted to negotiate with the United States, the majority of Mexican leaders, as well as much of the Mexican public, favored war. So when U.S. president James K. Polk sent a representative to Mexico to propose a deal by which Mexico would not only recognize the independence of Texas but give California and New Mexico to the United States for $25 million, Herrera refused to see him. This angered Polk, who was now waiting for a chance to declare war against Mexico.

Meanwhile, Herrera's opposition to war caused tension between himself and the Mexican military. There was a revolt, and on December 30, 1845, Herrera was forced to resign the presidency, which was taken over by General Mariano Paredes y Arillaga. A leader with a very hostile attitude toward the United States, Paredes would be in office for only one year before being overthrown. Replacing Paredes was a familiar face in Mexican politics. Having convinced his people once again that only he could save Mexico, and having tricked the United States into allowing him past its naval blockade to enter the country, Santa Anna now returned to power.

The Mexican American War began in 1846 after U.S. troops stationed along the Rio Grande were attacked by a Mexican force. During the war, Herrera served as military commander of Mexico City, the nation's capital. The U.S. army won battle after battle, successfully fighting its way to the gates of Mexico City. There, in August 1847, they paused and suggested an armistice (halt in fighting during which peace negotiations may take place). Considered a sane and steady influence, Herrera was called upon to take part in peace talks. It soon became clear, however, that Santa Anna would not back down from his unreasonable demands, and the armistice was called off. The U.S. Army captured Mexico City on September 14, and the war was over. About five months later, with the signing of the Treaty of Guadalupe officially ending the war, Mexico lost almost half of its territory to the United States.

Understandably, many Mexicans were dissatisfied with the terms of the treaty and with their leaders who had negotiated it. They again turned to Herrera, electing him president in 1848. Herrera took over the presidency while the country was in a period of great instability. Mexico was in financial crisis since it had only the $15 million recently received from the United States as part of the treaty terms in the government's bank account. Herrera also had to deal with rebellions in Yucatán and other areas of the country. Yet, he ruled as well as, or better than, anyone could have expected, working especially hard on managing Mexico's debts by reducing the military budget.

In 1851, Herrera turned over the presidency to the duly elected Mariano Arista in the first peaceful transition of power that had been seen in Mexico since independence. (Unfortunately, Arista would later be forced from office in a military takeover.) Herrera died four years later in Tacubaya.

Sources: Crawford, Mark, Encyclopedia of the Mexican American War. Santa Barbara, CA: American Bibliographical Center-Clio Press, 1998; Frazier, Donald, ed. The United States and Mexico at War. New York: Simon and Schuster, 1997.

MATTY MEETING THE TEXAS QUESTION.

the United States had a smaller army than Mexico, it also had a much larger population from which to recruit volunteers. Mexico's economy was still primarily agriculturally based, but the United States was an industrialized nation and could fairly easily produce the weapons, ammunition, and supplies that would be needed. Mexico had no navy at all, while the United States had a fairly strong one. All of these factors led many Mexicans to believe that they could not win a war against their northern neighbor.

An annexationist in the White House

The 1844 election pitted Whig candidate Henry Clay (1777–1852), who was opposed to the annexation of Texas and to war with Mexico, against Democrat James K. Polk (1795–1849; see biographical entry). Polk was such an enthusiastic expansionist and annexationist that his campaign slogan was "All of Texas and All of Oregon!" (At this time, the

United States also was arguing with Great Britain over where to draw the boundary between the northwestern territory of Oregon and the British colony of Canada.) Polk also had his eye on California and New Mexico.

When Polk won the election, the Mexicans were in a difficult position. They could not abandon their hard-line stance, but they hoped that the United States would back down on the annexation issue. That did not happen, however, and on March 1, 1845, soon after Polk's inauguration, Congress passed a bill annexing Texas. As a result, Mexico felt that it had no choice but to regard this as a direct insult. Stating that the United States had taken control of Mexican territory illegally, the Mexican ambassador to the United States immediately cut off diplomatic relations (the formal ties between friendly nations) and returned to Mexico City. Texas now became the twenty-eighth state, adding an area of 267,339 square miles to the United States.

Taylor sent to Corpus Christi, Slidell to Mexico City

That summer, Polk took a bold military step when he ordered General Zachary Taylor (1784–1850; see biographical entry), a rugged frontiersman and veteran of several Indian wars, to lead about four thousand troops (nearly half the U.S. Army at that time) into Texas. Taylor set up camp at Corpus Christi near the Nueces River. For the moment, everyone knew, the Mexicans were unlikely to react unless the U.S. forces actually crossed the Nueces and entered the 200-mile stretch between it and the Rio Grande, the disputed border between Texas and Mexico. In early November, Polk made a major diplomatic move by sending Louisiana congressman John Slidell (1793–1871) on a special mission to Mexico. Slidell was to offer the Mexicans $5 million for what is now New Mexico and $25 million for California, on the condition that Mexico recognize the Rio Grande as the border between the two nations.

The benefits that such a deal would offer the United States were great. It would nearly double the size of the nation and would, through the ports of California, provide access to precious trade routes with Asia. (In fact, Great Britain and Rus-

sia also were interested in those ports, so the United States needed to act fast.) Learning of Slidell's arrival in Mexico City and of what he proposed, Herrera called a meeting of his cabinet made up of the top leaders of various government departments. The cabinet members were outraged, since they believed that the *yanquis* (Yankees) had already stolen Texas, and now they wanted even more territory. Several of the cabinet members thought Mexico should declare war immediately, but Herrera persuaded them to wait. He was in favor of negotiating with the United States, but the majority of cabinet members felt that agreeing to any kind of meeting with Slidell would send the wrong message to the United States, the message that Mexico had given in on the loss of Texas.

So, Herrera refused to see Slidell, who returned empty-handed to Washington, D.C. Polk considered the Mexicans' refusal to even meet with Slidell an insult. He felt sure the U.S. public would support a war with Mexico, and now he just needed an excuse to start one.

Although sent to Mexico to negotiate buying some of the country's territory, Louisiana congressman John Slidell returned to the United States empty-handed. *Photograph reproduced by permission of the Corbis Corporation.*

Most Americans support expansion

Newspapers all around the country were printing editorials in favor of expansionism. To many U.S. citizens, it seemed not only desirable but inevitable that their nation would push past its current borders into Mexico. This assumption was based largely on the racist belief that white people, those of unmixed European ethnic heritage, were meant to dominate and "civilize" this vast, richly endowed continent. In words that were to ring throughout the rest of the nineteenth century and into the twentieth, journalist John O'Sullivan wrote (as quoted in *Manifest Destiny and the Imperialism Question*, edited by Charles L. Sanford) in the *De-*

mocratic Review that it was "our 'manifest destiny' to overspread the continent allotted by Providence [God] for the free development of our expanding millions [of people]." Most Americans believed that due to their mixed blood, Mexicans were lazy and ignorant, and certainly not fit for leading North America into the future. As quoted in Howard Zinn's *A People's History of the United States,* the respected journal *American Review* urged Mexico to bow before "a superior population, insensibly oozing into her territories, changing her customs, and out-living, out-trading, [and] exterminating the weaker blood." As recorded by Karl J. Bauer in *The Mexican War,* even the liberal-minded poet Walt Whitman declared in the *Brooklyn Eagle* that "Mexico must be thoroughly chastised. Let our arms now be carried with a spirit which shall teach the world that, while we are not forward for a quarrel, America knows how to crush, as well as how to expand!"

Despite those confident words, the army that would be expected to "chastise" Mexico if war did come was not particularly impressive. In Mexico, soldiering was an honorable profession, and boys grew up dreaming of attending the National Military Academy on Chapultepec Hill near Mexico City. By contrast, the United States had traditionally depended on volunteers, or militias (armies made up of private citizens that could be called upon by the federal government in times of war). Many U.S. citizens had a low opinion of professional soldiers, and considered soldiering a last resort for those who lacked the skills to get better jobs. (In fact, a large percentage of soldiers were recent immigrants to the United States who often faced prejudice and unemployment.) Being a U.S. soldier was, indeed, a life full of hardships and danger, for the pay was low, the food and supplies scanty, and the discipline harsh. At this period just before the Mexican American War began, U.S. troops numbered only about 7,200 (well below the authorized number of 8,613), most of them scattered across the country to defend the frontier.

"Old Rough and Ready"

Fortunately, the army did have some good officers. One of these was General Zachary Taylor, who had earned the nickname "Old Rough and Ready" because of his very casual,

Manifest Destiny: John O'Sullivan's Famous Term

One of the forces that led to the Mexican American War was expansionism, the belief that U.S settlers could, should, and would expand across their national boundaries into the rest of the continent. Journalist John L. O'Sullivan (1813–1895) coined the famous term "manifest destiny" to describe that spirit as well as the idea that U.S. citizens had both a right and a duty to force their ideals on others. The term first appeared in the following article, which appeared in his own journal, the *United States Magazine and Democratic Review* in July 1845.

ANNEXATION

It is time now for opposition to the Annexation of Texas to cease, all further agitation of the waters of bitterness and strife, at least in connexion with this question. It is time for the common duty of Patriotism to the Country to succeed;—or if this claim will not be recognized, it is at least time for common sense to acquiesce with decent grace in the inevitable and the irrevocable.

Texas is now ours. Already, before these words are written, her Convention has undoubtedly ratified the acceptance, by her Congress, of our proffered invitation into the Union. The next session of Congress will see the representatives of the new young State in their places in both our halls of national legislation, side by side with those of the old Thirteen [a reference to the original thirteen colonies]. Let their reception into "the family" be frank, kindly, and cheerful, as befits such an occasion.

Why, were other reasoning wanting, in favor of now elevating this question of the reception of Texas into the Union, out of the lower region of our past party dissensions, up to its proper level of a high and broad nationality, it surely is to be found, found abundantly, in the manner in which other nations have undertaken to intrude themselves into it, between us and the proper parties to the case, in a spirit of hostile interference against us, for the avowed object of thwarting our policy and hampering our power, limiting our greatness and checking the fulfilment of our manifest destiny to overspread the continent allotted by Providence for the free development of our yearly multiplying millions.

Texas has been absorbed into the Union in the inevitable fulfilment of the general law which is rolling our population westward; the connexion of which with that ratio of growth in population which is destined within a hundred years

even sloppy, dress and plain manners. Born in Virginia, but raised in Kentucky, the short, heavy Taylor was a veteran of battles against the Creek and Seminole Indians that had taken place in the southeastern United States several decades before. His calm, relaxed demeanor as well as his courage and toughness made him popular among the troops. (Taylor's horse, Old Whitey, was also known for its calm, hardly blinking an eye in the midst of gunfire and booming cannons.) Alto swell our numbers to the enormous population of two hundred and fifty millions *(if nor more), is too evident to leave us in doubt of the manifest design of Providence in regard to the occupation of this continent. It was disintegrated from Mexico in the natural course of events, by a process perfectly legitimate on its own part, blameless on ours; and in which all the censures due to wrong, perfidy and folly, rest on Mexico alone.*

California will, probably, next fall away from the loose adhesion which, in such a country as Mexico, holds a remote province in a slight equivocal kind of dependence on the metropolis. Imbecile and distracted, Mexico never can exert any real governmental authority over such a country. Already the advance guard of the irresistible army of Anglo-Saxon emigration has begun to pour down upon it, armed with the plough and the rifle, and marking its trail with schools and colleges, courts and representative halls, mills and meetinghouses. A population will soon be in actual occupation of California, over which it will be idle for Mexico to dream of dominion. And they will have a right to independence—to self-government—to the possession of the homes conquered from the wilderness by their own labors and dangers, sufferings and sacrifices—a better and a

truer right than the artificial title of sovereignty in Mexico a thousand miles distant, inheriting from Spain a title good only against those who have none better. Their right to independence will be the natural right of self-government belonging to any community strong enough to maintain it.

Away, then, with all idle French talk of balances of power on the American Continent. There is no growth in Spanish America! Whatever progress of population there may be in the British Canadas, is only for their own early severance of their present colonial relation to the little island three thousand miles across the Atlantic; soon to be followed by Annexation, and destined to swell the still accumulating momentum of our progress. And whatsoever may hold the balance, though they should cast into the opposite scale all the bayonets and cannon, not only of France and England, but of Europe entire, how would it kick the beam against the simple solid weight of the two hundred and fifty or three hundred millions—and American millions—destined to gather beneath the flutter of the stripes and stars, in the fast hastening year of the Lord 1845?

Source: Manifest Destiny (1845). *[Online] Available* http://www.hkuhist2.hku.hk/firstyear/Roberts/roberts E05.htm *(accessed on January 31, 2003).*

though popular with civilians and soldiers, Taylor was not seen as favorable with the army's commander-in-chief, General Winfield Scott (1786–1866; see biographical entry), who faulted him for his unprofessional appearance and lack of skill in tactics and strategy.

Another of Taylor's weaknesses was his neglect of sanitation measures in camp. Paying little attention to the connection between dirt and disease had dire consequences at the Corpus Christi army encampment during the last few months of 1845. There the troops lived a miserable existence, battling rattlesnakes, rain, and mosquitoes, sleeping in rotting tents, and drinking impure water. Thus in January, when Polk, who was tired of waiting for the Mexicans to make a move, ordered Taylor to take his troops across the Nueces and march toward the Rio Grande, about eight hundred soldiers suffering from a range of illnesses that included dysentery, fever, and snakebites had to be left behind. Taylor made the trip with about three thousand troops. Among them was a young lieutenant named Sam Grant, who would one day play an important role in the Civil War as General Ulysses S. Grant (1822–1885), and would also become the eighteenth president of the United States. David Nevin's book *The Mexican War* quotes Grant as he describes the journey from Corpus Christi and later remembers that his horse was a newly broken (trained) mustang who often disagreed with his rider "as to which way we should go and sometimes whether we should go at all."

A tense stand-off on the Rio Grande

Reaching the Rio Grande on March 28, Taylor's force made camp on a spot across from the Mexican town of Matamoros. Two days later, General Pedro de Ampudia (1805–1868) arrived in Matamoros with two thousand Mexican troops. He ordered Taylor to return to the Nueces River within twenty-four hours or face the consequences. Instead of retreating, Taylor responded by beginning work on a fort that was to be called Fort Texas. On April 11, General Mariano Arista (1802–1855) arrived on the scene and took charge of Matamoros. He soon ordered that sixteen hundred cavalry cross the river and take up positions a few miles from Fort Texas. This was intended as a menacing show of force, but in the end it actually gave Polk and Taylor the opening for which they had been waiting.

With the enemy camped so close to Fort Texas, Taylor sent out a sixty-three-member patrol to gather information on the Mexicans' position. A clash broke out on April 26, when the U.S. soldiers were surrounded at a ranch house by Mexican troops. It is not clear which side shot first, but in the

exchange of gunfire, eleven U.S. soldiers were killed and the others (except for four who escaped), wounded or captured. On May 10, Polk received a message from Taylor. As quoted in John S. D. Eisenhower's book *So Far from God,* Taylor's message says that there was no doubt about it, the general "Hostilities may now be considered as commenced."

An expedition of Mexican troops descending the Rio Grande right before the beginning of the Mexican American War. *Photograph reproduced by permission of the Corbis Corporation.*

The United States declares war

The next day, Polk sent to Congress a declaration of war against Mexico. In it he boldly claimed that Mexico had "invaded our territory and shed American blood upon American soil" and that the United States was now "called upon by every consideration to vindicate with decision the honor, the rights, and the interests of our country." The war measure passed the House of Representatives the next day by a vote of 173 to 14. It cleared the Senate next, and was signed by Polk

The United States Declares War on Mexico

After hearing that some soldiers under General Winfield Scott had been attacked and killed by Mexican troops in a disputed area of Texas near the Rio Grande, President James K. Polk sent the following declaration of war to the U.S. Congress.

Washington, May 11, 1846.

To the Senate and the House of Representatives:

The existing state of the relations between the United States and Mexico renders it proper that I should bring the subject to the consideration of Congress. In my message at the commencement of your present session, the state of these relations, the causes which led to the suspension of diplomatic intercourse between the two countries in March, 1845, and the long-continued and unredressed wrongs and injuries committed by the Mexican Government on citizens of the United States in their persons and property were briefly set forth.

The strong desire to establish peace with Mexico on liberal and honorable terms, and the readiness of this Government to regulate and adjust our boundary and other causes of difference with that power on such fair and equitable principles as would lead to permanent relations of the most friendly nature, induced me in September last to seek the reopening of diplomatic relations between the two countries. Every measure adopted on our part had for its object the furtherance of these desired results. In communicating to Congress a succinct statement of the injuries which we had suffered from Mexico, and which have been accumulating during a period of more than twenty years, every expression that could tend to inflame the people of Mexico or defeat or delay a pacific result was carefully avoided. An envoy of the United States repaired to Mexico with full powers to adjust every existing difference. But though present on Mexican soil by agreement between the two Governments, invested with full powers, and bearing evidence of the most friendly dispositions, his mission has been unavailing. The Mexican Government not only refused to receive him or listen to his propositions, but after a long-continued series of menaces have at last invaded our territory and shed the blood of our fellow-citizens on our own soil.

on May 13. The United States was now officially at war with Mexico. Congress quickly voted that $10 million go to finance the war effort. The regular army was to be increased to 15,540 troops, and the president was authorized to call up 50,000 volunteers. (By the end of the war, a total of about 100,000 served in the army, including approximately 60,000 volunteers.)

Despite dissent, most support the war

A few members of Congress did not agree with Polk's view of what had happened on the Rio Grande, or with this

The grievous wrongs perpetrated by Mexico upon our citizens throughout a long period of years remain unredressed, and solemn treaties pledging her public faith for this redress have been disregarded. A government either unable or unwilling to enforce the execution of such treaties fails to perform one of its plainest duties.

We have tried every effort at reconciliation. The cup of forbearance had been exhausted even before the recent information from the frontier of the Del Norte. But now, after reiterated menaces, Mexico has passed the boundary of the United States, has invaded our territory and shed American blood upon the American soil. She has proclaimed that hostilities have commenced, and that the two nations are now at war.

As war exists, and, notwithstanding all our efforts to avoid it, exists by the act of Mexico herself, we are called upon by every consideration of duty and patriotism to vindicate with decision the honor, the rights, and the interests of our country.

In further vindication of our rights and defense of our territory, I invoke the prompt action of Congress to recognize the existence of the war, and to place at the disposition of the Executive the means of prosecuting the war with vigor, and thus hastening the restoration of peace.

In making these recommendations I deem it proper to declare that it is my anxious desire not only to terminate hostilities speedily, but to bring all matters in dispute between this Government and Mexico to an early and amicable adjustment; and in this view I shall be prepared to renew negotiations whenever Mexico shall be ready to receive propositions or to propositions of her own.

I transmit herewith a copy of the correspondence between our envoy to Mexico and the Mexican minister for foreign affairs, and so much of the correspondence between that envoy and the Secretary of State and between the Secretary of War and the general in command on the Del Norte as is necessary to a full understanding of the subject.

JAMES K. POLK.

Source: Steven R. Butler, ed. A Documentary History of the Mexican War. Richardson, TX: Descendants of Mexican War Veterans, 1995, pp. 67–71.

dramatic step the United States was taking. As quoted in Don Nardo's *The Mexican American War,* Representative Joshua Giddings (1795–1864) of Ohio called this "an aggressive, unholy and unjust war," and vowed that he would not participate in "the murder of Mexicans upon their own soil, or in robbing them of their country." Future president Abraham Lincoln (1809–1865), then a young congressman from Illinois, agreed with Giddings and challenged Polk to reveal the exact spot upon which American blood had been shed on American soil. In Concord, Massachusetts, writer Henry David Thoreau (1817–1862) was jailed because he refused to pay his taxes, as-

Thoreau's "Civil Disobedience": Inspired by the Mexican American War

Among the minority of voices speaking out against the war with Mexico was that of Henry David Thoreau, a New England writer and philosopher. Thoreau spent a night in jail for having refused to pay taxes that would go to support the war. In 1849, Thoreau was inspired by this experience to write the following essay (originally titled "Resistance to Civil Government") in which he asserts that citizens may sometimes have a moral duty to disobey their country's laws. The essay would become one of the most influential in U.S. history.

I heartily accept the motto, "That government is best which governs least"; and I should like to see it acted up to more rapidly and systematically. Carried out, it finally amounts to this, which also I believe—"That government is best which governs not at all"; and when men are prepared for it, that will be the kind of government which the will have. The objections which have been brought against a standing army, and they are many and weighty, and deserve to prevail, may also at last be brought against a standing government. The standing army is only an arm of the standing government. The government itself, which is only the mode which the people have chosen to execute their will, is equally liable to be abused and perverted before the people can act through it. Witness the present Mexican war, the work of comparatively a few individuals using the standing government as their tool; for in the outset, the people would not have consented to this measure. This American government—what is it but a tradition, though a recent one, endeavoring to transmit itself unimpaired to posterity, but each instant losing some of its integrity...

The mass of men serve the state thus, not as men mainly, but as machines, with their bodies. They are the standing army, and the militia, jailers, constables, etc. In most cases there is no free exercise whatever of the judgement or of the moral sense; but they put themselves on a level with wood and earth and stones; and wooden men can perhaps be manufactured that will serve the purpose as well. Such command no more respect than men of straw or a lump of dirt.

There are thousands who are in opinion opposed to slavery and to the war, who yet in effect do nothing to put an end

serting that his money would not be used to support a war against Mexico. Against his wishes, however, Thoreau's friends soon got him out of jail by paying his taxes themselves. But the experience inspired him to write "Civil Disobedience," an essay on the idea that good citizenship sometimes calls for disobeying laws; it would become one of the most famous and influential writings in American history.

Just as Polk had expected, most U.S. citizens did not agree with these few dissenters, no matter how convincing to them; who sit down with their hands in their pockets, and say that they know not what to do, and do nothing; who even postpone the question of freedom to the question of free trade, and quietly read the prices-current along with the latest advices from Mexico, after dinner, and, it may be, fall asleep over them both. What is the price-current of an honest man and patriot today? They hesitate, and they regret, and sometimes they petition; but they do nothing in earnest and with effect. They will wait, well disposed, for other to remedy the evil, that they may no longer have it to regret.

I do not hesitate to say, that those who call themselves Abolitionists should at once effectually withdraw their support, both in person and property, from the government of Massachusetts, and not wait till they constitute a majority of one, before they suffer the right to prevail through them. I think that it is enough if they have God on their side, without waiting for that other one. Moreover, any man more right than his neighbors constitutes a majority of one already.

I have paid no poll tax for six years. I was put into a jail once on this account, for one night; and, as I stood considering the walls of solid stone, two or three feet thick, the door of wood and iron, a foot thick, and the iron grating which strained the light, I could not help being struck with the foolishness of that institution which treated me as if I were mere flesh and blood and bones, to be locked up. I wondered that it should have concluded at length that this was the best use it could put me to, and had never thought to avail itself of my services in some way. I saw that, if there was a wall of stone between me and my townsmen, there was a still more difficult one to climb or break through before they could get to be as free as I was.

Is a democracy, such as we know it, the last improvement possible in government? Is it not possible to take a step further towards recognizing and organizing the rights of man? There will never be a really free and enlightened State until the State comes to recognize the individual as a higher and independent power, from which all its own power and authority are derived, and treats him accordingly.

Source: Civil Disobedience, by Henry David Thoreau. *[Online] Available http://www.cs.indiana. edu/statecraft/civ.dis.html (accessed on January 31, 2003).*

their words and moral convictions might now seem. Pro-war rallies were held in New York, Philadelphia, Baltimore, and other cities, and young men lined up to volunteer for military service—more, in fact, than were even needed. It had, after all, been several decades since the United States had fought Great Britain in the War of 1812, and the memories of suffering and bloodshed caused by that conflict and by the American Revolution (1775–83) seemed lost in the wave of patriotism that rolled over the land. But there was plenty of patriotism on the other side of the border, too, as the Mexicans prepared for what they considered a fight for land that belonged to them. The Mexican army was forty thousand strong and, despite incompetence among many of its officers and miserable conditions endured by its enlisted men, its soldiers would soon demonstrate their considerable courage and toughness. The fight ahead would be neither as short nor as easy as some U.S. citizens assumed.

For More Information

Books

Bauer, Karl J. *The Mexican War.* New York: Macmillan, 1974.

Downey, Fairfax. *Texas and the War with Mexico.* New York: American Heritage Publishing, 1961.

Eisenhower, John S. D. *So Far from God: The U.S. War with Mexico, 1846–1848.* New York: Random House, 1989.

Frazier, Donald, ed. *The United States and Mexico at War.* New York: Simon and Schuster, 1997.

Nardo, Don. *The Mexican-American War.* San Diego, CA: Lucent Books, 1991.

Nevin, David. *The Mexican War.* Alexandria, VA: Time-Life Books, 1978.

Zinn, Howard. *A People's History of the United States.* New York: Harper and Row, 1980.

Web Sites

PBS Online. *U.S.-Mexican War: 1846–1848.* [Online] Available http://www.pbs.org/kera/usmexicanwar/ (accessed on January 31, 2003).

The War Begins in Northern Mexico

On May 13, 1846, the United States officially declared war against Mexico. Although the war declaration stated that the United States was taking this step because American blood had been shed upon American soil, the real issue was the disputed territory of Texas. Despite the Mexicans' claim that this region belonged to them, the United States had annexed (made it a state) Texas in March 1845. And now the original boundary between Texas and Mexico, the Nueces River, also was part of the controversy, for the United States wanted the Rio Grande river, located much farther south inside Mexico, to form the boundary. The United States also hoped to acquire the Mexican territories of California and New Mexico, and would soon send part of its army marching in that direction.

The San Patricio Battalion

A vocal minority opposed the war with Mexico, but most U.S. citizens agreed with it. Young men were signing up in droves for what they expected to be a fairly harmless adventure that would be over quickly. The rugged frontier general known as "Old Rough and Ready," Zachary Taylor (1784–1850; see biographical entry), already was stationed with several thousand troops on the Rio Grande, just across from the Mexican town of Matamoros. They had been there for several months now, peering curiously across the narrow river at the Mexican citizens and soldiers on the other side. A few soldiers, however, went beyond looking and actually crossed the river.

In the middle of the nineteenth century, military service was not considered a top career choice by most U.S. citizens. In fact, it was often thought of as a last resort for those who could not find other jobs. As a matter of fact, 47 percent of army soldiers at this time were recent immigrants, who often faced prejudice and discrimination when seeking employment, but who could at least find refuge in the military. Of this percentage, many were Irishmen whose Catholic faith often set them apart and marked them for unfair treatment in a society that was predominantly Protestant.

Mexico, on the other hand, was a Catholic society. Mexican leaders were well aware of the situation of Irish soldiers in the U.S. Army. Knowing they might not feel as loyal to their new, adopted country as others, and hoping to lure them over the river to fight for Mexico, they managed to sneak flyers into the American encampment on the Rio Grande. Mexico offered a warm welcome to any and all deserters from the U.S. Army. Each of them was promised not only a chance to practice their faith freely but also more than 300 acres of free land on which to settle. More than two hundred men, most of them Irish, accepted this offer and swam the Rio Grande to Mexico. Led by former U.S. Army sergeant John Riley, these men would form the San Patricio Battalion (see biographical entry) and fight against their former U.S. comrades in several important battles of the war. Condemned as traitors by the United States, they were celebrated as heroes by the Mexican people and are still warmly remembered in Mexico.

The Battle of Palo Alto

On April 26, the first fight of the war—the one in which, supposedly, American blood had been shed upon American land—had taken place when a group of sixty-three

U.S. soldiers on a scouting mission had been attacked by Mexican troops. About three weeks later, war would be declared. Even before the official declaration was signed, however, two more significant battles would take place.

On May 1, Taylor marched about twenty-two hundred of his troops from Fort Texas (their base on the Rio Grande) to Point Isabel, a supply depot (a place where weapons, ammunition, and other supplies are stored) about 26 miles away. Hoping to catch Taylor on his return to Fort Texas, Mexican general Mariano Arista (1802–1855) moved his soldiers into position on the wide, flat plain, known as Palo Alto, that lay between Fort Texas and Port Isabel. There, on May 8, the two armies clashed.

The American cannons and "flying artillery" (a kind of light cannon mounted between two big wheels, which could be moved quickly and easily) let loose a deadly rain of fire on the Mexicans. The Mexican cannons, on the other hand, were ineffective because they were fired too low, so that the cannon-

An illustration of the Battle of Palo Alto, the first battle of the Mexican American War. *Photograph reproduced by permission of Getty Images.*

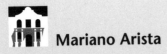

Mariano Arista

One of the highest ranking officers in the Mexican army at the start of the Mexican American War, the stocky, red-haired Mariano Arista played a prominent role in the first two battles of the conflict. He is often cited as an example of the weak leadership that contributed to Mexico's repeated battle losses, despite the fact that their troops far outnumbered that of the United States.

Born in the central Mexican town of San Luis Potosí, Mariano Arista joined the Spanish colonial army as a cadet (the lowest rank) when he was fifteen. A few years later, he joined the army of Agustín Iturbide, who was leading a revolt against Spanish rule. By 1821, the year that Mexico won its independence, Arista had reached the rank of lieutenant colonel. He was soon promoted to the rank of brigadier general in the new Mexican army.

Due to his participation in failed political rebellion in 1833, Arista spent three years in exile in the United States. He returned to Mexico in 1836 to serve under the dynamic general and leader Antonio Lopéz de Santa Anna, who had established himself as a conservative dictator. Arista regained his general's rank and served in various high military positions for the next few years.

Arista had retired from the military when, in 1846, the United States declared war on Mexico. President Manuel Paredes y Arillaga called him back into military service, giving him command of Mexico's Army of the North. By this time, the U.S. Army, led by General Zachary Taylor, had entered territory that both countries claimed as their own (the land between the Nueces River, which had been the traditional boundary between Texas and Mexico, and the Rio Grande river, located about 100 miles south).

General Pedro de Ampudia had been commanding the Mexican troops stationed at Matamoros, directly across from the fort that Taylor's troops had just built. Known for his harshness and cruelty, Ampudia was very unpopular with the people of Matamoros, so they requested a change of leadership. Paredes sent Arista to take over for Ampudia, who now became second in command. This resulted in constant quarreling between the two rival

balls tended to land well in front of the U.S. troops and roll harmlessly toward them, giving them time to dodge the attack. The Mexicans took very heavy losses throughout the day. Toward evening, the high, sharp-edged "saw" grass through which both armies had trudged caught fire, and resulted in a truce being called. In the morning, Taylor's men were surprised to see that Arista's soldiers had retreated from the battlefield.

offices, which helped to weaken the Mexican war effort.

The Mexican and U.S. armies met for the first time even before the U.S. war declaration had been signed. On May 8, Arista led an attack on Taylor's troops at Palo Alto. The United States had superior artillery (large guns, such as cannons) that was devastatingly effective, and the Mexicans were finally forced to retreat. They set up a new position at a place called Resaca de la Palma and another battle took place on May 9, but again the Mexicans were outgunned. Arista ordered a retreat to Matamoros, then quickly moved his army farther south.

These two disastrous battles were very discouraging to the Mexican leaders and public, and Arista took much of the blame. He had gone into the conflict with too much confidence in his own army, and too little regard for the U.S. troops. In addition, it was said that he had stayed away from the fighting, writing letters in his tent as the battles raged. Thus Santa Anna transferred command to General Francisco Mejía and had Arista court-martialed (called before a military court). At the trial, Arista successfully defended his actions and was excused from blame for the losses.

After the war, Arista became Mexico's Secretary of War and Marine Affairs. In 1850, he was elected president and was inaugurated in 1851 in the first peaceful transition of power the country had seen since independence. Like his predecessor, José Joaquín Herrera, Arista ruled as a moderate, and his administration was known for its honesty. But in 1853, Arista was forced from office when the Mexican army rebelled against him, and Santa Anna once again took power.

Now in poor health, Arista moved to Spain. In 1855, while traveling to France on an English steamboat, he died. He was buried in Spain but, according to his wishes, his heart was removed from his body and buried in Mexico. About twenty-five years later, Arista was declared a national hero and his remains were returned to his native country.

Sources: Crawford, Mark. Encyclopedia of the Mexican American War. *Santa Barbara: CA: American Bibliographical Center-Clio Press, 1998; Frazier, Donald, ed.* The United States and Mexico at War. *New York: Simon and Schuster, 1997.*

The two armies meet again at Resaca de la Palma

Historians would later claim that this early battle signaled the beginning of the end for Mexico's Army of the North, exposing their weaknesses. Even though the Mexican army was made up of much greater numbers, the soldiers used cannons and ammunition that were of poorer quality than those on the U.S. side, and the Mexican guns were older and less effective. Despite the considerable skills of the Mexican cavalry (soldiers mounted on horseback), their horses were not as big and strong as those used by the U.S. cavalry, and the Mexican horses did not hold up as well in battle. According to U.S. reports, the Mexicans sustained four hundred casualties (those killed, wounded, or missing) at the Battle of Palo Alto, while the United States had less than ten men killed and about forty wounded. However, among those ten killed was Major Sam Ringgold (1800–1846), the man who, eight years earlier, had championed the idea of the flying artillery and who had trained two battalions in its use.

The two armies met again the next day at a place called Resaca de la Palma, about 5 miles south of Palo Alto. Arista had taken his troops to this spot, hoping that the rugged terrain and dense, thorny brush, which the Mexicans called chaparral, would keep the U.S. troops at bay. Nevertheless, Taylor's troops attacked, engaging in what soon became hand-to-hand combat, in which men used knives and bayonets rather than longer-range weapons. The Mexicans stubbornly resisted the attack, but were finally pushed back. The U.S. soldiers overran the Mexican camp and carried off all the cannons and supplies as well as six hundred mules and hundreds of muskets (the old-fashioned kind of gun used by the Mexicans). More tragically, the Mexicans had lost more than eight hundred men, while only about one hundred U.S. soldiers were killed.

Taylor's reputation for coolness under fire was reinforced when it was reported that at one point during the fighting, when urged to take cover, he had said, "Let us ride a little nearer [to the enemy]. The balls will fall behind us." According to Fairfax Downey's book, *Texas and the War with Mexico*, a popular song also honored the U.S. victory, and Taylor's role in it: "In the thickest of the fight old Zachary appeared. / The shot flew about him as thick as any hail. / And the only injury he there received / Was a compound fracture of his brown coat tail."

A week later, Taylor took control of the town of Matamoros, from which the Mexican troops had already fled. Now the United States was firmly in control of the disputed land between the Nueces and the Rio Grande rivers. However, while the action in northern Mexico would settle down for a time, things were heating up in California.

Californians rebel against Mexico

During the three centuries in which Mexico was ruled by Spain, the area that is now the state of California was called *alta* (upper) California while the lower part (which is still part of Mexico) was called *baja* (lower) California. Mexican colonists had proved somewhat reluctant to settle in the remote alta California region, which featured a wide variety of terrains, from desert to fertile valley to forested mountains. By the nineteenth century, there was a network of missions and forts strung along the Pacific Coast between San Francisco and San Diego, but only about eight thousand Mexicans living in scattered communities.

In the decades leading up to the Mexican American War, U.S. settlers were moving by the thousands into the western territory acquired through the Louisiana Purchase (the agreement by which the United States bought 800,000 square miles of land from France). They also were moving beyond that area into the Oregon Territory, the boundaries of which were still being disputed with Great Britain. Some of these settlers recognized the rich potential of the land just south of Oregon, and they began to trickle into California in small numbers.

By the time of the Mexican American War, there were about seven hundred U.S. citizens living in California, most of them without Mexico's official consent. News of the conflict developing in Texas and northern Mexico troubled them deeply, for the Mexican government already was hostile to them and a war would only make things worse. Determined to hold on to their land, a group of U.S. citizens living in the Sacramento Valley (east of San Francisco) banded together with some *Californios* (California residents of Mexican descent) who also were unhappy with their government. In June 1847, they launched a rebellion against Mexico.

Three Women of the Mexican American War

Sarah Borginnis

Not much is known about the early life of this woman, who was born Sarah Knight in Tennessee or Missouri in 1812. It is thought that as a young woman she married a soldier in the U.S. Army, traveling with him as wives often did in those days, cooking his meals and washing clothing for both him and other soldiers. Remembered as a strong woman who stood six feet, two inches tall, Borginnis was nicknamed "the Great Western" after a famous steamship of the period.

What is definitely known about Borginnis is that she was with the troops of General Zachary Taylor when they were sent first to Corpus Christi, Texas, and then to the Rio Grande in the disputed Mexican territory. During the early battles of Palo Alto and Resaca de la Palma, the Mexicans also were bombarding nearby Fort Texas. Reportedly issued a gun, Borginnis was among the fort's defenders. She also nursed the wounded, and set up a tent to serve food and coffee to the soldiers. At one point, it is said, a bullet pierced the bonnet she wore on her head, while another knocked a tray out of her hands.

Borginnis also was present at the Battle of Buena Vista. In honor of her bravery and contributions, Taylor made her a brevet (honorary) colonel, the first woman to receive this rank from the U.S. Army. In the years following the war, Borginnis married and lost a series of husbands and operated hotels or taverns in Texas and New Mexico.

She ended her life in Yuma, California, where she may have worked as a prostitute. She died in 1866 of complications from a tarantula bite, and was buried with full military honors in the Fort Yuma cemetery.

Ann Chase

Called by some the "heroine of Tampico," Ann Chase served as a spy for the United States during the Mexican American War.

Born in 1809 in northern Ireland, Chase lived in the United States for ten years before marrying Franklin Chase, a merchant who was serving as the U.S. Consul (government representative) in the coastal city of Tampico, Mexico. When the United States declared war against Mexico in 1846, all U.S. citizens were required to leave Mexico. Her husband returned to the United States, but because of her British citizenship, Ann Chase was able to remain in Tampico to run the family's trading company.

Chase's house was located on the same plaza as the Mexican army barracks and she often overheard comments and statements from military officials. Sometime around July 1846, she started reporting what she heard to the U.S. Navy Gulf Squadron, which had ships positioned off the Mexican coast. These messages were probably delivered by British naval officers.

In November 1846, the United States captured Tampico. Chase played a key role in this event by providing a plan of the port as well as information on the fortifications (protective systems) the Mexicans had in place. Visited by a Mexican who she believed was a spy, she deliberately gave the man misinformation, telling him that the United States would soon invade with up to thirty thousand troops. This led to the Mexicans evacuating their troops from Tampico, at which point Chase sent word that the U.S. forces could now easily take the town. On November 14, Chase flew an American flag from her roof as the United States conducted its bloodless capture of Tampico.

Susana Dickinson

The only adult Anglo (white) survivor of the Mexican attack on the Alamo, Susana Dickinson was born Susana Wilkerson in Tennessee around 1814. When she was fifteen, she married Almaron Dickinson, and in the early 1830s she moved with him to join the colony of U.S. settlers at Gonzales, Texas. Her daughter Angelina was born in 1834.

In the fall of 1835, determined to establish Texas as an independent republic, the residents of Gonzales chased the Mexican army from their town. Dickinson's husband subsequently left to join the volunteers gathered at San Antonio; she and Angelina joined him a few months later. When news arrived that the army of Mexican general Antonio López de Santa Anna was on its way to San Antonio, the Dickinsons and other volunteers moved into the Alamo, an old Spanish mission.

The Mexicans attacked on March 6, 1836, killing all of the Alamo's 189 defenders. On the day of the attack Dickinson had been nursing Jim Bowie, a famed frontiersman and leader of the volunteers, who had fallen ill with pneumonia and who was killed in his sickbed. One of very few inside the Alamo who were allowed to live, Dickinson was questioned by Santa Anna and released. Carrying her baby, she made her way toward Gonzales and was picked up by Texas scouts. Arriving in the town, Dickinson informed Sam Houston, leader of the Texan army, of the massacre at the Alamo.

Twenty-two years old, illiterate, and now a widow, Dickinson was denied a request for a $500 donation from the Texas government. In late 1837, she married Francis Williams, but the two divorced the following spring. Dickinson went through three more husbands before achieving a stable marriage with Joseph Harnig in 1857. She died in Austin, Texas, in 1883.

Sources: Frazier, Donald, ed. The United States and Mexico at War. New York: Simon and Schuster, 1997; Nevin, David. The Mexican War. Alexandria, VA: Time-Life Books, 1978; "Susana Dickinson (1814–1883)." Lone Star Junction. [Online] Available http://www.lsjunction.com/people/dickinson.htm (accessed on January 31, 2003); Women Were There: The Wars of 1812 and 1846 and the Spanish American War. [Online] Available http://userpages.aug.com/captbarb/ femvets3.html (accessed on January 31, 2003).

John Charles Frémont aided the "Bear Flaggers" in their quest for independence from Mexico. *Photograph courtesy of The Library of Congress.*

Frémont aids the Bear Flaggers

As it happened, an ambitious and dynamic U.S. Army officer, Colonel John Charles Frémont (1813–1890; see biographical entry), was in the area at this time. A member of a branch of the army called the U.S. Topographical Engineers, he had led sixty men on a westward expedition to explore and survey the region. Even though Frémont had not been officially authorized by the U.S. government to do so (although some historians believe he may have been sent on some sort of secret mission to aid the Californians), he offered the settlers not only the support of his troops but himself as leader of their rebellion. Naming themselves the "Bear Flaggers" because of the flag they had adopted (which featured a single star, a grizzly bear, and the words "California Republic"), the group easily and bloodlessly took control of the area, declared themselves an independent nation, and established a government in Sonoma.

Meanwhile, a squadron of U.S. Navy forces were hovering off the coast of California under the command of Commodore John D. Sloat (1781–1867), who had been ordered to guard American interests in California. Learning of the Bear Flag Rebellion and assuming that Frémont's actions must have been ordered by the U.S. government, Sloat moved to block all of the major ports along the California coast. On July 7, his forces took command of the cities of San Francisco and Monterey, then worked their way south to occupy Santa Barbara, San Pedro, and San Diego.

U.S. forces take Los Angeles

When Sloat finally met with Frémont, he was shocked and greatly troubled to learn that Frémont had not been authorized by the U.S. government to lead a rebellion in California. Soon after meeting with Frémont, Sloat became too ill to continue his command. He was replaced by Commodore Robert F. Stockton (1795–1866), who had no qualms about continuing with the naval operations already underway. With the help of the Bear Flaggers, now renamed the California Battalion, Stockton's forces took control of Los Angeles on August 13. These U.S. sailors, now performing the same duties that would normally be the role of infantry soldiers, began to build forts and set up governments in all of California's major coastal towns.

Meanwhile, the Mexicans were organizing their own small but formidable resistance to U.S. occupation in California. Along with General José Castro (c. 1810–1860), California's governor Pío Pico (1801–1894) quickly organized an army from among the pro-Mexican forces in the area, particularly around Los Angeles. This task was made easier because the U.S. officer put in charge of Los Angeles, Lieutenant Archibald Gillespie (1812–1873), had made himself very unpopular by forcing the city's residents to follow a number of harsh rules. On September 29, General José María Flores led less than one hundred Californios in successfully recapturing Los Angeles from the forty-eight U.S. troops who had been left to defend it.

General Kearny travels west

At around the same time that the Bear Flag Rebellion was taking place in California, General Stephen W. Kearny

California governor Pío Pico helped to organize a small but formidable resistance to the U.S. occupation of California. *Photograph reproduced by permission of the Granger Collection.*

(1794–1848; see biographical entry) was in Fort Leavenworth, Kansas, preparing what would be called the Army of the West to march toward the Pacific Ocean. Soon after war with Mexico was declared, Kearny had been ordered to open another front (area of conflict or fighting) farther west. The United States was intent on expanding its boundaries to include California and New Mexico as well as Texas, and they needed this extra front to secure those lands.

By July, Kearny had gathered an army of about fifteen hundred, most of them rugged veterans of frontier life and not actual military experience. They set out for their first goal, Santa Fe, and moved quickly, despite intense summer heat and difficult, dusty terrain. Sometimes covering as many as 30 miles per day, they marched 1,000 miles in six weeks, reaching Santa Fe on August 18. The town's Mexican defenders had fled as soon as they heard that U.S. troops were approaching, so Kearny took the town with no resistance. Proclaiming himself governor of New Mexico, Kearny announced that its eighty thousand inhabitants were now U.S. citizens. As a gesture of goodwill towards the residents, Kearny hosted a ball a few days later that was attended by five hundred people.

Kearny did not, however, spend much time dancing in Santa Fe. His next goal was California. Getting there through territory that had rarely been traveled would not be easy. Soon after leaving Santa Fe, Kearny ran into the famous frontier scout Christopher "Kit" Carson (1809–1868) and hired him as a guide. Although Kearny had set out with three hundred men, he sent two hundred of them back to Santa Fe after Carson told Kearny that Stockton had control of the situation in California. Kearny would later regret this decision, however.

Doniphan's amazing journey

Kearny's occupation force at Santa Fe included the First Regiment of Missouri Mounted Volunteers, led by Colonel Alexander Doniphan (1808–1887). As he was departing for California, Kearny ordered Doniphan and his troops to march south from Santa Fe to Chihuahua in order to help secure that part of northern Mexico. Despite their lack of military experience, this group of tough, determined volunteers clad in buckskins (the simple clothing made of deerskin that many frontier residents wore) made the difficult journey in good time and with little trouble. At Brazito, about halfway to Chihuahua, they were surprised by a huge force of Mexican troops but defeated them in less than an hour. The Mexicans suffered about two hundred casualties, including fifty men killed, while Doniphan's force had only seven wounded. Close to Chihuahua, Doniphan and his men fought and won another battle at which they were outnumbered three to one, killing three hundred Mexican soldiers and losing only three of their own. After the war, Doniphan and his Missourians became famous for having trekked an incredible 3,600 miles during the war, and for proving what effective soldiers volunteers could be.

The fight for Los Angeles

Kearny reached California in early December, still unaware of the turn of events at Los Angeles. When he met with representatives of Gillespie's force and found out that the Mexicans had retaken that town, Kearny regretted having sent two-thirds of his original expedition back to Santa Fe. Nevertheless, he immediately marched his small force into action, attacking Californio troops under Pico at San Pascual. Exhausted by their journey, Kearny's soldiers did not perform well and the battle was a disaster for the Americans, with eighteen killed and about the same number wounded, including both Kearny and Gillespie. None of Pico's troops were killed.

Retreating to San Diego, Kearny joined his forces with the sailors and marines under Stockton, as well as about four hundred men led by Frémont, who had just arrived from Monterey, and spent the next few weeks preparing to take

Doniphan's Incredible Journey

One of the most celebrated leaders of the Mexican American War, Alexander Doniphan led the First Regiment of Mounted Missouri Volunteers on an incredible land and sea journey that covered more than 5,000 miles and included two battles.

Born in Kentucky in 1808, Alexander Doniphan was the son of a Revolutionary War (1775–83) veteran. In 1830, Doniphan moved to Missouri and established a law practice. Big and tall with reddish hair, a ready smile, a calm manner and a good sense of humor, he won many friends. Known for maintaining a moderate stance on controversial issues, Doniphan served three terms in Missouri's state legislature.

In May 1846, when the Mexican American War began, Missouri's governor asked Doniphan to organize a military unit of volunteers (due to the relatively small size of the U.S. Army, Congress had authorized the calling up of fifty thousand volunteer soldiers to help fight the war). Doniphan enlisted eleven hundred men, who elected him to the rank of colonel even though he had signed up as a private (the lowest rank). Doniphan immediately marched his men to Fort Leavenworth, Kansas, where General Stephen W. Kearny was assembling the Army of the West and preparing to march into and conquer New Mexico and California.

Like their leader, most of Doniphan's regiment had little or no military experience, but they were tough veterans of frontier life. With their mismatched uniforms and casual attitude toward military discipline, they did not much look or act like soldiers, but they were ready for whatever might lie ahead. After a brief two-week training period, they set out with Kearny in early June to Santa Fe, New Mexico, a journey of nearly 1,000 miles across a harsh, desert landscape that was made even more difficult by a shortage of food and water. Kearny's army arrived at Santa Fe on August 18 and easily occupied the town, since its Mexican defenders had already fled.

Over the next month, Kearny had to establish a civil government and set of laws for New Mexico. Doniphan's legal background proved helpful for this task, and he was the main author of the territory's new constitution and laws. In late September, Kearny departed for California, leaving Doniphan in charge of the military forces still in Santa Fe.

In December, Doniphan was ordered to proceed with his regiment to Chihuahua, Mexico, where they were to meet up with troops under General John E. Wool. The first stop on their three-month journey was El Paso del Norte (now the city of Juarez, Mexico), which they reached by taking a shortcut across a treacherous 95-mile wide desert called the Jornada del Muerte (Journey of Death).

On Christmas Day, when about half of Doniphan's regiment (the group

Alexander Doniphan. *Photograph reproduced by permission of Getty Images.*

had been split and traveled by two different routes) was 30 miles north of El Paso del Norte, they heard that Mexican troops were approaching. They quickly organized themselves into defensive positions, from which they were able to defeat a Mexican force of about twelve hundred. The Mexicans suffered two hundred casualties in the battle, while Doniphan's force had only seven men wounded and none killed. Doniphan' regiment took control of El Paso del Norte on December 27.

Learning that Wool had given up the plan to meet in Chihuahua, Doniphan decided to proceed there anyway. The regiment set out on February 8, marching south through deep sand, surviving on very little water, and fighting off prairie fires along the way. When they were 15 miles north of Chihuahua near the Rio Sacramento ranch, they fought another battle against a much larger Mexican force. Again the casualties were lopsided, with the Mexicans losing six hundred men to death or injury, while only one U.S. soldier was killed and eleven wounded.

Having occupied Chihuahua on March 2, Doniphan's regiment was ordered to return to the United States. After a 750-mile march to the coastal town of Matamoros, they boarded ships that carried them to New Orleans, then took steamboats up the Mississippi River to Missouri. The regiment had made a circular journey of 5,500 miles, enduring many hardships without complaint and winning two battles in which they were far outnumbered. They were famous both at home and across the rest of the United States. Doniphan was acclaimed as a great leader, but he never used his celebrity to gain political office, as other heroes of the Mexican American War had done. Instead he settled near St. Louis and spent the rest of his career as a lawyer and bank president. He died in 1887.

Sources: Crawford, Mark. Encyclopedia of the Mexican American War. *Santa Barbara, CA: American Bibliographical Center-Clio Press, 1998; Frazier, Donald, ed.* The United States and Mexico at War. *New York: Simon and Schuster, 1997; Launius, Roger D.* Alexander William Doniphan: Portrait of a Missouri Moderate. *Columbia: University of Missouri Press, 1997.*

control of Los Angeles again. On January 7, at San Luis Rey, the U.S. troops managed to fend off an attack by Flores's force of about five hundred. The next day, the two armies met again at La Mesa and the United States again emerged victorious. At this point the small Californio force was fatally weakened, and Kearny's troops met no resistance when they marched into and occupied Los Angeles. In a controversial action typical of his career, Frémont took the liberty of negotiating a surrender with Flores, whom he encountered in San Luis Obispo as the Mexican general was trying to escape to the north. Frémont had no authority to negotiate this treaty, but since it was already signed it was deemed acceptable, even though it was unusually favorable to the Mexicans, demanding only that they stop fighting.

Friction between Kearny and Frémont

Although there were no more battles in California between Mexico and the United States, another conflict was now developing there among the U.S. leaders. Kearny had orders from President James K. Polk designating Kearny as governor of California, but Stockton, who was about to leave California for Mexico, ignored these orders and named Frémont governor. Kearny kept quiet in order to avoid trouble, but soon new orders arrived from Washington, D.C., that clearly designated Kearny as the man in charge of California until its people were ready to govern themselves. Much to Frémont's dismay and anger, Kearny took charge of the California Battalion, which soon disbanded after most of its members resigned.

In the summer of 1847, after the war was over, Kearny and Frémont returned to Washington, D.C., where the latter was court-martialed (tried in a military court) for his actions during the war, including disregarding the orders of his superior officers. Frémont was found guilty. Pardoned by Polk, Frémont nevertheless resigned from the army. Although he would go on to become one of California's first two senators and even run for president of the United States, Frémont never really recovered from what he viewed as an unfair turn of events. Meanwhile, he watched as Kearny received all the credit for conquering California.

PORTRAIT OF SANTA ANNA IN MILITARY COSTUME.

Santa Anna returns to power

Frémont might have looked to General Antonio López de Santa Anna (1794–1876; see biographical entry) for an example of how to bounce back from adversity. Exiled to Cuba after the humiliating defeat at the Battle of San Jacinto, when the small but scrappy army of the Republic of Texas had not only beaten the Mexican forces but captured Santa Anna himself, the dynamic Mexican general was on the comeback trail. And he was being helped, at least at first, by the United States government. After the disastrous battles of Palo Alto and Resaca de la Palma, Mexican president Mariano Paredes y Arrillaga (1797–1849) became very unpopular. In July, Paredes was taken prisoner after part of the Mexican army staged a rebellion against his administration. Mexico was once again in desperate need of leadership. Sensing an opportunity to regain power, Santa Anna convinced Polk that

General Antonio López de Santa Anna returning to Mexico with two aides after being exiled to Cuba.
Photograph reproduced by permission of the Corbis Corporation.

if the United States would allow him to travel back to Mexico, he would take over the presidency and begin peace talks immediately. He also promised to sell the United States the disputed territory for $30 million. The fact that Polk agreed to Santa Anna's proposal is a testament to the persuasiveness of this flamboyant man.

Santa Anna arrived in Mexico City in September and soon installed himself as president. Instead of starting peace talks with the United States, however, Santa Anna began to put together a huge army, which he based at the town of San Luis Potosí. He spent the next several months gathering together what would be a force of twenty-five thousand men, not an easy task when they had not only to be fed and equipped, but also outfitted in fancy uniforms. (In fact, more money was actually spent on the uniforms.) It was not until February 1847 that Santa Anna would send his troops on a 300-mile march to the Battle of Buena Vista, where they would have a disastrous encounter with the U.S. Army.

U.S. troops prepare for more battles

News of the victories at Palo Alto and Resaca de la Palma reached the United States in late May, bringing relief and excitement to a population that was still unsure about the enemy it faced and what the outcome of the war might be. Now, most people were sure that the United States would win the war. Taylor not only became a hero to the general public but received a promotion to the rank of major general. Military recruiting officers were flooded with volunteers. The volunteer units received little training and elected their own leaders, often basing their decisions on factors other than military skill or experience. The realities of fighting in Mexico would turn out to be much harsher than most had expected, and many would quit as soon as their short terms of service were finished. Still, many of the volunteers were generally men who had grown up on the frontier. They were used to hardship, and they knew how to handle guns. As a result, they turned out to be fairly good soldiers.

The biggest risk that U.S. troops faced was not bullets or cannonballs. It was disease. Of the nearly thirteen thousand U.S. deaths resulting from the Mexican American War,

only about seventeen hundred came in battle. More than eleven thousand men died from infectious diseases that included malaria, yellow fever, typhoid, cholera, measles, mumps, smallpox, and dysentery. Even more died after returning to their homes. In addition to the poor sanitary conditions and the threat of sickness, soldiers had to face difficult journeys either by ship, in which case they were packed like sardines in small spaces, or on foot through dust, heat, or even torrential rains.

Given these conditions, perhaps it is understandable that there was a lot of rowdy behavior in Matamoros, where fourteen thousand U.S. soldiers were stationed in the summer of 1847. Much to the dismay of the veteran army officers, the troops, especially the volunteers, did a lot of drinking, gambling, and fighting. Members of the regular army considered the volunteers an undisciplined, ill-behaved group, while the volunteers sneered at the regulars for acting superior.

U.S. soldiers washing clothes in a military camp. Because the living conditions in the camp were so unsanitary, many more soldiers died from diseases than from actual battle injuries. *Photograph reproduced by permission of the Granger Collection.*

The Soldiers' Lives: Not What They Expected!

Before the Mexican American War began, the U.S. Army numbered only about eighty-six hundred officers and soldiers. Because the military profession was not much respected by most U.S. citizens, becoming a soldier was often a last resort for those who could not find other jobs. Thus about 40 percent of the army was made up of recent immigrants, who often were discriminated against when it came to finding work.

When the United States declared war on its southern neighbor, however, it suddenly became desirable, and maybe even fashionable, to join the military. Congress was immediately authorized to call up fifty thousand volunteers, and young men signed up in droves. They were inspired to join the military by the prospect of defending their country against what they considered foreign aggression. They also were attracted to the idea of traveling to an exotic place and enjoying, what they envisioned to be the romantic and adventurous life of a soldier. Many of the men who signed up had never been away from home before.

The realities of military service

The young men who enlisted in the military were in for a big surprise when they finally received their orders. The first troops began arriving in Texas and northeastern Mexico in early 1846, camping first at Corpus Christi on the Nueces River (the traditional border between Texas and Mexico) and later moving south to the Rio Grande river, which the United States was now claiming as the border. It was not long before the realities of military service in this difficult environment began to emerge.

These realities included harsh weather—that included either stifling heat or driving rain—dust, and insects. The soldiers' food was generally bad, and their tents inadequate for the climate and terrain. Army discipline was harsh and in some cases even cruel, especially as tensions arose between volunteers and "regulars," the term used for professional soldiers. Waiting around for battles to begin was boring. When ordered to march, soldiers had to carry 30 pounds or more of gear on their backs over a landscape that featured jagged rocks, treacherous ditches and holes, and sharp saw-grass. Of course, when the soldiers began to fight a whole new set of realities confronted them, for they were surrounded by the terror, confusion, blood, and pain that occur in all wars.

Disease takes a high toll

Perhaps the worst hardship faced by troops who served in the Mexican American War was illness. While a little more than fifteen hundred soldiers and officers were killed in battle, another eleven thousand or so lost their lives to various diseases. In addition, ten thousand men were discharged from the army with various types of medical conditions, and many of these probably died in the months following the war. Both the ignorance of individual soldiers—especially the volunteers, who had little or no military experience—about how to take care of themselves under difficult conditions and unsanitary camp conditions led to widespread disease.

Use of the same water for drinking, cooking, and bathing created ideal conditions for the spread of water-born diseases like cholera and typhoid fever. In the swampy coastal areas, malaria (which no one yet realized was spread by mosquitoes) and dengue fever were common and, all across the country, the men also contracted yellow fever, dysentery, measles, mumps, smallpox and tuberculosis.

Once a soldier was sick or wounded, he was not assured of proper medical care. Doctors and other medical staff were in short supply and often poorly trained. They were sorely overworked, especially in the heat of battle, and lacked both adequate supplies and knowledge of effective techniques. Thus men waited long periods for attention, damaged limbs were often hastily amputated, and instruments were used for many patients without being cleaned. Medical staff often used old-fashioned treatments, like bleeding and blistering, which not only did not help but increased the suffering and sped up the deaths of many sick and wounded men.

Mexican soldiers face even worse hardships

Mexican soldiers endured even worse conditions than those in the U.S. Army. While most officers in the Mexican army came from the ranks of the country's wealthy *criollos,* (those of pure Spanish ancestry), most of the regular troops were poor *mestizos* (people of mixed Spanish and Native American heritage) or Indians. The wide disparity between officers, many of whom displayed much more concern for gaining personal glory than for the welfare and comfort of their troops, and soldiers created an atmosphere of distrust and resentment.

Punishments for misdeeds both great and small were harsh. Food, pay, medical care, and even uniforms were scarce and sometimes nonexistent. In fact, the Mexican army depended very much for its survival on a group of women called *soldaderas,* made up of soldiers' wives, sisters, and girlfriends, who fed and nursed the men and kept their clothing and quarters clean. These women also took part in battles, and the U.S. troops were shocked to find their bodies among the dead.

Despite these conditions, the Mexican army fought with remarkable bravery. In their view, the United States had a deep hatred for the Mexican culture and especially for the Catholic religion, the state religion of Mexico. The Mexicans also believed that the United States had invaded their country and meant to bring it into submission. However, the Mexican soldiers were not going to let that happen without a fight. It is true that most U.S. troops did, indeed, have a low opinion of the Mexican people, and they were surprised by the courage that the Mexicans displayed on the battlefields.

Sources: Frazier, Donald, ed. The United States and Mexico at War. *New York: Simon and Schuster, 1997; Nardo, Don.* The Mexican-American War. *San Diego, CA: Lucent Books, 1991.*

An illustration of the Battle of Monterrey. Among the U.S. soldiers taking part in this grueling three-day battle were several men who would later gain fame as generals and leaders during the American Civil War. *Photograph reproduced by permission of Getty Images.*

The Battle of Monterrey

Meanwhile, U.S. government leaders were assessing the war situation to determine their next step. They agreed that to achieve their goal of acquiring a large piece of Mexican territory, they would have to strike at the heart of Mexico: its capital, Mexico City. The very experienced and competent General Winfield Scott (1786–1866; see biographical entry) would take a leading role in that effort. For the time being, however, Taylor focused his efforts on targets closer to his own army. The first was the town of Monterrey, located about 100 miles south of the Rio Grande.

Taylor headed toward Monterrey with 6,640 troops, arriving on September 21, in the middle of a heavy rainstorm. They were met by more than 5,000 Mexican soldiers under the command of Major General Pedro de Ampudia (1805–1868), who had been ordered to defend the town. The U.S. Army went into battle with a low opinion of the enemy's fighting spirit and ability, and they were surprised when the Mexicans fiercely resisted giving up Monterrey. The U.S. forces had to overrun two strongly fortified hills as well as a formidable building called the Bishop's Palace that stood just outside the city. Once they had done that, they had to wage a hand-to-hand fight toward the central plaza, with people firing at them continuously from rooftops and windows. Among the U.S. soldiers taking part in this grueling three-day battle were several men who would later gain fame as generals and leaders on both the Confederate and Union sides of the American Civil War (1861–65). These men included Jefferson Davis (1808–1889), Ulysses S. Grant (1822–1885), George Gordon Meade (1815–1872), and Albert Sidney Johnston (1803–1862). The U.S. Army deserters who made up Mexico's San Patricio Battalion also were present at the battle, heading an artillery attack against their former comrades.

A group of people on the porch of a hotel reading about the brutal behavior of U.S. soldiers in Monterrey. *Photograph courtesy of The Library of Congress.*

U.S. soldiers behave brutally in Monterrey

Finally, amid fears that the U.S. forces would soon begin blowing up Monterrey's churches, the city surrendered. On the U.S. side, 128 soldiers had been killed and 368 wounded, while the Mexicans reported 430 total casualties (killed, wounded, and missing). In a treaty agreement that seemed too lenient to some people, the Mexican troops were allowed to march out of the city with their horses and small arms (pistols and other personal guns) and an eight-week ceasefire was declared. After the Mexican troops had left, one of the most shameful incidents of the war occurred, as U.S. soldiers began to run wild through the city. They burned homes, stole goods, raped women, and even killed some civilians before their officers could get them under control.

These brutalities were reported in U.S. newspapers, causing widespread revulsion and sparking renewed protests against the war. In the *Liberator,* a newspaper founded by abolitionist (a person who fights for an end to slavery) William Lloyd Garrison, an editorial condemned this as a conflict "of aggression, of invasion, of conquest, and rapine—marked by ruffianism and other features of national depravity." Taylor admitted that some horrible things had happened, but pointed out that his soldiers had themselves endured very harsh conditions and fierce, brutal fighting. No, he admitted, this did not excuse their behavior, but at the same time, he took no disciplinary action against them.

Despite the misgivings of a minority of war protesters in the United States, Taylor's army had now brought northern Mexico under stronger U.S. control. After the next major battle, which would take place at Buena Vista in five months, the stage would be set for a total U.S. victory over Mexico.

For More Information

Books

Bauer, Karl J. *The Mexican War.* New York: Macmillan, 1974.

Butler, Stephen R. *A Documentary History of the War with Mexico 1846–1848.* Richardson, TX: Descendents of Mexican War Veterans, 1994.

Butler, Stephen R., and Lawrence R. Clayton. *The March to Monterrey: The Diary of Lt. Rankin Dilworth.* El Paso: The University of Texas at El Paso, 1996.

Downey, Fairfax. *Texas and the War with Mexico.* New York: American Heritage Publishing, 1961.

Eisenhower, John S. D. *So Far from God: The U.S. War with Mexico, 1846–1848.* New York: Random House, 1989.

Ferrell, Robert H., ed. *Monterrey is Ours! The Mexican War Letters of Lieutenant Dana, 1845–1847.* Lexington: University Press of Kentucky, 1990.

Frazier, Donald, ed. *The United States and Mexico at War.* New York: Simon and Schuster, 1997.

Hogan, Michael. *The Irish Soldiers of Mexico.* Guadalajara, Mexico: Fondo Editorial Universitario, 1997.

Miller, Robert Ryal. *Shamrock and Sword: The St. Patrick's Battalion in the U.S.-Mexican War.* Norman: University of Oklahoma Press, 1989.

Nardo, Don. *The Mexican-American War.* San Diego, CA: Lucent Books, 1991.

Nevin, David. *The Mexican War.* Alexandria, VA: Time-Life Books, 1978.

Zinn, Howard. *A People's History of the United States.* New York: Harper and Row, 1980.

Web Sites

Descendants of Mexican War Veterans. *The U.S.-Mexican War: 1846–1848.* [Online] Available http://www.dmwv.org/mexwar/mexwar1.htm (accessed on January 31, 2003).

The Mexican-American War Memorial Homepage. [Online] Available http://sunsite.unam.mx/revistas/1847/Summa.html (accessed on January 31, 2003).

PBS Online. *U.S.-Mexican War: 1846–1848.* [Online] Available http://www.pbs.org/kera/usmexicanwar/ (accessed on January 31,2003).

The Conquest of Mexico City

Eager to expand into the Mexican territories of Texas, California, and New Mexico, and using the excuse that Mexico had shed American blood in the U.S. state of Texas (though Mexico did not recognize it as part of the United States), the United States declared war against Mexico in March 1846. In the months that followed, U.S. troops under General Zachary Taylor (1784–1850; see biographical entry) won several battles against much larger Mexican forces. They were proving that regular army soldiers and volunteers could work together to produce victories. Nevertheless, the war was far from over.

After tricking the U.S. government into allowing him to return to Mexico from Cuba, where he had been exiled, the dynamic Mexican general Antonio López de Santa Anna (1794–1876; see biographical entry) had gone back on his promise to make peace with the United States. Instead, he had taken over as president of Mexico and gone straight to work on building up the Mexican army. Far from planning peace with the enemy, Santa Anna was promising his people that he would crush the U.S. invaders, whom the Mexicans viewed as brutal, faithless people bent on destroying the Mexican culture and especially the Roman Catholic religion.

General Winfield Scott to lead invasion

U.S. president James K. Polk (1795–1849; see biographical entry) and his advisors were convinced that to win the war, the United States must strike at the heart of Mexico by gaining control of the country's capital, Mexico City. Taylor had achieved much success in the interior reaches of northeastern Mexico, but now Polk turned to a different general to lead the push toward Mexico City.

General Winfield Scott (1786–1866; see biographical entry) was commander-in-chief of the U.S. Army and a much-respected veteran of the War of 1812 (1812–14) as well as several major struggles against Native Americans. He was the author of *Infantry Tactics*, the army's first manual for training soldiers, and he was an expert in military strategy. A tall, strong man of sixty-one, Scott was nicknamed "Old Fuss and Feathers" because he believed in proper dress, formal manners, and strict discipline. He could not have been more different from Taylor, who dressed like a farmer and often reviewed his troops while slouching casually on his horse. It is not surprising that the two generals disliked each other intensely.

Part of their dislike was political. Both were ambitious men who had their eyes on the U.S. presidency. This put Polk in a difficult position, too, because Scott and Taylor were members of the Whig political party, while Polk was a Democrat. Either or both of these generals could become big heroes through their actions in this war, which could put the Whigs back in the White House. Polk would have much preferred to use military leaders from his own party, but none were available. All he could do was hope that neither Scott

General Winfield Scott was chosen to lead the invasion of Mexico City, which the United States needed to capture in order to end the war. *Photograph courtesy of The Library of Congress.*

nor Taylor gained enough glory to get himself elected president after the war.

Scott was to lead an invasion of Mexico City that would begin from the coastal city of Vera Cruz, Mexico's most important port, located 200 miles east of the capital. He planned an amphibious assault (with forces arriving by both water and land) that would turn out to be the largest such operation conducted before World War II (1941–45). To succeed, Scott would need to use some of the troops currently serving under Taylor, so in January 1847, Taylor received an order to transfer most of his regular soldiers and some of his volunteers to Scott's army. Taylor was dismayed, for his army was now reduced by about half to between five and six thousand soldiers, and he would be facing the enemy sooner than Scott. In February 1847, Taylor began pushing his army westward into the interior of Mexico, where the Sierra Madre mountains lay.

The Battle of Buena Vista

Meanwhile, Santa Anna had an army of twenty thousand based at San Luis Potosí, located about 250 miles south of Saltillo, which Taylor's forces had occupied in November 1846. When a U.S. letter was intercepted, Santa Anna learned about Scott's attack plan and also that Taylor's troops had been reduced. Hungry for a victory in northeastern Mexico before he turned his attention to Scott's planned invasion, Santa Anna decided that this would be a good time to attack Taylor. Thus, he marched his army north, losing about five thousand of his men along the way to disease and desertion.

The two armies would meet in an area of very rugged terrain about 150 miles south of Monterrey. The road on which Taylor's troops were traveling went through a narrow pass near a ranch called Buena Vista that would give its name to the battle fought here. There were mountains on one side of the pass and impassible gullies (ditches) on the other, making it difficult terrain for either attack or defense. Taylor's force reached the area on February 22, and took up a defensive position in the pass, beyond which Santa Anna's troops were waiting. The next day, Santa Anna sent Taylor a very formally worded message demanding that the United States surrender. As reported in Don Nardo's *The Mexican American War*, Taylor responded,

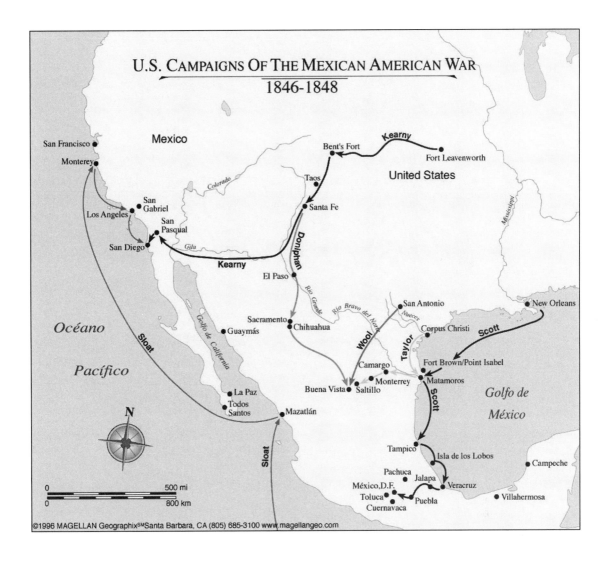

U.S. CAMPAIGNS OF THE MEXICAN AMERICAN WAR
1846-1848

A map showing the various military campaigns that took place during the Mexican American War.
Photograph reproduced by permission of the Corbis Corporation.

"Tell Santa Anna to go to hell!" But the general's more refined and restrained young aide (and future son-in-law), William "Perfect" Bliss, rephrased Taylor's message to read, "I decline acceding [agreeing] to your request."

That afternoon, the two armies took part in some minor skirmishes, then both spent a rainy night preparing for a bigger clash the next day. In the morning, the U.S. troops watched as the Mexican army—dressed in beautiful uniforms, flying colorful banners, and blessed by priests who walked among the troops—prepared itself for battle. Soon, however, fancy uniforms and colorful banners became unimportant as

General Zachary Taylor leading the American troops into battle at Buena Vista.

Photograph reproduced by permission of The Library of Congress.

the air filled with smoke and flying bullets. The U.S. troops had protected themselves well with a system of trenches, and they were able to push back the Mexicans' repeated attacks.

As night fell, the two armies agreed to take a break from fighting. The next morning, the U.S. troops were surprised to find that the Mexican army had left the battlefield. They were making a slow retreat back to San Luis Potosí, probably because they could not afford to lose any more men. The Mexicans had left behind 500 dead bodies, and it is estimated that their total casualties were close to 3,000. The U.S. side also had high casualties with 267 killed, 465 wounded, and 23 missing.

A sigh of relief

The U.S. soldiers were relieved when they saw that the Mexicans had retreated and by the realization that things might have turned out differently. This relief is evident in Fairfax Downey's *Texas and the War with Mexico*. In this book, Downey recounts the recollections of Lew Wallace, who served as a soldier in the Mexican American War and later wrote the novel *Ben Hur*:

> "I looked up the road and saw distinctly the dust of the re-treating column. Oh, what a feeling of relief came over me. I set up a shout of *victory*. It was a mockery however. I had the day before felt very much as I should suppose a *whipped* man would feel—and I've no doubt—had it been just as convenient for us as for Santa Anna to *vamos* [go] we would have been off for Monterrey."

Despite the heavy casualties, the United States counted the Battle of Buena Vista as a victory. Once again, a force made up largely of volunteers had performed well against a much larger army and in very difficult terrain. As a result, important territory had been secured. Taylor could bask in the glow of his now even brighter fame, which would propel him into the White House in 1848, while Scott took up the difficult task of conquering Mexico City.

Scott prepares to invade from the coast

Scott spent the early months of 1847 assembling his "Army of Invasion," a force of almost fourteen thousand that included both regiments raised in the United States and those transferred from Taylor's army. He was eager to get his army moving into the Mexican interior before April, which signaled the beginning of the dreaded yellow fever season. This deadly disease—called *el vomito negro,* or black vomit, by the Mexicans because that was one of its symptoms—was carried by mosquitoes, although this fact was not yet known. Yellow fever was common along Mexico's swampy coast in the spring and summer, and Scott knew that it could take a devastating toll on his soldiers, who would have no immunity to it.

Finally, the force was ready for action, sailing first from the city of Tampico, which had been under U.S. control since October, at the mouth of the Rio Grande to Lobo Island, midway to Vera Cruz. From there they headed to their landing point, Collado Beach, about 3 miles southeast of Vera Cruz, on March 9. Specially made surf-boats carried about ten thousand soldiers to shore, the first time such a feat had been accomplished. As they arrived, the soldiers and sailors could see the impressive, stately, and very well-fortified city in the near distance.

The attack on Vera Cruz

Against the advice of some of his officers, Scott decided not to launch an infantry (foot soldier) attack on Vera Cruz, knowing that too many lives would be lost in the attempt to climb over the city's high walls. Instead, Scott planned to bomb Vera Cruz. However, before the bombardment began, Scott sent a message to General Juan José Landero (1802–1869), who was leading the Mexican defense of Vera Cruz, offering to allow its noncombatant (nonfighting) residents to leave. Scott received no reply, and on March 22, the army began to bomb the city with its heavy cannons. Soon the navy joined the effort, firing from six heavy guns mounted on ships just off the coast.

The U.S. forces had cut off all supply lines into the city, including its water supply, which quickly began to cause much suffering. In addition, many buildings, including private homes, were being destroyed by the bombs, and civilians (nonmilitary people) were being killed along with soldiers. The weapons and ammunition used by the Mexican defenders were of poor quality, and they were not able to respond effectively to the attack. In fact, on the U.S. side, only 19 soldiers were killed in this battle, with 81 wounded, whereas 180 Mexicans were killed.

Finally, on March 28, Landero handed Vera Cruz over to the U.S. forces. The surrender agreement specified that the city's residents would not be prevented from practicing their religion. As had been shown in previous battles, the Mexicans had a deep-seated fear that the U.S. invaders, whom they considered antireligious and especially anti-Catholic, would punish them for their faith.

Santa Anna marches north

News of the Mexican army's defeat at Vera Cruz came as a huge shock to the residents of Mexico City, creating great worry and anger against the Mexican leaders who had al-

American troops landing at Vera Cruz after the city was bombed from ships anchored just off the city's coast. *Photograph reproduced by permission of Getty Images.*

lowed this to happen. All that now lay between them and the U.S. forces was 225 miles of the National Highway, the road that led straight from Vera Cruz to their doorsteps. Like the people of Vera Cruz, those of Mexico City feared that the godless U.S. soldiers would destroy churches, murder priests, and rape nuns. It was essential that Mexico crush the invaders before they reached the capital, and this was just what Santa Anna and his army of twenty thousand promised to do. Meanwhile, anxious to get his troops out of the dangerous coastal region, Scott set out on April 8, with a force of eighty-five hundred soldiers. They were bound for Mexico City.

The National Highway was a good example of the unexpected beauty and achievement that U.S. soldiers and officers, most of whom considered Mexico's people and culture inferior to their own, witnessed as they marched through the Mexican countryside and paused in its towns and cities. Originally built by the Spanish, who had conquered Mexico in the sixteenth century and occupied it for almost three hundred years, the National Highway was generally well paved, evenly graded, and equipped with gutters to drain off rain water. It was certainly far superior to most U.S. roads of the period. And it provided a convenient route for the U.S. Army as it began its march toward its first goal on the way to Mexico City, the town of Jalapa.

The Battle of Cerro Gordo

Determined to halt the U.S. advance, Santa Anna positioned his army at a narrow mountain pass near the village of Cerro Gordo, only 12 miles west of Vera Cruz. Nearby were many extremely steep hills. The Mexicans chose to fortify only one of them, called El Telégrafo, because they assumed the U.S. troops would not be able to make these nearly vertical ascents with their heavy guns. Arriving on the scene on April 17, however, U.S. Army engineers led by Lieutenant Robert E. Lee (destined to become the leading general of the Confederate Army in the American Civil War; 1861–65) devised a special conveyer system to move both equipment and men up the steep hills. They did so rapidly and without the Mexicans detecting them. The next day, the U.S. forces were able to attack the Mexicans from three sides in a movement that soon caused great losses among Santa Anna's troops.

Realizing that his army had been out-maneuvered and unwilling to sustain more losses, Santa Anna ordered a hasty retreat. Many Mexican soldiers had already begun to flee, and Santa Anna himself left in such a hurry that he had to abandon many personal belongings, including his wooden leg (perhaps a spare). In this short battle, only 63 U.S. soldiers were killed and 353 wounded, while the Mexicans sustained an estimated 1,000 casualties. The United States captured 3,000 Mexican soldiers, who were released after their guns were taken and they had promised not to fight again, as well as 43 cannons, 4,000 smaller weapons, and a big load of ammunition and other supplies.

The U.S. troops were surprised to find the bodies of many Mexican women among those left on the battlefield at Cerro Gordo. These women were called *soldaderas*—mothers, wives, and girlfriends—who followed the Mexican army, pro-

viding a great service to its leaders by feeding, clothing, and nursing the soldiers and sometimes even taking part in battles. Once again, the U.S. soldiers were astounded to find this evidence of Mexican bravery, devotion, and patriotism.

Back in the United States, those who opposed the war were growing both in number and volume. They wanted to know why it was necessary to attack Mexico City, since they believed that enough blood, especially Mexican, had already been shed. Among those making strong antiwar statements at this time were former slave Frederick Douglass (1817–1895) and well-known writer and activist, and abolitionist (person who wanted to end slavery) William Lloyd Garrison (1805–1879). In fact, as quoted in Howard Zinn's *People's History of the U.S.A.*, Garrison's *Liberator* newspaper published a statement that might even have been considered treasonous (disloyal or traitorous to one's nation) since it seemed to call for a Mexican victory. The statement read: "We wish [Scott] and his troops no bodily harm, but the most utter defeat and disgrace."

The Battle of Cerro Gordo, in which Antonio López de Santa Anna ordered a hasty retreat after realizing that his army had been outmaneuvered by U.S. troops. *Photograph reproduced by permission of Getty Images.*

A Few Voices Speak Out Against the War

Despite the general popularity of the Mexican American War, there was a small but significant group of voices that spoke out against it. Some of the most prominent are described here.

Henry David Thoreau

A native of New England, Henry David Thoreau (1817–1862) was a prominent essayist who urged people to cast off society's conventions and commune with nature to achieve peace and enlightenment. After the war, Thoreau would gain fame as the author of a famous book called *Walden, or Life in the Woods* (1854) in which he chronicled his experiences living for two years in a small cabin on Walden Pond, near his hometown of Concord, Massachusetts.

It was during his time on Walden Pond, in the summer of 1846, that Thoreau made a dramatic antiwar protest. Like many U.S. citizens, Thoreau believed that the war was closely linked with slavery, which he believed was morally wrong. In order to protest, Thoreau refused to pay his taxes because he did not want any of his own money to be used to finance a war associated with slavery. He did not pay taxes for six years. While walking into Concord one day to have a shoe repaired, Thoreau happened to meet the town's police officer, Sam Staples. When Staples told Thoreau that if he did not pay his taxes soon he would be sent to jail, the writer replied that he had no intention of paying until the war was over and slavery abolished. In regard to jail time, said Thoreau, as quoted in Catherine Reef's *Henry David Thoreau: A Neighbor to Nature,* he could spend it "as well now as any time, Sam."

Staples did indeed take Thoreau to jail. During the night, someone (probably one of Thoreau's relatives) paid his taxes and, much against his wishes, he was released in the morning. The experience later inspired Thoreau to write "Civil Disobedience," an important and very influential essay in which he stresses the necessity of following one's own conscience even if it means breaking laws that one considers unjust. Thoreau's contention that this is an effective and peaceful way to bring about positive change in society has since inspired other leaders, such as India's Mohandas Gandhi (1869–1948) and U.S. civil rights activist Martin Luther King Jr. (1929–1968).

Ralph Waldo Emerson

A celebrated essayist and poet, as well as Thoreau's friend, Ralph Waldo Emerson (1803–1882) also disapproved of the war. Although they were of the same opinion, Emerson did not condone Thoreau's action, and contrary to popular belief, is not the person who bailed Thoreau out of jail. It is said that when Emerson later asked Thoreau why he had taken this action, Thoreau replied, "Why did you not?"

Abraham Lincoln

An Illinois Congressman who was destined to become president of the United States during one of the most turbulent periods in its history, Abraham Lincoln

(1809–1865) opposed the Mexican American War even after others loudly proclaimed that this made him a traitor. In December 1847, Lincoln introduced to Congress a series of resolutions that challenged President James K. Polk (1795–1849) to prove "whether the particular spot of soil on which the blood of our citizens was so shed was, or was not, our own soil." Lincoln was referring to the claim found in Polk's war message to Congress that American blood had been shed on American soil; in fact, the area in which several U.S. soldiers had been killed by Mexican troops was claimed by both countries. Polk never responded to what would become known as Lincoln's "spot resolutions."

Lincoln also spoke out against the war in January 1848 (when peace negotiations were underway), questioning why the United States had gotten into the conflict in the first place. He was not re-elected to Congress, and many believed that his opposition to the war had made him unpopular. Nevertheless, Lincoln was elected president in 1860, presiding over the bloody Civil War (1861–65) which pitted the northern states against the southern Confederacy and even cost Lincoln his own life when he was assassinated by a southern sympathizer.

Joshua Giddings

An Ohio congressman and an ardent abolitionist, Joshua Giddings (1795–1864) felt that the war was the result of a conspiracy by southerners to expand the practice of slavery into any new territories that might be gained through the conflict. He was one of only fourteen members of Congress (all of them from the Whig Party, whose members generally condemned slavery) to vote against the war. Convinced that the war was one of pure and unjustified aggression, Don Nardo's book, *The Mexican American War,* quotes Giddings as stating that "In the murder of Mexicans upon their own soil, or in robbing them of their country, I can take no part either now or hereafter."

William Lloyd Garrison and Horace Greeley

A Massachusetts journalist and abolitionist with extreme views about the immorality of slavery, William Lloyd Garrison (1805–1879) agreed with those who believed the war was just an excuse to expand the practice. He published many antiwar editorials and poems in his magazine, *The Liberator.* Another journalist who spoke out against the war was Horace Greeley (1811–1872), who wrote in the *New York Tribune* that "We can easily defeat the armies of Mexico, slaughter them by the thousands but what then? Who believes that a score of victories over Mexico will give us more liberty, a purer morality?"

Sources: Crawford, Mark. Encyclopedia of the Mexican-American War. *Santa Barbara, CA: American Bibliographical Center-Clio Press, 1998;* Nardo, Don. Mexican-American War. *San Diego, CA: Lucent Books, 1991; Reef, Catherine.* Henry David Thoreau: A Neighbor to Nature. *Frederick, MD: Twenty-first Century Books, 1992.*

The army pauses at Puebla

With the Mexican army now retreating to the south, Scott could continue on his way to Jalapa, which the U.S. forces occupied with no fighting on April 19. Troops under General William Worth (1794–1849) also took the town of Perote, and Puebla was occupied about a month later. The Army of Invasion would rest here for most of the summer of 1847, waiting for replacements for the seven regiments of volunteer soldiers whose terms of service had ended. One new arrival on the scene was state department representative Nicholas P. Trist (1800–1874; see biographical entry), a Spanish-speaking diplomat sent by Polk to try to negotiate a peace treaty with Santa Anna. Scott strongly objected to this move, causing a major feud with Trist that was only overcome later, when the two men became good friends. In any case, Santa Anna did not respond to the offer.

Additional troops arrived in June, and in the first week of August, future U.S. president Major Franklin Pierce (1804–1869) brought more, boosting Scott's army from somewhere between six and seven thousand to about fourteen thousand. Unfortunately, due to the great toll of disease, about two thousand soldiers were too ill to fight, and many more were recovering from illness but still very weak. Besides disease, another problem that Scott faced had to do with his supply line from Vera Cruz. Although the bulk of the Mexican army had retreated to Mexico City, many guerilla (small groups of soldiers who operate outside of the regular army) fighters were still around, and they continually attacked the transports carrying men and supplies between Vera Cruz and Puebla.

Scott makes his move

Against the advice of many, Scott decided that now was the time to stop worrying about the supply lines, gather his available troops together, and move. Between August 7 and 10, almost eleven thousand U.S. troops once again set out for Mexico City.

The U.S. army entered the Valley of Mexico on August 11. Located 7,000 feet above sea level, Mexico City was situated in a volcanic crater 46 miles long and 32 miles wide, and surrounded by six swampy lakes as well as marshes and villages. A city of about two hundred thousand residents, the capital was defended by nearly thirty thousand soldiers and many fortifications. Ruling out other approaches as too easily attacked, Scott chose to reach the city from the south, the muddiest and most difficult route. He stopped the army at San Agustin, located 9 miles from Mexico City. Then he sent his trusted army engineer Robert E. Lee to scout out the area and find a good way to get the army into the city.

"I almost despair..."

Lee found that a 15-square-mile expanse of jagged lava rock known as the pedragal lay just south of the city. The Mexicans would never expect the U.S. forces to try to cross it, for it was full of treacherous bumps and dips. Lee, however, discovered an old mule trail that could be adapted to the army's uses. Work began immediately on expanding the mule trail into a road, while the U.S. soldiers gazed with nervous apprehension at the majestic city in the distance. Their fears are evident in an excerpt from a letter written by the Fifth Infantry's Captain E. Kirby Smith to his wife and quoted in David Nevin's *The Mexican American War*: "I almost despair when I reflect upon the destitute situation in which you will be left, with the three children dependent upon you, should I fall in the coming battle."

The Battles of Contreras and Churubusco

Just as Lee had foreseen, the troops were able to cross the pedragal successfully. After reaching the other side they took their positions, and on August 19, attacked a Mexican force near the village of Contreras. The United States won this battle as well as another the next day at the very well-fortified town of Churubusco. There the U.S. soldiers had to storm a convent that the Mexicans had been using to store weapons. These two battles were extremely costly for the Mexicans, who suffered 4,000 casualties, or about one-third of their total force. The United States had about 150 killed and a little more than 800 wounded.

Among the defenders of the convent at Churubusco was the two-hundred-and-sixty-member San Patricio Battal-

The American assault at Contreras. The United States won this battle as well as another the next day at the well-fortified town of Churubusco. *Photograph reproduced by permission of Getty Images.*

ion, which was down to only seventy-five men (including its leader, John Riley) by the end of the fight. At a hearing held immediately after the battle, fifty members of the battalion were given the death penalty for treason (betraying or being a traitor to one's own country). Riley and the others, who had joined the Mexican army before war was officially declared, were sentenced to be whipped and branded with a "D" to mark them as deserters. The fifty who were to be executed would be hanged on a hill overlooking Mexico City, just after U.S. troops had conquered the capital.

On August 21, as the U.S. forces prepared to attack Mexico City and the Mexican army prepared to defend it, Scott sent a letter to Santa Anna proposing that the two nations begin peace negotiations. As quoted in *The Mexican American War* by Don Nardo, Scott stated that "Too much blood has already been shed in this unnatural war between the two great Republics of this Continent. It is time that the

differences between them should be amicably and peacefully settled." Santa Anna agreed to the ceasefire, and a truce went into effect the next day. At Santa Anna's request, former Mexican president José Joaquín de Herrera led a team representing Mexico in peace talks. However, the talks were halted because of Santa Anna's unreasonable demands, and the truce ended on September 7.

The U.S. Army takes El Molino del Rey and Casa Mata

On September 8, Scott ordered an attack on El Molino del Rey, located only about 2 miles from Mexico City. Part of Santa Anna's elaborate system of fortifications, this group of stone buildings was rumored to house a cannon factory. Worth led 3,400 soldiers in the attack, meeting unexpectedly fierce resistance before they were finally able to overcome the

U.S. general Winfield Scott ordered an attack on El Molino del Rey after hearing rumors of a Mexican cannon factory being located in the city. The battle proved costly for the American side, especially since it turned out that the information regarding the cannon factory was false.
Photograph reproduced by permission of Getty Images.

Mexican defenders. The U.S. force also quickly took nearby Casa Mata. The assault, however, proved very costly for the U.S. side, especially since it turned out that there was no cannon factory in El Molino del Rey. After the battle, it was reported that 23 percent of those fighting for the United States had been killed, wounded, or were missing. This was the highest rate of casualties of any single battle of the war, and resulted in Worth being criticized for poor planning.

The only remaining obstacle between Scott's army and Mexico City was the famous landmark, Chapultepec Hill, located on the western edge of the capital. A 600-yard-long, 195-feet-high slab of volcanic rock, this hill was home to the National Military Academy (housed in a palace that had once belonged to the Spanish rulers of Mexico) and a source of great pride to the Mexicans. Chapultepec had been a symbol of their history and heritage since the days of Montezuma, the great Aztec leader who had once ruled over this land and these people's ancestors. Scott knew that capturing the hill was the next, and most inevitable, step in conquering Mexico City.

The fight for Chapultepec Hill

On September 12, Scott's troops began bombing both Chapultepec Hill and the city beyond it. The heavy cannons kept up their devastating work throughout the whole day and night, causing much damage and many deaths (both military and civilian). The next morning, the bombing stopped and the infantry set out on foot. Troops led by Worth, General Gideon Pillow (1806–1878), and General John A. Quitman (1799–1858) attacked Chapultepec Hill from the north, west, and southeast, respectively. Since most of Santa Anna's soldiers were inside the city wall, the hill was defended by only about eight hundred troops, who were under the command of General Nicolás Bravo. Most of Bravo's soldiers were experienced veterans, but about fifty of them were cadets from the National Military Academy. These cadets were thirteen- to seventeen-year-old boys clad in their traditional gray uniforms and tasseled blue hats. Although they had been ordered to leave, this dedicated group had stayed to defend their school and their nation.

As the U.S. soldiers charged toward the hill, the Mexicans fired down on them until they were at the hill's base,

out of the range of the Mexican guns. There the U.S. troops waited until tall ladders were brought to allow them to climb up the hill. As they ascended, many were shot down or fell to the ground when the Mexicans above pushed the ladders backwards. At about the same time that the U.S. soldiers began making it up to the top of the hill, the Mexicans were running out of ammunition, and the hand-to-hand fight that then took place was brutal.

Soon almost all of the Mexican defenders of Chapultepec Hill had fallen even though they outnumbered the U.S troops. Among the last to die were six cadets who fought ferociously until they were killed, earning for themselves a lasting place in Mexico's history. Finally only one of *Los Ninoes Heroes* (the boy heroes), Juan Escutia, was left. After being shot, he pulled down his country's flag and wrapped it around himself before he either jumped or fell from the palace roof. Two hours after the attack on Chapultepec Hill began, the surviving Mexicans surrendered to the U.S. troops.

American troops attacking the Fortress of Chapultepec, the last obstacle between Winfield Scott's forces and Mexico City. *Photograph reproduced by permission of Getty Images.*

The United States takes Mexico City

It was not long after this battle that U.S. troops launched a full-scale attack on Mexico City. By the end of the day, the U.S. side had suffered 850 casualties, while the Mexicans had sustained 3,000, including 800 taken prisoner. During the night, anticipating an even more disastrous battle the next day, Santa Anna and what was left of his army fled the city, retreating to the town of Guadalupe Hidalgo, just north of the capital. Scott rode into Mexico City in triumph at dawn on September 14. Two days later, Santa Anna resigned the presidency, stating that others were to blame for the country's bad fortune.

Technically, the war was over, but that did not mean that all of the trouble had disappeared. Still in charge of the Mexican army, Santa Anna made one last show of force on September 22, with an unsuccessful attack on the U.S. garrison at Puebla. U.S. supply lines were still harassed by guerillas, and snipers in Mexico City and elsewhere continued to shoot occasionally at the invaders who had overrun their country. Scott was now faced with the difficult task of setting up a temporary government in Mexico City, which had been left virtually leaderless and in chaos. In fact, the last U.S. troops would not leave Mexico until June 1848. However, the news that reached the United States, and caused the greatest rejoicing there, was that the war had ended and that the United States was triumphant.

For More Information

Books

Downey, Fairfax. *Texas and the War with Mexico*. New York: American Heritage Publishing, 1961.

Eisenhower, John S. D. *So Far from God: The U.S. War with Mexico, 1846–1848*. New York: Random House, 1989.

Frazier, Donald, ed. *The United States and Mexico at War*. New York: Simon and Schuster, 1997.

George, Isaac. *Heroes and Incidents of the Mexican War*. San Bernardino, CA: Borgo Press, 1982.

Hogan, Michael. *The Irish Soldiers of Mexico*. Guadalajara, Mexico: Fondo Editorial Universitario, 1997.

Nardo, Don. *The Mexican-American War*. San Diego, CA: Lucent Books, 1991.

Nevin, David. *The Mexican War.* Alexandria, VA: Time-Life Books, 1978.

Robinson, Cecil, ed. and trans. *The View from Chapultepec: Mexican Writers on the Mexican-American War.* Tucson: University of Arizona Press, 1989.

Zinn, Howard. *A People's History of the United States.* New York: Harper and Row, 1980.

Web Sites

Descendants of Mexican War Veterans. *The U.S.-Mexican War: 1846–1848.* [Online] Available http://www.dmwv.org/mexwar/mexwar1.htm (accessed on January 31, 2003).

The Mexican-American War Memorial Homepage. [Online] Available http://sunsite.unam.mx/revistas/1847/Summa.html (accessed on January 31, 2003).

PBS Online. *U.S.-Mexican War: 1846–1848.* [Online] Available http://www.pbs.org/kera/usmexicanwar/ (accessed on January 31,2003).

Peace, But at What Cost?

O n September 14, 1847, General Winfield Scott (1786–1866; see biographical entry) led U.S. troops in a triumphant march into Mexico City, which they had just taken from its Mexican defenders. The veteran military leader known as "Old Fuss and Feathers," because of his formal dress and belief in manners and strict discipline, had landed on the Mexican coast the previous March. At that time, the United States was already deep in a war over territory that would one day become the states of Texas, California, and New Mexico. Troops led by General Zachary Taylor (1784–1850; see biographical entry) had taken control of northern Mexico, while a combined army and navy force under General Stephen W. Kearny (1794–1849; see biographical entry) and Commodore Robert Stockton (1795–1866) had conquered California and New Mexico.

It had been Scott's role to finish the war by striking at the heart of Mexico, the nation's capital, Mexico City. From the east coast of Mexico, Scott led his Army of Invasion in a campaign that had been victorious at the battles of Vera Cruz and Cerro Gordo as well as the bloody conquest of Mexico

City. Now the dynamic Mexican military leader, Antonio López de Santa Anna (1794–1876; see biographical entry), had been vanquished from Mexico after he resigned the country's presidency on September 12. His troops had fled Mexico City, leaving its government in chaos and its people in fear and anxiety about the future. The war was over, but now the difficult work of peace would begin.

American troops attacking Mexico City. The United States knew that in order to end the Mexican American War, it would be necessary to capture Mexico's capital city. *Photograph reproduced by permission of Getty Images.*

A long wait for a peace treaty

Traveling with Scott's troops was Nicholas Trist (1800–1874; see biographical entry), a Spanish-speaking representative of the U.S. State Department (the government department that handles relations with other countries). Trist's job was to negotiate a peace treaty with Mexico. The problem was that there was no one on the Mexican side with whom he could meet. Having resigned the presidency, Santa Anna had no power to negotiate a treaty and his role in his country's downfall would soon send him into exile on the Caribbean island of Jamaica. Although Manuel de la Peña y Peña (1789–1850) had been chosen as interim (temporary) president, he lacked the approval of the Mexican congress. The atmosphere in Mexico City was tense and uncertain, while in the countryside guerrillas (soldiers operating outside of the army) continued to attack U.S. troops and supply wagons.

Meanwhile, some people called for the United States to take this opportunity to seize the entire country of Mexico, and not just the territory fought over in the war. This "All Mexico" movement included Secretary of State James Buchanon (1791–1869), Vice President George M. Dallas (1792–1864), and Stockton. A majority of U.S. leaders, however, realized that it would be too difficult for the United States to govern such a huge territory, especially one populated by people from a completely different culture, and who spoke a different language. Some critics of the All Mexico movement were motivated by racism (the belief that one's own race is superior to others) in wishing to avoid the "pollution" of white blood by intermarriage with Mexicans, while others pointed out that conquering Mexico would go against the American ideals of democracy and freedom of choice. Thus the All Mexico movement never gained much momentum.

On November 11, a new Mexican congress was elected. Pedro María Anaya, a general who had taken part in the defense of Mexico City, was chosen as the new interim president. Also chosen were commissioners who were to negotiate a peace treaty with the United States. These men began meetings with Trist in the village of Guadalupe Hidalgo, located just north of the capital. At about the same time, Trist received an order from President James K. Polk (1795–1849; see biographical entry) to return to the United States. Polk had grown impatient because it had taken the Mexicans so long to organize a government, and he did not know that the peace talks had finally begun. In a bold move for which he was later praised, Trist decided to disobey Polk's order and continue the negotiations. He did not want to lose what he knew was a good opportunity to work out an agreement with Mexico.

The Treaty of Guadalupe Hidalgo

The Treaty of Guadalupe Hidalgo was signed on February 2, 1848. It granted to the United States the territories of California and New Mexico, an area of 525,000 square miles and more than half of Mexico's total territory. It established a line about 3 miles south of San Diego as the California border, and the Rio Grande river as the border of Texas. Significantly, the United States agreed to pay Mexico $15 million for this land and to help with rebuilding. The terms of the treaty also forgave debts owed by Mexico to the United States. When news of the treaty reached the United States, a minority of voices screamed that the terms were outrageous. Why should the winner in a war pay the loser? But the treaty's supporters, including most U.S. leaders and newspaper editorial writers, insisted that this generosity would lead to better long-term relations between the United States and its close neighbor.

The treaty reached Polk two weeks later, delivered by reporter James L. Freaner of the *New Orleans Delta* newspaper, who made the journey from Mexico to Washington, D.C., in record time. Although he was initially angry with Trist for disobeying his order, Polk was pleased with the final treaty, and he immediately submitted it to Congress for approval. It was ratified (approved by both the House of Representatives and the Senate) on March 10, and signed by Polk on March 16. The Mexican government ratified the treaty on May 30, putting it officially into effect. Since the other remaining border issue, that of where to draw the line between Oregon and the British colony of Canada, had been peacefully resolved in June 1846, the boundaries of the United States were now (except for a few minor adjustments) established as they would remain. As claimed in the traditional song *My Country Tis of Thee,* the nation now stretched "from sea to shining sea."

Victory: A cause for pride or shame?

On July 4, 1848, the United States received notice that Mexico had ratified the Treaty of Guadalupe Hidalgo. On that same day in Washington, D.C., a ceremony was held to dedicate the cornerstone (the first piece of the foundation) of the Washington Monument, the landmark that would honor the first president of the United States, George Washington (1732–1799). According to Donald Frazier's book, *The United States and Mexico at War,* Massachusetts representative, Whig Party leader, and Speaker of the House (the top leader in the House of Representatives) Robert C. Winthrop claimed in his dedication

A reproduction of the Treaty of Guadalupe Hidalgo, which officially ended the Mexican American War and established the boundaries of the United States as they remain today. *Photograph reproduced by permission of the Corbis Corporation.*

speech that this day marked "the precise epoch at which we have arrived in the world's history." In other words, because the United States achieved victory in the war, the country must surely have gained respect in the eyes of the world.

The reason for Winthrop's belief was because of the where and how the war was fought. The Mexican American War was the first war that the still-young United States had fought on foreign soil. During this conflict, the United States had successfully moved more than one hundred thousand troops, as well as the huge quantities of weapons, equipment, and supplies needed to wage the war, across great distances, overcoming a myriad of difficulties that included harsh weather, disease, rugged terrain, and harassment from enemy guerillas. In almost every battle, the U.S. Army, with occasional help from the navy, had defeated much larger Mexican forces. Because of the victory, the United States had gained a huge parcel of territory that would eventually comprise the states of California, New Mexico, and Arizona, as well as parts of the states of Utah and Nevada. All these factors, many claimed, showed that this nation was no longer an experiment in democracy, a newborn society that might or might not survive.

Yet not everyone agreed that the United States deserved respect for the part it had played in the Mexican American War. For one thing, the financial cost had been high. The country spent $100 million to finance the war. The human cost was even more staggering. Out of 104,556 who had fought in the Mexican American War, 13,768 had died, mostly due to disease. The resulting 13 percent mortality rate was, and still is, the highest of any U.S. war. But some critics argue that the price paid in money and lives is nothing compared to the cost of the honor and integrity of the United States. The nation that trumpeted the ideals of freedom, democracy, and justice for all had invaded and conquered a much weaker country. For no more noble reason than greed, the United States had taken Mexican lives and stolen Mexican land.

Those who had spoken out against the war before it began now predicted that it would take a heavy toll on the international reputation of the United States. The famous essayist and philosopher Ralph Waldo Emerson (1803–1882) predicted that the country would now be seen as militaristic and imperialistic (eager to extend its power over weaker nations). In his memoirs, as quoted in John S. D. Eisenhower's *So Far from God,* future U.S. president Ulysses S. Grant (1822–1885), who served as a young lieutenant during the Mexican American War, would call it "the most unjust war ever waged by a stronger against a weaker nation."

The slavery debate heats up

Related to the question of whether the United States had suffered a moral defeat, even as returning soldiers were welcomed home as heroes with parades and celebrations, was that of slavery. Since the seventeenth century, Africans had been transported under horribly inhumane conditions to North America and forced to work on farms and plantations (very large farms), most of them in the southern

United States. Supporters of slavery claimed it was the only way to provide enough agricultural workers to keep the U.S. economy going. Racist attitudes meant that Africans and other people of non-European heritage did not deserve to be treated humanely or offered the same rights as white people.

By the middle of nineteenth century, however, attitudes were beginning to change, especially in the more industrial North. In fact, a division was growing between the northern and southern states, as more northerners began to express the view that slavery was morally wrong. An abolitionist movement, whose members worked to end slavery, had emerged and was growing in numbers and influence. In the South, however, the economy was still based on agriculture, and farmers and plantation owners still depended on slaves to work their fields and harvest the cotton, rice, and other crops. White southerners felt pride in their own customs and lifestyle and did not want anything to change, and they resented the interference of northerners in their affairs.

After the Mexican American War, the famous essayist Ralph Waldo Emerson predicted that the United States would be viewed as a militaristic and imperialist nation. *Photograph courtesy of The Library of Congress.*

A delicate balance of power

Throughout the nineteenth century, new states were being formed. Some of them allowed slavery and some did not, and this was an important difference because it meant that the balance of power between slave and free states (or, as it worked out, southern and northern states) could shift. Southerners wanted the new states to allow slavery so that the South, as a whole, would have more power in Congress. Northerners wanted the new states to make slavery illegal, to give the North more power. In 1845, Texas had been admitted as a slave state, which displeased northerners but made southerners happy.

Slavery was an important issue from the earliest days of the Mexican American War. Many of those who opposed the war, especially northerners, had seen slavery as the major reason for the conflict. They called attention to the fact that Polk had been willing to compromise with Great Britain on where to draw the border between Canada and Oregon, but insisted on going to war with Mexico over the border of Texas. To northerners, this meant that Polk favored the southern states and wanted to expand slavery to whatever new territories might be acquired through the war.

Now that the war was over and at least two new territories had been won for the United States, a debate about whether or not they would allow slavery quickly developed. In 1848, Zachary Taylor's fame as a hero of the Mexican American War led to his election as president of the United States. He had run as the candidate of the Whig Party, winning the nomination over his old military rival, Winfield Scott. Although Taylor was a southerner and a slave-owner, the Whig Party was generally dominated by northerners who opposed slavery. Although he urged both California and New Mexico to apply for statehood, it was uncertain whether or not he wanted them to be admitted as slave or free states.

An uneasy compromise

In 1850, a compromise drafted by Kentucky senator Henry Clay resolved the debate, at least temporarily, by offering something to both the North and the South. California would be admitted as a free state, while both slaveholders and those who opposed slavery would be allowed to settle in the new territories of New Mexico and Utah. Slavery would be abolished in the District of Columbia (Washington, D.C.), but the Fugitive Slave Law, which benefited slaveholders by allowing them to recapture slaves who had escaped to the North, would be strictly enforced.

Despite the compromise, the slavery debate would become increasingly heated over the next decade. In 1861, the tension between the North and the South would lead to the outbreak of the Civil War, the bloody struggle that would divide the nation for four years and that would decide the slavery issue once and for all. The Mexican American War had been one of the key events that brought about that devastating and decisive conflict.

Kentucky senator Henry Clay temporarily resolved the slavery debate in 1850 by drafting a compromise in which California would be admitted to the Union as a free state and both slaveholders and those opposing slavery would be allowed to settle in the territories of New Mexico and Utah. *Photograph courtesy of The Library of Congress.*

Future leaders gained experience and fame

The impact of the Mexican American War was felt in other ways as well. Historians have called the war an important training ground for men who later became important U.S. military and political leaders. Zachary Taylor gained so much fame and popularity as "Old Rough and Ready," the brave and unpretentious general who led his troops to glorious victory in Mexico, that, despite a complete lack of political experience, he was elected president in 1848. (Taylor died unexpectedly two years later.) Franklin Pierce (1804–1869), who had commanded twenty-four troops during the attack on Mexico City, became the nation's fourteenth president in 1853, serving for one term. Jefferson Davis (1808–1889), who had served with distinction under Taylor in the Battle of Buena Vista, later became president of the Confederate States

A photo of future president Ulysses S. Grant as a lieutenant during the Mexican American War. Many future U.S leaders served during the war.
Photograph reproduced by permission of the Corbis Corporation.

of America. This short-lived nation formed by eleven slaveholding states unsuccessfully opposed the Union Army during the Civil War.

The Mexican American War played a crucial role in producing a crop of extremely competent officers who served on both sides of the Civil War. The most distinguished are undoubtedly Robert E. Lee (1807–1870) and Ulysses S. Grant (1822–1885), who served side by side in Mexico but led armies against each other during the later conflict. In the Mexican American War, Lee was an army engineer who contributed to the U.S. victory at the Battle of Cerro Gordo (see Chapter 5), while Grant was a young lieutenant who marched through Texas under Taylor (see Chapter 4). Each of these two old military comrades rose to the top ranks of their respective armies during the Civil War, and Grant also served two terms (1869–77) as president of the United States. Other Mexican American War veterans who made names for themselves in the Civil War included Union generals George McLellan (1826–1885) and George Meade (1815–1872) and Confederate generals Thomas "Stonewall" Jackson (1824–1863) and George Pickett (1825–1875).

A devastating impact on Mexico

It should come as no surprise that the Mexican American War had a huge and negative impact on Mexico. This impact was both immediate and long-lasting. What may be more surprising is the contrast between the place of this war in the U.S. memory and its place in the Mexican memory. Most U.S. citizens know little about the conflict that so profoundly changed both their nation's boundaries and its character. Mexicans, on the other hand, have kept close to their hearts the bitter memory of what they considered a brutal, illegal invasion of their country. The war caused thousands of deaths and widespread destruction of property, and disrupted the normal flow of trade and agricultural production. It led to political chaos (Mexico had seven presidents and ten ministers of foreign affairs during the two years of the war), but its damage went even deeper than that.

As in all wars, it was ordinary Mexicans who bore the heaviest burden of suffering, particularly in those areas that became part of the United States. When the Mexican American War ended, there were about seventy-five thousand Mexican citizens living in the territory that had been ceded to the United States. They were given the choice of moving farther south into Mexico or staying where they were. If they stayed, they could keep their Mexican citizenship or become U.S. citizens, but if they did not make a choice within one year they would automatically become U.S. citizens.

What this meant was that many families were torn in half, and that many more felt stranded between two countries, belonging in neither. In a dialogue recorded as part of the documentary *The U.S.-Mexican War, 1846–1848,* produced by KERA Dallas-Fort Worth and the Public Broadcasting System, scholar Antonia J. Casteña notes that these people's "lives, cultures, languages, livelihoods, governments, structures, and ways of being were totally altered, changed, turned upside down within a very short period of time." Those who stayed in the United States faced prejudice and discrimination from a society that would continue, well into the twentieth century, to favor those of white European heritage. Those who left the place they considered home and settled inside the new Mexican border would share in the years of turmoil their nation still faced.

A long-lasting resentment

The Mexican American War cost Mexico a great deal in material ways, through the loss of lives, land, and property, but it also took a heavy psychological toll on the country. Soon after the war ended, a group of young men, all Mexican army veterans who had fled with Santa Anna when the U.S. forces overtook Mexico City, came together to write a book. Collecting both documents from the war and notes on their own experiences and reflections, they published *Apuntes para la historia de la Guerra entre México y los Estados Unidos* (Notes on the History of the War Between Mexico and the United States). These former soldiers wanted to understand what had taken place and try to determine why Mexico had been defeated, so the country could learn from its mistakes. The same men would one day take part in a civil war (1858–60) that would bring liberal president Benito Juarez (1806–1872) to power. (This conflict would be followed by an armed struggle against France from 1864 to 1867 and by the Mexican Revolution [1910–11], when the harsh thirty-five-year reign of dictator Porfirio Díaz [1830–1915] was brought to an end.)

Mexicans had been a proud people, but now they felt a new sense of shame and insecurity. They also felt a deep resentment against the nation and people who had invaded Mexico, killed so many Mexicans, and taken away nearly half of its territory. That resentment would last for more than a hundred years, even as the United States and Mexico became close friends and trading partners. In *The U.S.-Mexican War, 1846–1848,* contemporary Mexican Jesús Velasco-Márquez, a professor at the Instituto Technológico Autónomo de Mexico, reflected on his feelings about the Mexican American War: "I feel tremendously sad that we lost our original territory, and that the experience of having an invader in our country was so brutal. But on the other hand, I do believe that as Mexicans, this painful experience forced us to reevaluate our country."

A time of change in the United States

The Mexican American War took place at a time of great change in the United States. Advances in technology and communication, the growth of cities, and the great flow of immigrants from Europe made the middle- to late-nineteenth century both an exciting and a confusing time. As these dramatic changes occurred, the people of the United States were reaching out and expanding both their physical borders, as they moved westward to explore and settle the great expanses of their land, and their view of the world and the role of their country in it. U.S. citizens believed it was their "manifest destiny" (see Chapter 1), or their God-given right, to impose their beliefs and way of life on others. This philosophy

had been used to justify the declaration of war against Mexico. It would be used again in the coming decades as thousands of U.S. settlers streamed into the American West, shoving aside the Native Americans who had lived in those lands for centuries.

Before and during the Mexican American War, critics had claimed that this territory being fought over was too full of deserts, rocks, and mountains to be of much use to people looking for good farmland. However, there was much lush and fertile land waiting there, especially in California, and other treasures hiding beneath the rocks. In January 1948, gold was found at Sutter's Mill, located near Sacramento, the present-day capital of California. The discovery led to the California Gold Rush, when adventurers and fortune-seekers known as Forty-Niners (named for the year in which most of the action took place) headed west, hoping to become millionaires. During the next century, additional discoveries of other mineral deposits—including silver, copper, uranium,

Forty-Niners mining for gold during the California Gold Rush. *Photograph reproduced by permission of Archive Photos, Inc.*

A Journalist's First-Hand Account

The Mexican American War was the first conflict that was brought to the doorsteps of U.S. citizens by reporters from city and hometown newspapers, many of whom actually joined the army and then chronicled the war first-hand. Below is an article by journalist George Kendall, whose account of the fall of Mexico City on September 14, 1847, appeared in the New Orleans *Picayune*.

Another victory, glorious in its results and which has thrown additional luster upon the American arms, has been achieved today by the army under General Scott—the proud capital of Mexico has fallen into the power of a mere handful of men compared with the immense odds arrayed against them, and Santa Anna, instead of shedding his blood as he had promised, is wandering with the remnant of his army no one knows whither.

The apparently impregnable works on Chapultepec, after a desperate struggle, *were triumphantly carried; Generals Bravo and Mouterde, besides a host of officers of different grades, taken prisoners; over 1000 noncommissioned officers and privates, all their cannon and ammunition, are in our hands; the fugitives were soon in full flight towards the different works which command the entrances to the city, and our men at once were in hot pursuit.*

General Quitman, supported by General Smith's brigade, took the road by the Chapultepec aqueduct toward the Belén gate and the Ciudadela; General Worth, supported by General Cadwalader's brigade, advanced by the San Cosme aqueduct toward the garita of that name. Both routes were cut up by ditches and defended by breastworks, barricades, and strong works of every description known to military science. Yet the daring and impetuosity of our men overcame one defense after another, and by nightfall every work to the city's edge was carried.

Source: American Eras: Westward Expansion, 1800–1860. *Farmington Hills, MI: Gale Group, 2001.*

and, much later, oil—would greatly increase the value of the Southwest's vast expanses.

A war worth remembering

The Mexican American War has been called a war of "firsts" for the United States. It was the first war in which graduates of the U.S. Military Academy at West Point participated, allowing these young men their first taste of combat and giving many of them experience that would serve them well in the coming Civil War. This was the first of any war, anywhere in the world, that was photographed and the first on which newspaper correspondents (many of them soldiers hired by hometown newspapers) regularly reported from the battlefields. The recent development of faster presses and the telegraph made this work possible, and it meant that people knew more about what was really happening, and what soldiers were really experiencing, than they ever had before.

Perhaps most profoundly, though, the Mexican American War marked the first time that the young nation had fought a war on foreign soil, and one that was seen by many as a war of aggression rather than defense. Perhaps it is true that the United States was simply destined to expand, and that this war helped establish its dominance in world affairs. Or perhaps it was true that the honor of the United States had been forever tarnished when U.S. military forces crossed Mexico's borders and claimed its land. Historians would continue to debate these questions, while the majority of U.S. citizens forgot all about them. But for those who understand its importance, as well as the historical, cultural, and social impact of the southwestern United States on the entire nation, the Mexican American War is worth remembering.

For More Information

Books

Bauer, Karl J. *The Mexican War.* New York: Macmillan, 1974.

Butler, Stephen R. *A Documentary History of the War with Mexico 1846–1848.* Richardson, TX: Descendents of Mexican War Veterans, 1994.

Conner, Seymour V., and Odie B. Faulk. *North America Divided: The Mexican War 1846–1848.* New York: Oxford University Press, 1971.

Del Castillo, Richard. *The Treaty of Guadalupe Hidalgo: A Legacy of Conflict.* Norman: University of Oklahoma Press, 1990.

Downey, Fairfax. *Texas and the War with Mexico.* New York: American Heritage Publishing, 1961.

Eisenhower, John S. D. *So Far from God: The U.S. War with Mexico, 1846–1848.* New York: Random House, 1989.

Frazier, Donald, ed. *The United States and Mexico at War.* New York: Simon and Schuster, 1997.

Meyer, Michael C., and William L. Sherman. *The Course of Mexican History.* New York: Oxford University Press, 1982.

Nardo, Don. *The Mexican-American War.* San Diego, CA: Lucent Books, 1991.

Nevin, David. *The Mexican War*. Alexandria, VA: Time-Life Books, 1978.

Robinson, Cecil, ed. and trans. *The View from Chapultepec: Mexican Writers on the Mexican-American War*. Tucson: University of Arizona Press, 1989.

Zinn, Howard. *A People's History of the United States*. New York: Harper and Row, 1980.

Web Sites

Descendants of Mexican War Veterans. *The U.S.-Mexican War: 1846–1848*. [Online] Available http://www.dmwv.org/mexwar/mexwar1.htm (accessed on January 31, 2003).

The Mexican-American War Memorial Homepage. [Online] Available http://sunsite.unam.mx/revistas/1847/Summa.html (accessed on January 31, 2003).

PBS Online. *U.S.-Mexican War: 1846–1848*. [Online] Available http://www.pbs.org/kera/usmexicanwar/ (accessed on January 31, 2003).

Biographies

John Charles Frémont

Born January 21, 1813
Savannah, Georgia

Died July 13, 1890
New York, New York

American explorer and politician

Nicknamed "the Pathfinder," John Charles Frémont gained fame several years before the Mexican American War through his vividly written reports of his exploring and surveying expeditions through the American West. An officer in the army's Topographical Corps (the division of the army that had been assigned the job of surveying the unmapped areas of the United States), he happened to be in California just as tensions between its Mexican rulers and the U.S. settlers who had moved there were coming to a head. In a series of controversial actions, Frémont played a key role in the Bear Flag Rebellion, an uprising of these settlers, and in the subsequent U.S. takeover of California.

Discovering his life's work

Born in Savannah, Georgia, John Charles Frémont was the illegitimate child of Anne Pryor, who had caused a scandal in her hometown of Richmond, Virginia, by running away from her elderly husband to live with her lover. Frémont's father, who went by the name Charles Frémont but

John Charles Frémont.
Photograph courtesy of The Library of Congress.

whose actual name was Louis-René Frémon, was a French-Canadian who earned a meager living by teaching dancing and French. Besides John Charles, Charles Frémont and Anne Pryor had two more children, another boy and a girl. After the elder Frémont died when John Charles was five, Anne Pryor took her children to live in Charleston, South Carolina, where she rented out rooms to support them.

John Charles Frémont grew to be a smart, charming, and handsome young man with dark hair and blue eyes. A Charleston lawyer for whom Frémont had worked as a clerk paid his tuition at the College of Charleston, where he excelled in math and science. But in 1831, due to a love affair that distracted him from his studies, Frémont was expelled from the college. He was just three months short of graduation. (Five years later, he did earn his bachelor's degree.) He taught mathematics in a private secondary school until 1833, when he was lucky enough to attract the attention of a powerful man.

Joel Poinsett was a South Carolina politician who had recently returned from a five-year post as the U.S. government's representative in Mexico. Poinsett got Frémont a job teaching mathematics to U.S. Navy sailors on the U.S.S. *Natchez,* and he spent the next two years traveling around South America on the ship. In 1835, Poinsett found another good job for Frémont; he was to help survey land to be used for the planned Charleston, Louisville, and Cincinnati Railroad. The next year, Frémont worked on surveying land in Georgia, Tennessee, and North Carolina that would become a Cherokee Indian reservation. These assignments awakened Frémont's deep interest in nature and exploration.

A good assignment and a fateful meeting

Perhaps the best opportunity of Frémont's career came in 1838. Now secretary of war, Poinsett arranged for Frémont to be commissioned a second lieutenant in the U.S. Corps of Topographical Engineers. As a result, Frémont was soon assigned to accompany the great French scientist Joseph Nicolas Nicollet in an expedition to the region between the upper Mississippi and Missouri rivers (in what is now Minnesota and North and South Dakotas). While serving as

Nicollet's assistant, Frémont gained a wealth of information and an education in geology, astronomy, botany, and map-making, as well as such practical skills as how to use scientific instruments and how to plan an expedition.

Returning to Washington, Frémont met Missouri senator Thomas Hart Benton (1782-1858), one of the nation's strongest advocates of expansionism (the movement of U.S. citizens past the nation's current borders and into the continent's western reaches). Benton was extremely interested in Frémont's travels to the West. During the course of his visits with Benton, Frémont fell in love with the senator's fifteen-year-old daughter, Jessie. Benton was dismayed at this turn of events and tried to remedy the situation by sending Frémont on a surveying expedition to the Des Moines River in what is now Iowa.

Conducted during the spring and summer of 1841, the expedition did not end the romance. In October, Frémont eloped with Jessie. Benton was furious at first but came to accept the marriage, eventually growing very close to his new son-in-law. In fact, Benton was to become Frémont's most loyal and powerful supporter and sponsor in the years to come.

The first major expedition

In early 1842, Frémont set out on an especially challenging assignment. He was to travel west from the Mississippi River up to South Pass, Wyoming, the same route that U.S. settlers were beginning to use as they moved along the Oregon Trail to the Pacific Northwest. Frémont was to explore the Wind River mountain chain in Wyoming. Traveling with a crew of twenty-one that included the renowned mountain man and scout Christopher "Kit" Carson (1809-1868), Frémont made a careful scientific survey of the region, and also climbed what he thought (wrongly, as it turned out) was the highest mountain in the Rockies, and which he named Frémont Peak.

Returning to Washington in October, Frémont worked closely with his wife, a skilled writer, to produce a lively report relating the explorer's many adventures. Vivid with descriptions of the West's awesome beauty, it also contained an excellent map. The report was very well-received by

Christopher "Kit" Carson

The subject of many a tall tale and frontier legend, Christopher "Kit" Carson was also an authentic western hero. He earned his living, and much of his fame, as a mountain man and expert frontier scout, but he also served as an officer during the Mexican American War. A member of the California Battalion, led by Colonel John C. Frémont, Carson helped capture California from the Mexicans.

Carson's ancestors had originally settled in the mountains of North Carolina and Virginia, but by the time he was born his family had migrated to Madison County, Kentucky. They soon moved even farther west, to the Missouri frontier. Carson received little education and in fact, could not read for most of his life. At the age of fifteen he was apprenticed to a saddlemaker. Less than two years later, the teenaged Carson ran away to join a group of traders who were heading for the thriving town of Santa Fe in what was then still Mexican territory.

For the next few years, Carson worked at a number of odd jobs around the Southwest. In 1829, he joined forces with trapper Ewing Young, who taught him the difficult art of hunting and harvesting beaver (at this time there was a great demand for beaver pelts, which were made into a special kind of man's hat) as they worked along the streams of what would become the U.S. states of Arizona and California.

Like many other frontier trappers, Carson married a Native American woman of the Arapaho tribe, who died after giving birth to a daughter. Carson took the girl, named Alice, to Missouri to be raised by his relatives. In 1843, after another short-lived marriage to a Cheyenne woman, Carson married fifteen-year-old Josefina Jaramillo in Taos, New Mexico.

During the summer of 1842, Carson was on his way back to Missouri when he happened to meet Frémont on a steamboat. A member of the U.S. Corps of Topographical Engineers, Frémont had been assigned to explore and map an area of the West that included the Wind River mountain range in what is now Wyoming. He hired Carson as a guide, and the two began a mutually respectful partnership that would last through several future expeditions.

Frémont's detailed and colorful report of this first expedition brought fame to both him and Carson. The next year, Carson again accompanied Frémont to a journey that took their party across what is now Utah and over the Sierra Nevada mountains to California, then back by way of Colorado. In 1846, Frémont and Carson were on their third expedition together when they became involved in an uprising of U.S. settlers living in California. With Frémont's help, which may have been but probably was not authorized by the U.S. government, these settlers declared themselves independent from Mexico and established the short-lived Bear Flag Republic.

Soon the Mexican American War was underway in northeastern Mexico, and navy officer Robert Stockton arrived to take

Christopher "Kit" Carson. *Photograph courtesy of the Library of Congress.*

charge of the conquest of California. He organized the Bear Flaggers into an army unit called the California Battalion, with Frémont as its commander. Carson was given the rank of second lieutenant. Having taken control of town after town along the California coast, Stockton and Frémont sent Carson east toward Washington, D.C., with a message informing President James K. Polk that California was now in U.S. hands.

When he reached New Mexico, Carson encountered General Stephen W. Kearny, who had just led the U.S. Army of the West in capturing Santa Fe and who was now on his way to California. Unaware that the Mexicans had recaptured Los Angeles, Carson told Kearny that the United States was firmly in control of California. Upon hearing this news, Kearny sent most of his force back to Santa Fe, and ordered Carson to guide him to California.

Nearing Los Angeles, Kearny heard that the Mexicans had regained the city. Although worn out by their travels, Kearny insisted on leading his small force into a disastrous battle at San Pascual. That night, with the U.S. troops surrounded by the Mexicans, Carson and another officer made a daring and difficult escape. They managed to reach San Diego and request that Stockton send Kearny some more troops. With these reinforcements, the U.S. force was able to retake Los Angeles. This time, California really was in the hands of the United States.

After the war, Frémont was court-martialed for disobeying superior officers. Frémont's disgrace led to Carson's removal from the army. He went on to become an agent for the Office of Indian Affairs, working as a liaison between the federal government and Native Americans, who were being forced out off their traditional lands and, in many cases, resisting violently. In this position Carson, despite his reputation as someone who had fought with and killed many Indians, often criticized his superiors for their lack of knowledge of Indian concerns.

Carson took part in the American Civil War (1861–65), organizing the New Mexico Volunteer Infantry Regiment and fighting at the Battle of Val Verde. In 1867, Carson settled in southern Colorado with his family. His beloved wife died the next year and Carson, who had been in ill health for some time, soon followed her in death.

a U.S. public that was hungry to hear any and all details about the West.

Within only a few months, Frémont was off on another expedition. This one moved beyond South Pass to the Great Salt Lake, in present-day Utah, and the adjacent Great Basin. From there, Frémont traveled up the Snake River, then followed the Columbia River to its mouth on the Pacific Ocean, at Vancouver. On his return trip, he headed south into the Mexican territory of California, stopping at Sutter's Fort, a prosperous settlement founded by Swiss settler John Sutter (1803–1880). Frémont then continued south to Los Angeles and turned east to pass through Santa Fe and parts of what are now Nevada and Utah.

Frémont arrived home in August 1844, and he and Jessie immediately started working on a report of this second major expedition. This one was as good, and as popular, as the first, with lots of helpful information on the terrain, plants, animals, weather, and Native Americans that settlers could expect to encounter in this region. The report was required reading for members of Congress, and demand was such that ten thousand copies were printed. As a result, Frémont became even more famous than he was previously.

Heading west again

Soon Frémont was ready to embark on yet another expedition. Leaving in June 1845 from St. Louis, Missouri, Frémont headed west with seventy-four men, including Kit Carson. Their journey would take them along the southern end of the Great Salt Lake and across the Great Basin and the Sierra Nevada range to California. All of the men carried weapons, and in view of what happened later, historians have wondered about the real purpose of Frémont's expedition. Some have speculated whether he really intended to make a scientific study of the terrain, or instead, had secret government orders to take on a military role in California.

A few months before Frémont's departure, mounting tensions between the United States and Mexico came to a head when the United States annexed Texas, which the Mexicans considered their territory. The Mexicans had vowed to

go to war if the annexation occurred, and during the summer of 1845 General Zachary Taylor (1784–1850) had taken four thousand U.S. Army troops to Corpus Christi, on the edge of the disputed territory. Eager expansionists, including President James K. Polk, were hoping to wrest from Mexico not only Texas but the more western lands of California and New Mexico, especially since they knew that Great Britain also was interested in doing so. There were already about seven hundred U.S. citizens living in California, and they were unhappy with the way the Mexican government treated them.

Frémont's group reached Sutter's Fort in December, after a challenging winter crossing of the Sierra Nevadas. There they would rest before turning east again. In early March, Frémont took his men to the town of Monterey to purchase supplies. He also met with the U.S. consul (representative) there, Thomas Larkin (1802–1858). At this point, the Mexican government became suspicious of Frémont. Thus, Monterey's military commander, General José Castro (1810–1860), ordered

John Charles Frémont leading an expedition to California. It has been speculated that Frémont may have had secret government orders to take on a military role upon reaching California.
Photograph reproduced by permission of Archive Photos, Inc.

him to leave the country. Frémont responded with defiance, moving his men into a log cabin on a nearby mountain peak and raising the U.S. flag as a challenge to the Mexican authorities. Frémont soon headed north into Oregon Territory, even though his original orders said that he was to have returned to Washington by the end of 1845, and began to explore the Klamath Lake area.

The Bear Flag Rebellion

On May 9, Lieutenant Archibald Gillespie (1812–1873) arrived at Frémont's camp. Gillespie had ridden north to find Frémont after meeting with Larkin in Monterey in which he had delivered a message to Larkin from Secretary of State James Buchanan (1791–1868). Buchanan had advised Larkin to try to bring about a peaceful takeover of California. The question remains, however, what Gillespie told Frémont when he arrived at Frémont's camp. Over the years, it has been part of Frémont's legend that he received secret orders to lead a military uprising against Mexico, and Frémont himself later implied that this was true. Yet no one knows for sure. What is known is that Frémont hurried back to Sutter's Fort after his meeting with Gillespie.

Only four days after Gillespie's arrival at Frémont's camp, the United States declared war against Mexico. But this news would not reach California for some time. In the meantime, a group of settlers who were determined to shake off Mexican rule had appealed to Frémont to help them. On June 14, under his direction, they converged on Sonoma, a sleepy town about 40 miles north of San Francisco, and arrested its Mexican commander, General Mariano Vallejo (1807–1890). Then they raised a flag patched together from scraps of old clothes that featured a red star and a bear standing on its hind legs. Thus the Republic of California was born, though it would last for only twenty-five days.

The conquest of California begins

Having taken charge of this group that would become known as the Bear Flaggers, Frémont began adding the title

"Military Commander of the U.S. Forces in California" to his name. Toward the end of June, Polk promoted him to the rank of lieutenant colonel. On July 7, the U.S. Navy arrived in Monterey with the news that the war had begun. Commodore John Sloat (1781–1867) took over the town. He soon met with Frémont and was shocked to learn that Frémont had acted without official orders.

Due to illness, Sloat left California a few weeks later and was replaced by Commander Robert Stockton (1795–1866), who was much more sympathetic to Frémont. He gave Frémont permission to organize the Bear Flaggers, who now numbered more than four hundred, into a military unit called the California Battalion. Along with Stockton's sailors, who were now serving more as infantry (foot soldiers), Frémont's battalion marched south and took control of town after town with no resistance or bloodshed. They also easily took the larger towns of San Diego and Los Angeles, for by now California's Mexican governor Pío Pico (1801–1894) had fled.

At this point it seemed to Stockton and Frémont that the conquest of California was complete. They wrote messages to Polk announcing their success and sent Carson east to deliver them to Washington. Meanwhile, Stockton had put Gillespie in charge of Los Angeles. The lieutenant's arrogance and extremely strict rules made the city's residents angry and resentful, so it was not difficult for Castro, who was still in the area with a number of troops, to organize an uprising. Greatly outnumbered, Gillespie surrendered on September 23, and Los Angeles was again under Mexican control.

Kearny arrives on the scene

Meanwhile, General Stephen Watts Kearny (1794–1848) was on the march, in command of the Army of the West. Having taken control of Santa Fe, Kearny was headed to California with 300 troops. Along the way he met Carson, who—unaware of what had happened in Los Angeles—told him that California was already in U.S. hands. Thus, Kearny sent all but 110 of his soldiers back to Santa Fe, an action he would soon regret.

Reaching California, Kearny learned of the Los Angeles uprising. Disregarding his troops' fatigue after their long journey, he marched them into battle almost immediately. In the San Pascual Valley, northeast of San Diego, they fought troops under General Andrés Pico (1810–1876), the governor's brother. After being reinforced by Stockton's men, the U.S. forces were able to beat back the Mexicans in a two-day battle. In the process, however, they suffered considerably more casualties than their foes; twenty-one U.S. soldiers were killed, as opposed to only one Mexican.

Kearny and Stockton now led their combined troops toward Los Angeles, which they easily conquered. Frémont, meanwhile, had been moving his force south and had stopped at a ranch just north of Los Angeles. There he heard that the last Mexican army was now ready to surrender. Frémont met with General Pico and, even though he had not been ordered to do so, worked out a peace agreement that offered the Mexicans very lenient terms. Kearny was angry, but had to accept the agreement since it had already been signed. On January 14, Frémont rode triumphantly into Los Angeles.

Tension leads to a court-martial

Kearny was even more incensed when Stockton named Frémont governor of California. Frémont moved into a Los Angeles mansion and repeatedly ignored Kearny's orders to report to him at Monterey. When he finally did, Kearny showed him official papers from Washington that named Kearny as governor of California. In June, Kearny ordered Frémont to travel east with him. When they reached Fort Leavenworth, Kansas, Frémont was arrested and charged with "mutiny, insubordination, and conduct prejudicial to discipline." In other words, he had disregarded his superior officer and acted on his own authority.

At his court-martial (military) trial in Washington, D.C., that winter, Kearny made himself look even worse by verbally attacking Frémont. On January 31, 1848, Frémont was found guilty and sentenced to dismissal from the army. Polk cancelled the sentence, but three weeks later an outraged Frémont resigned from the army anyway. He still considered himself the conqueror of California and could not believe that the U.S. government had turned against him.

An up-and-down life

The next year, Frémont undertook another expedition through the West, this one with the purpose of investigating a location for a possible railroad to the Pacific coast. This trip turned out disastrously, since Frémont unwisely chose to try to cross southern Colorado's Sangre de Cristo mountains in mid-winter. Eleven of his men died from cold and starvation. When Frémont finally reached California, he heard that gold had been discovered there. He had earlier purchased 70 square miles of land in the Sierra foothills, called Mariposa, and soon made a fortune in gold mining.

In 1850, Frémont was elected as one of California's first two senators but served only a six-month term. In 1853, he undertook another expedition to scout out a southern railway route. Three years later, the brand new Republican Party nominated Frémont as its first presidential candidate, mostly due to his opposition to the extension of slavery to the new territories. After losing the election, Frémont returned to California, but he came east again when the American Civil War (1861–65) began. President Abraham Lincoln (1809–1865) made him a major-general in charge of the army's western division, and later of its Mountain Department based in West Virginia. Frémont did not perform well in either assignment and was soon forced out.

In 1864, Frémont was briefly a candidate for president a second time but pulled out before the election. The same year, he lost control of his Mariposa estate. Frémont moved to New York and invested in a number of railroad schemes, but these all ended badly. For a while, Jessie Frémont supported the family with her writing. In 1879, Frémont was named territorial governor of Arizona, an office he held until 1883. Four years later, the Frémonts returned to California to live. In 1890, Frémont was on a visit to New York when he died in a boarding house.

Although he was often faulted for what many saw as his efforts to grab glory for himself, Frémont also was admired for his bold, adventurous spirit and determination. His reports detailing his expeditions not only provided a wealth of useful information but inspired many U.S. settlers with the same sense of adventure. In some ways Frémont was a personification of expansionism, for he acted on the belief that the rich expanses of the North American continent were there for white U.S. citizens to take. His role in the Mexican American War was undoubtedly shaped by that belief.

For More Information

Books

Egan, Ferol. *Frémont: Explorer for a Restless Nation.* New York: 1977.

Nardo, Don. *The Mexican-American War.* San Diego, CA: Lucent Books, 1991.

Nevin, Allan. *Frémont: Pathmaker of the West.* Lincoln, NE: 1992.

Roberts, David. *A Newer World: Kit Carson, John C. Frémont, and the Claiming of the American West.* New York: Touchstone, 2000.

Rolle, Andrew. *John Charles Frémont: Character as Destiny.* Normal, OK: 1991.

Web Sites

John Frémont. [Online] Available http://www.johnfremont.com/ (accessed on January 27, 2003).

Spence, Mary Lee. "John Charles Frémont." *Utah History Encyclopedia. Utah History To Go.* [Online] Available http://historytogo.utah.gov/jcfremont.html (accessed on January 27, 2003).

Sam Houston

Born March 2, 1793
Rockbridge County, Virginia

Died July 26, 1863
Huntsville, Texas

American politician

As one of the most important and colorful figures in the early history of Texas, Sam Houston seemed to embody the state's bigness and independent spirit. A tall, friendly man who was both flashy and courageous, Houston was devoted both to Texas and to the United States as a whole. Soon after Texas declared itself the Lone Star Republic, Houston led a Texan army against a much bigger and more experienced Mexican force at the Battle of San Jacinto. The Texan victory in the battle brought a temporary peace to the region that would be shattered ten years later, when, following the admission of Texas to the union, the United States declared war against Mexico.

A teenager called "the Raven"

Sam Houston was born in Rockbridge County, Virginia, near the town of Lexington. The fifth in a family of nine children, he was the son of Major Samuel Houston, a veteran of the American Revolution (1775–83) who continued to make his living as a soldier after the war was over. Houston remembered his mother, Elizabeth Paxton Houston, as a woman of intelligence, morality, and strength. As a child, Houston hated school but loved reading, especially adventure stories. He received only about a year and a half of formal education.

When Houston was fourteen years old, his father died while inspecting frontier military outposts. Just before his death, the elder Houston had made plans to move his family to the frontier state of Tennessee, where he had acquired 419 acres of land. After his father's death, Houston's mother packed her children and belongings into a wagon and headed west. When they reached their new home, Houston's brothers began the hard work of starting a farm in an undeveloped area. Although old enough to help with the daily chores, Houston found farming boring and did little to help his brothers. His brothers often scolded Houston for his laziness around the house. Since Houston was not aiding his brothers with the farm, the family arranged for him to work as a clerk in a store when he turned sixteen.

Deciding he had had enough of his brothers bossing him around, and having found neither school nor clerking to his liking, Houston escaped across a river into land inhabited by Native Americans of the Cherokee nation. He spent the next three years living with the Cherokees, an experience that he would always remember fondly. Adopted by a chief named Ooloteka (also known as John Jolly) who gave him the name "the Raven," Houston learned the Cherokee language and customs and developed what would be a lifelong respect for them and concern for their welfare.

Soldiering with Andrew Jackson

Returning to the white community and his family in 1812, Houston opened a school, even though many people laughed at the idea of Sam Houston as a schoolteacher, charging his students a tuition fee of $8.00 per term. But after a year, he was off on his next adventure, which was serving as a soldier in the U.S. Army. The United States was now involved in a second war with Great Britain, the War of 1812 (1812–14), this one begun primarily because England had interfered with U.S. ships and sailors on the high seas. Assigned to serve under a fellow Tennessee native, General Andrew Jackson (1767–1845), Houston took part in the U.S. Army's attempt to bring a rebellious band of Creek Indians under control. At the Battle of Horseshoe Bend in March 1814, Houston was severely wounded but nevertheless contributed to the U.S. victory. His courage and ability were noticed by Jackson, and the two men began a strong friendship that would last until Jackson's death.

A young lawyer and politician

Houston served under Jackson for several more years, based at Nashville, Tennessee, and serving as a sub-agent (a representative between them and the U.S. government) to the Cherokees. In 1818, Houston decided to leave the army and become a lawyer. Even though the process of preparation for the bar exam (the test by which attorneys become qualified) usually took much longer, Houston passed after only six months of study. He set up a law practice in Lebanon, Tennessee. Houston's large size, physical vigor, and fondness for dramatic, unconventional clothing made him stand out. He also was admired for his skill as a public speaker, and in 1819, he was elected attorney general of Tennessee (the top position in the state's legal system). This election launched Houston's political career.

In 1823, Houston was elected to represent his district of Tennessee in the United States Congress. He held this position for the next four years. Houston was only thirty-five years old when, in 1827, he was elected governor of Tennessee. Two years later, he married Eliza Allen, a young woman from a wealthy family. It seemed that he was now at his personal and professional peak. Only three months after the wedding, however, Eliza left Houston and returned to her parents' home. The short marriage was over, but no one ever knew why since neither Eliza nor Houston would talk about it. Some historians speculate that Eliza had been forced into the marriage by her father and did not like being married to Houston, while others guess that either Houston or his wife had been unfaithful.

A troubled time

Whatever the reason for the breakup, it left Houston devastated. To his friends' surprise, he resigned the governorship and went to live among the Cherokee again, this time in the western part of what would later become the state of Arkansas. Known among his Native American friends as a very heavy drinker, Houston opened a trading post and married a Cherokee woman named Tiana Rogers. During this period he made several trips to Washington, D.C., to ask the U.S. government to help the Cherokees.

On one of these trips, Houston was insulted by something Ohio representative William Stanberry had said about him on the floor of the House of Representatives. In his speech, Stanberry had accused Houston of being dishonest in his dealings with the Indians. Encountering Stanberry on the street, Houston attacked him with a cane. Stanberry charged Houston with assault, and he was brought before the House to answer the charges. Relying on his public speaking skills, Houston was so successful in defending himself that he got away with only a mild reprimand. This success also inspired him to start a new life in the white community.

Texas: A land of opportunity

Like many U.S. citizens, Houston was attracted to Texas, the sprawling, sparsely populated part of Mexico that was adjacent to the southeastern United States. Under Spanish control for several hundred years, this area called Tejas y Coahuila was now ruled by Mexico, which had gained its independence from Spain in 1821. At around the same time, a land speculator (someone who buys land and then sells it again for a profit) named Moses Austin (1761–1821) had struck a deal with the Mexican government. U.S. citizens would be allowed to settle in Mexico, provided they become Mexican citizens, obey the country's laws, and join the Roman Catholic Church (Catholicism was Mexico's official religion). Austin's son Stephen (1793–1836) took over as leader of this movement after his father's unexpected death.

By the early 1830s, "Texas fever" was raging as pioneers streamed in, looking for the fresh start and opportunities that seemed to lie in the rolling hills and wide-open grasslands of Texas. Houston caught the fever too, moving to the town of Nacogdoches in 1832 and setting up a law practice. Soon he also was involved in Texas politics. This was a turbulent period in the region's history, for trouble was brewing between the U.S.-born Texans and the Mexican government. The Texans ignored many Mexican laws, especially those banning slavery and the Mexican law requiring the registration of guns. The Texans also refused to go along with the Mexicans' wish for them to blend in with the local culture. Few bothered to practice Catholicism or even learn to speak Spanish. Most also considered themselves superior to the native Mexicans, who resented these arrogant newcomers.

Called to lead fellow Texans

In 1833, Houston was chosen to take part in a special convention at which Texans voted to ask the Mexican government to allow them to form a separate state within Mexico. Stephen Austin went to the Mexican capital, Mexico City, to deliver the proposal, only to find the Mexicans so suspicious of the Texans that they not only turned down the request but arrested Austin and kept him in prison for eighteen months. The Mexican government was now headed by a former military hero named Antonio López de Santa Anna (1794–1876), who had made himself the country's dictator (absolute, all-powerful ruler).

Determined to squash the Texans' rebelliousness before it grew, Santa Anna sent Mexican troops to take over Texas towns. But this, of course, only made the Texans more angry. Violent clashes occurred across Texas as settlers battled Mexican troops. In the town of Gonzales, the Texans forced a sizable Mexican army to retreat. As defiant men began to sign up to defend the land they now considered theirs, what became known as the Texas Revolution got underway.

Houston's military experience and dynamic personality made him a natural choice to lead the still-tiny Texas army, so he took charge of the four hundred-man force. For some time, however, Houston played a low-key role as he found that individual units were reluctant to take his advice and to act in unison. One of these groups was, in early 1836, holed up at the Alamo, an old Spanish mission located just across the river from San Antonio. Some months earlier, the Texans had managed to chase the Mexican troops out of San Antonio, but it was rumored that Santa Anna would soon send more to retake the town.

Disaster at the Alamo

Houston believed the Alamo would be a deathtrap if the Mexicans surrounded it, and he ordered its less than two hundred defenders under the command of Colonel James O'Neill to abandon the place and burn it down. O'Neill, who was soon to be replaced by Colonel William Travis, refused to follow this order. In late February, Santa Anna arrived at San Antonio with several thousand troops and quickly took control of the town. He ordered Travis to surrender, and when Travis refused, the Mexicans raised the red flag. This meant that there would be no mercy for any Texans who managed to survive the coming battle.

On the morning of February 24, the Mexicans began bombing the Alamo. The same day Travis, whose appeal for more troops would not reach Houston in time, issued a message "to the people of Texas and all Americans in the world," vowing that he would "never surrender or retreat" and that he would seek "Victory or Death!" Legend has it that Travis offered his men a chance to escape with honor from the Alamo. It is believed that perhaps only one man chose to leave. On March 6, Santa Anna ordered a full-scale attack on the Alamo. His troops quickly penetrated the mission's walls and began slaughtering its defenders, who included the legendary frontiersman Jim Bowie (1796–1836), known for the big knife that carried his name, and Davy Crockett (1786–1836), a veteran Indian fighter and former Tennessee congressman.

All of Travis's men were killed, and their bodies burned in a heap. Only the wife of one of the men, Susana Dickinson, was allowed to escape. Carrying her baby in her arms, she managed to reach Houston and deliver the horrifying news. Just days before, Houston had taken part in a historic meeting where Texan delegates had written up a constitution for their new country, which they had christened the Lone Star Republic. When he received Travis's call for reinforcements, Houston had set out for San Antonio but had only gotten as far as Gonzales when he heard what had happened at the Alamo.

The Runaway Scrape

There was soon more bad news. On March 19, 350 Texans under the command of Colonel James Fannin (1804–1836) were forced to surrender to a Mexican force at Goliad. Although other Mexican officers disagreed, Santa Anna ordered the prisoners shot. News of the massacres at the Alamo and Goliad spread among the Texas settlers like wildfire, setting off a northward scramble for safety that came to be known as the Runaway Scrape. Meanwhile, Houston planned a new, cautious strategy of retreating to regroup his troops, to continue to train them for battle, and to wait for Santa Anna to make a mistake.

The ranks of the Texan army soon were bolstered by fresh volunteers, fueled by the desire to teach the Mexicans a lesson. Eager for revenge, they grumbled about Houston's order to retreat. That was the last thing they wanted to do, but Houston held firm. One day he had two graves dug, announcing that they were for the first two men who chose to desert his army. Houston now moved his force eastward (toward the site that would one day become the city of Houston), just ahead of Santa Anna, who was trying to locate and squash the leaders of the Texas independence movement.

A surprising victory on the San Jacinto River

His army now just under eight hundred soldiers, Houston halted at the place where the San Jacinto River meets the Buffalo Bayou. They camped in a grove of oak trees, and watched as Santa Anna's much larger force arrived in the area and set up their own camp. Still Houston did not make a move, even as Santa Anna received reinforcements. For his part, Santa Anna was more convinced than ever that the Texan army was incompetent and Houston, a coward. On the afternoon of April 21, tired of waiting for a U.S. attack that never came, Santa Anna allowed his troops a *siesta* (nap).

Houston took advantage of this opportunity. Just after 4:30 P.M., he ordered his troops to attack the Mexican camp. Taken utterly by surprise, with cries of "Remember the Alamo! Remember Goliad!" ringing in their ears, the Mexicans could barely defend themselves. A large number of them fled in panic toward the nearby river, where many drowned or were shot in the water. The Battle of San Jacinto lasted only eighteen minutes, with the Texan soldiers brutally slaughtering every Mexican they could get their hands on, even when their officers ordered them to stop.

Houston had been severely wounded in the lower leg by a bullet that also took the life of his white horse, Saracen. (Another horse also had been shot from under him during the battle.) Refusing any pain medication that would have made him sleepy, he surveyed the battlefield. Only nine Texans had been killed, while more than six hundred Mexicans were dead and another seven hundred taken prisoner. Santa Anna was missing, but a few days later he was found disguised as a farm worker and brought into camp. This attempt to conceal his identity failed, however, when some Mexican prisoners saw their general and the leader of their country and yelled, "El presidente!" (the president).

Serving as president of Texas

Although many U.S. officers and soldiers wanted Santa Anna executed for ordering the massacres at the Alamo and Goliad, Houston believed the Mexican general could be more valuable alive than dead. Thus Santa Anna was kept a prisoner for several months, during which period he signed treaties that required him to leave Texas, quit fighting, and persuade the Mexican government to accept the independent status of the Lone Star Republic. When Santa Anna finally returned to Mexico in disgrace, however, his government promptly ruled the treaties invalid.

Houston's reputation, by contrast, could not have been better. In September 1836, he was elected, by an overwhelming majority, president of Texas. His term was fairly calm and peaceful, as large numbers of settlers poured into Texas, and Houston worked actively to develop smooth relations with Native Americans in the area as well as the still-hostile Mexicans. Houston's presidency was followed by that of Mirabeau Lamar (1798–1859), a man of much more extravagant visions who involved Texas in some foolhardy schemes, especially his attempt to convince the residents of Santa Fe, New Mexico, to join the Lone Star Republic. This resulted in the imprisonment of several hundred Texan soldiers in Mexico.

By 1841, when Houston regained the presidency of Texas, there was much talk of Texas becoming part of the

United States. It seemed that defending Texas from Mexico, which continued to stage periodic small-scale attacks across the border, was just too difficult for the small republic. In addition, most Texans still identified strongly with the ideals and culture of the United States. Within the United States, however, the possible annexation (being made a state) of Texas posed problems.

The annexation of Texas

The practice of slavery had become a controversial issue, with citizens of the northern states calling for it to be abolished (made illegal) while the southerners defended it as necessary to their livelihood. The states were evenly divided between those that allowed slavery and those where it was illegal. Texas was sure to be admitted to the union as a slave state, which would upset the balance. Thus, southerners pushed for, and northerners opposed, its annexation. Mean-

Texan leader and soldier Sam Houston accepting the surrender of the Mexican officers Antonio López de Santa Anna and Perfecto de Cos after the Battle of San Jacinto during the Texan War of Independence.
Photograph reproduced by permission of Getty Images.

while, U.S. leaders hesitated to take a firm stance either way because they did not want to alienate voters in either the South or the North.

Houston's opinion, however, was very firm. He was in favor of statehood for Texas. By the time he left office in 1844, he had made it clear to the United States that its arch-rival, Great Britain, was making very friendly overtures to Texas. This was a good strategy, for nobody in the United States wanted the British to get a foothold in North America again. Now there was much more pressure to annex Texas. In 1845, Texas did become a state, much to the delight of Houston and most Texans.

At around the same time, Houston's personal life also was taking a turn for the better. By 1840, Houston had divorced his first wife and his second had died. So he was free to marry Margaret Lea, with whom he would have a very happy, twenty-three-year marriage that produced eight children. Much younger than her husband, Margaret also was very religious and was able to convince Houston to stop drinking.

War with Mexico

In the summer of 1845, President James K. Polk (1795–1849; see biographical entry) sent U.S. troops to Texas. Less than a year later the United States, using as its excuse an incident in which a Mexican force had attacked and killed some U.S. soldiers, declared war on Mexico. Despite their much larger army, the Mexicans suffered from poor leadership and inferior weapons, and they lost battle after battle. In September 1848, General Winfield Scott (1786–1866; see biographical entry) rode in triumph into the Mexican capital, Mexico City, which his troops had captured. The war was over.

With the signing of the Treaty of Guadalupe Hidalgo, the United States not only tightened its grip on Texas but gained the territories of California and New Mexico, an area of 525,000 square miles and more than half of Mexico's total land. Most U.S. citizens were happy with the treaty, but Houston did not much like it. He agreed with those who thought the United States should take over all of Mexico.

The sanctity of the Union

Houston served as one of his state's two U.S. senators from 1845 until 1859. During this period the slavery issue became more and more divisive. Despite his status as a devoted southerner from a slave state, Houston believed that slavery should one day be abolished, and he voted for measures that prevented its extension into the new states that were now being formed. Like his friend and mentor Andrew Jackson, Houston believed that the Union must be preserved above all, no matter how strong the disagreements between individual states might be.

Elected governor of Texas in 1859, Houston made many Texans unhappy by warning them of the danger of seceding from (leaving) the Union, which was now a strong possibility. In late 1860 and early 1861, eleven southern, slaveholding states did secede and form the Confederate States of America, leading to the outbreak of the Civil War (1861–65). Texas was one of those states, but Houston refused to sign the oath of allegiance to the Confederacy. Turning down an offer from President Abraham Lincoln (1809–1865) of federal troops to aid him, Houston was forced to leave office. He also had to endure the taunts of "Traitor!" that he heard from some of his fellow Texans.

Still a devoted supporter of Texas, despite what he saw as its mistakes, Houston returned to his home in Huntsville. Houston died on July 26, 1863, and the last words on his lips were the two names most precious to him, "Margaret" and "Texas." His role in the history of Texas, a state that was to become a vital part of the United States in the late-nineteenth and twentieth centuries, was acknowledged when one of its most important cities was given his name.

For More Information

Books

De Bruhl, Marshall. *Sword of San Jacinto*. New York: Random House, 1993.

Friend, Llerena. *Sam Houston: The Great Designer*. Austin: University of Texas Press, 1954.

Fritz, Jean. *Make Way for Sam Houston*. New York: Putnam's Sons, 1986.

James, Marquis. *The Raven: A Biography of Sam Houston*. New York: Grosset and Dunlap, 1929.

Roberts, Madge Thornall. *Star of Destiny: The Private Life of Sam and Margaret Houston*. Denton: University of North Texas Press, 1993.

Robson, Lucia St. Clair. *Walk in My Soul: The Story of Tiana of the Cherokee, the Young Sam Houston, and the Trail of Tears*. New York: Ballantine Books, 1985.

Williams, John Hoyt. *Sam Houston: A Biography of the Father of Texas*. New York: Simon & Schuster, 1993.

Wisehart, M. K. *Sam Houston: American Giant*. Washington: Robert B. Luce, 1962.

Periodicals

Nevin, David. "'Fight and Be Damned!' Said Sam Houston." *Smithsonian* 23, No. 4 (July 1992): 82.

Dingus, Anne. "Sam the Man." *Texas Monthly* 21, No. 3 (March 1993): 110.

Web Sites

"Houston, Sam." *Handbook of Texas Online*. [Online] Available http://www.tsha.utexas.edu/handbook/online/articles/view/HH/fho73.html (accessed on January 27, 2003).

"Sam Houston." *PBS: New Perspectives on the West*. [Online] Available http://www.pbs.org/weta/thewest/people/d_h/houston.htm (accessed on January 27, 2003).

"Sam Houston 'The Raven' (1793–1863)." *The Lone Star Junction*. [Online] Available http://www.lsjunction.com/people/houston.htm (accessed on January 27, 2003).

"Sam Houston 'The Raven' (1793–1863)." *Lone Star Internet, All About Texas*. [Online] Available http://www.lone-star.net/mall/main-areas/txtrails.htm (accessed on January 27, 2003).

"Sam Houston." *Texas State Library and Archives Commission*. [Online] Available http://www.tsl.state.tx.us/treasures/giants/houston-01.html (accessed on January 27, 2003).

Stephen Watts Kearny

Born August 30, 1794
Newark, New Jersey

Died October 31, 1848
St. Louis, Missouri

U.S. Army general and politician

One of three top U.S. generals in the Mexican American War, Stephen Watts Kearny led the Army of the West in a bloodless takeover of Santa Fe in the territory of New Mexico. Proceeding farther west to California, he merged his troops with those of navy commander Robert Stockton (1795–1866) and army officer John Charles Frémont (1813–1890; see biographical entry) in a combined force that succeeded in putting down a rebellion of *Californios* (Mexican citizens living in California). Although he was sometimes criticized for being overly stern, domineering, and inflexible, Kearny was admired for his courage and leadership ability.

A young officer on the frontier

Stephen Watts Kearny was the fifteenth and youngest child of Philip and Susanna Watts Kearny. His father, who was of Irish ancestry (the family name had originally been O'Kearny), was a successful wine merchant and landowner in Perth Amboy, New Jersey, before the start of the American Revolution (1775–83). He sided with the Loyalists (those who

Stephen Watts Kearny.
Photograph courtesy of The Library of Congress.

wanted what became the United States to remain a colony of Great Britain), however, and after the war his land was confiscated. The family moved to New York City and then to Newark, New Jersey, where Kearny was born.

Kearny attended public schools, entering Columbia College, which later became New York City's Columbia University, in 1811. But the next year marked the start of the War of 1812 (1812–14), a conflict between the United States and Great Britain that started over disputes related to free trade and sailors' rights on the high seas. Kearny joined New York's militia (an army made up of volunteers who offer their services in emergencies) and was appointed a first lieutenant in the Thirteenth Infantry.

At the Battle of Queenston Heights—which took place near what later became Queenston, Ontario, in October 1812—Kearny was wounded and captured by the British. He was soon exchanged for a British prisoner, however, and was promoted to the rank of captain about a year later. Following the war, Kearny continued his army career. After 1819, he served almost exclusively on the western frontier, the undeveloped area west of the Appalachian mountains, to which U.S. settlers were moving in great numbers throughout the nineteenth century.

Moving up through the ranks

During the next several decades, Kearny established a good reputation through his leadership of expeditions to find good locations for, and to build, new frontier forts. These included Camp Missouri (later called Fort Atkinson) near present-day Omaha, Nebraska, and Camp Cold Water (later called Fort Snelling) near St. Paul, Minnesota. In 1825, he took part in an expedition to the mouth of the Yellowstone River, and three years after that he took command of Fort Crawford (located near present-day Prairie du Chien, Wisconsin).

Kearny earned the rank of major in 1829, and in the same year was transferred to the newly built Jefferson Barracks in Missouri. A tall, slender man with a dignified bearing, he was often invited to visit friends in nearby St. Louis. At the home of General William Clark (1770–1838), who gained fame as one of two leaders (the other was Captain Meriwether Lewis; 1774–1809) of the Lewis and Clark Expedition, Kearny met Clark's stepdaughter, Mary Radford. Married in September 1830, the two would go on to have eleven children, several of whom died before reaching adulthood.

By the end of the year, Kearny had moved to what would become the state of Oklahoma, where he supervised the rebuilding of Fort Towson, which had recently been destroyed. In 1833, he was made a lieutenant colonel in the new Dragoon Regiment, which was very similar to a cavalry (soldiers mounted on horseback) unit. After leading an expedition to the Iowa territory and beginning construction of Fort Des Moines, Kearny was made colonel and put in command of the Dragoon Regiment. He established his headquarters at Fort Leavenworth in Kansas territory.

Continuing his march up through the army ranks, Kearny was put in charge of the Third Military District, with headquarters in St. Louis, in 1842. There he had the difficult responsibility of trying to protect the many settlers who were streaming into the frontier areas, and to keep peace with the Native Americans whose lives were being disrupted by this westward expansion movement. The settlers were moving into the west along the Oregon Trail, which wound for 2,000 miles from Independence, Missouri, to the Columbia River in Oregon Territory. In 1845, Kearny led an expedition along the trail to South Pass in the Wind River range of the Rocky Mountains.

War with Mexico begins

In May 1846, Kearny was one of two generals in charge of construction of the new Fort Kearny (originally located near present-day Nebraska City, Nebraska, but eventually moved to a location on the Platte River). The same month, however, an event occurred that would put Kearny on a new path. On May 13, the United States declared war on Mexico.

Almost ten years earlier, U.S. settlers living in the Mexican Territory of Texas had declared their independence and driven out the Mexican army. Mexico had never accepted the loss of this territory, and had threatened to declare war if the United States annexed Texas (made it a state). Annexation had occurred in March 1845, and tension mounted as U.S. president James Polk (1795–1849; see biographical entry) sent troops to Texas. Many U.S. leaders and citizens were eager to acquire not only Texas but the large Mexican territories of California and New Mexico. The situation had erupted into war when the United States had used a Mexican attack on a small band of U.S. soldiers in an area of disputed land as its excuse to declare war.

The strategy that Polk and his war planners devised had three parts. General Zachary Taylor (1784–1850; see biographical entry) would lead an army into northeastern Mexico, while U.S. troops also marched to the important trading center of Santa Fe, New Mexico, and then into California to take control of this vast area valued for its seaports and fertile farmland. Later, General Winfield Scott (1786–1866; see biographical entry) would command an invasion from the eastern coastal city of Vera Cruz, leading his army overland to capture Mexico City, the country's capital.

Commanding the Army of the West

Considered one of the army's most capable officers, the fifty-two-year-old Kearny was given command of the Army of the West in May 1846. At Fort Leavenworth, he assembled a fighting force of 1,660 that included not only his own dragoons, but a large number of volunteers whose toughness and skill with guns made up for their lack of military experience. Kearny and his troops set out in early June and made remarkably fast progress across the desert terrain. They marched 1,000 miles in six weeks, sometimes covering 30 miles per day.

On August 18, Kearny's army reached Santa Fe, a city of about eighty thousand residents. The Mexican troops assigned to defend Santa Fe had fled upon hearing of Kearny's approach, and no one opposed the U.S. takeover. After gaining control of the city, Kearny issued a statement proclaiming that the residents of New Mexico were now U.S. citizens and that their rights—especially the right to practice the Roman Catholic religion, which was an important issue to Mexicans—would be protected. Kearny would remain in Santa Fe for about a month. As military governor of New Mexico, he had to organize a government for the territory, including a system of laws.

The conquest of California gets underway

Meanwhile, some major events had taken place in California, but due to the slowness of communication during the nineteenth century, Kearny would not hear about them for some time. At this period, there were about seven hundred U.S. settlers living in California, most of them without the approval of the Mexican government. These settlers had grown increasingly nervous about the prospect of a war with Mexico and how they would be treated by the Mexicans if war broke out. Finally a group of them who were living in the Sacramento Valley decided to make a decisive move.

With the help of a U.S. military officer—Major John Charles Frémont, a member of the U.S. Corps of Engineers who was in the area on a surveying assignment—these settlers staged what came to be known as the Bear Flag Rebellion. Raising a flag that featured a picture of a grizzly bear, they declared themselves independent from Mexico. Frémont had led the revolt despite the lack of any official orders from the U.S. government to do so. (Although some historians have suggested that Frémont may have had secret orders to take a military role if necessary.)

At around the same time, a U.S. Navy squadron (group of warships) under the command first of Commander John Sloat (1781–1867) and then of Commodore Robert Stockton had taken control of ports along the California coast, beginning with San Francisco and Monterrey and finally including Santa Barbara, San Pedro, Los Angeles, and San Diego. At first, there had been little or no resistance from the Californios, who numbered only about eight thousand. In fact, Stockton and Frémont were so confident that they had California in hand that they sent the famous frontier scout Christopher "Kit" Carson (1809–1868) east to deliver this news to Washington, D.C.

On September 25, with Charles Bent installed as New Mexico's new civil governor and with about three hundred soldiers behind him, Kearny set out for California. On the way, Kearny and his group ran into Carson, who told Kearny that the situation in California was under control. Upon hearing this news, Kearny sent two hundred of his troops back to Santa Fe, an action he would soon regret. For what neither Carson nor Kearny knew was that a small group of Californios under the command of generals José Castro and José María Flores as well as Governor Pío Pico had staged their own revolt and recaptured Los Angeles. The fight for California was not yet over.

Finishing the fight for California

As he approached Los Angeles, Kearny met some U.S. troops who informed him that the city had been retaken by the Mexicans. As a result of this information, Kearny rushed his weary soldiers into battle instead of giving them time to rest from their long journey. This decision lead to Kearny's force being badly defeated at a December 6 battle near the village of San Pascual. While only one Mexican was killed during this fight, Kearny lost about one-third of his troops, and he was wounded twice himself. Only the arrival of some reinforcements from Stockton prevented an even worse outcome.

Kearny now led his men on to San Diego, where he combined forces with Stockton, bringing the total U.S. troop strength to about six hundred. On January 8 and 9, 1847, this force fought two battles at Los Angeles. The result was dramatically different from San Pascual, for only one U.S. soldier was killed while the Mexicans sustained heavy casualties. On January 10, Kearny and Stockton occupied Los Angeles. Then they headed toward Monterrey in pursuit of the last remaining Mexican fighters. Along the way, they heard that this small band had already surrendered to Frémont, whom they had encountered unexpectedly. In a bold step that was typical behavior for Frémont, he had already negotiated a treaty with the Mexicans. Although Frémont had not been authorized to do this, the treaty had been signed and would have to be accepted.

The fighting was over, but now the task of governing a large new territory had to begin. A disagreement quickly arose about who was to take charge of this effort. Kearny felt that his orders made it clear that he was to become the military governor of California. Stockton disagreed, however, and just before leaving to take part in other military actions in Mexico, he named Frémont governor. Frémont moved into a Los Angeles mansion and repeatedly ignored Kearny's demands that he come to Monterrey to meet with Kearny. Finally, more orders arrived from Washington that made it very clear that Kearny was in command, and Frémont had to relinquish his role.

Two careers end prematurely

Within a few months, Frémont had to answer for his actions. The war ended in May 1848, following the September 1847 conquest of Mexico City by Scott's troops and the signing of the Treaty of Guadalupe Hidalgo in February. In June, Kearny prepared to return to the eastern United States, and he ordered Frémont to accompany him. When the party reached Fort Leavenworth, Frémont was arrested for disobeying a superior officer. He was to be court-martialed (tried by a military court) in Washington, D.C. At the trial, Frémont made his situation worse by insulting Kearny. As a result, Frémont was found guilty and was sentenced to be discharged from the army. Although Polk pardoned Frémont, he decided to resign from the army anyway. Until the end of this life, Frémont felt that he had been wronged by Kearny and the army.

In the months following the war, Kearny returned to Mexico, serving brief terms as civil governor in Vera Cruz and Mexico City. In August, despite strong opposition from powerful Missouri senator Thomas Hart Benton (1782–1858), who was Frémont's father-in-law, Kearny was promoted to the rank of brevet (honorary) brigadier general.

While in Mexico, Kearny had contracted yellow fever, a deadly disease that was then common in Mexico's swampy coastal regions in the spring and summer. Because of his ailment, he returned to Jefferson Barracks in Missouri. As he grew more ill, he was moved into his father-in-law's home in St. Louis, where he died on October 31, 1848. Kearny's funeral, which included seven hundred people marching behind his casket, was said to be the largest that St. Louis had seen up to that time. It honored the thirty-six-year career of a military officer who had served his country well, mostly in securing the edges of the frontier for U.S. settlers.

For More Information

Books

Clarke, Dwight. *Stephen Watts Kearny: Soldier of the West.* Norman: University of Oklahoma Press, 1961.

Frazier, Donald, ed. *The United States and Mexico at War.* New York: Simon and Schuster, 1997.

Von Sachsen, Hans, et al. *Winning the West: General Stephen Watts Kearny's Letter Book.* Pekitanoui Publications, 1998.

Web Sites

"General Stephen Watts Kearny." *Department of Physics and Physical Science, University of Nebraska at Kearney.* [Online] Available http://rip.physics.unk.edu/Kearney/SWK.html (accessed on January 29, 2003).

"Kearny, Steven Watts." *Fact Monster.com.* [Online] Available http://www.factmonster.com/ce6/people/A0827256.html (accessed on January 29, 2003).

José Antonio Navarro

Born February 27, 1795
San Antonio de Bexar, Mexico

Died January 14, 1871
San Antonio, Texas

Politician

J oseé Antonio Navarro is considered one of the founders of the state of Texas. He was one of the few *Tejanos* (Texas citizens of Mexican heritage) to gain recognition for playing a key role in the early days of Texas, from the Texas Revolution—when Texas declared its independence from Mexico—and the establishment of the Lone Star Republic to Texas statehood and beyond. Throughout his political career, Narvarro was a strong defender of the rights of Mexican Americans in his beloved Texas.

Witness to a revolution

José Antonio Navarro's father, Angel Navarro, was a private in the Spanish army when he came to what was then the colony of New Spain, and which later became Mexico. Leaving the army, he established a trading business in the town of Saltillo in the province of Tejas y Coahuila. After marrying Maria Josepha Ruiz y Pena, Angel Navarro moved to San Antonio de Bexar where he opened a store and started a family that would eventually include twelve children.

José Antonio Navarro was the eighth of these children. At the age of ten he was sent to Saltillo to attend school, but when his father died three years later, he had to return to San Antonio, and he never received any more formal education. The young Navarro was working in his father's store when the violence that had been erupting across New Spain reached his own town.

Beginning in 1811, resentment over the harsh rule of the Spanish, whose rigid class system granted privileges to those who were wealthy and of direct Spanish descents, led to scattered rebellions. The first was led by Roman Catholic priest Miguel Hidalgo y Costilla (1753–1811), whose uprising of mostly poor, mixed-race followers was crushed by the Spanish. Eventually, however, the Spanish were beaten, and Mexico achieved its independence in 1821.

Before that day, however, the citizens of San Antonio de Bexar had fought their own battle with the Spanish. In 1813, the teenaged Navarro witnessed the brutal execution of some Spanish soldiers that the rebels had taken prisoner, an event that horrified him despite his admiration for the freedom fighters. Soon Spain sent a larger army to defeat the rebels, and Navarro was forced to flee, with his brothers and his uncle Francisco Ruiz, to the United States. After spending three years in Louisiana, Navarro returned to San Antonio de Bexar to establish himself as a merchant.

The White Dove

Now an adult, Navarro was six feet tall and muscular, although he walked with a limp from a childhood horseback-riding accident. He was a quiet, modest, serious young man who loved reading and who usually wore white clothing, which is why his brothers gave him the nickname "the White Dove." In his free time, he studied law books and developed an extensive knowledge of Spanish and, later, Mexican law.

In late 1820, just as Mexico's independence struggle was nearing its end, an American named Moses Austin (1761–1821) came to San Antonio de Bexar. He met with the town's Spanish representative and received permission to bring three hundred U.S. settlers to Tejas y Coahuila, which would come to be known in the United States as Texas. An expanding population, economic pressures, and expansionist spirit (the idea of U.S. citizens moving beyond their nation's current boundaries) had combined to make that rolling, sparsely populated land south of the border seem very attractive.

Not long after the meeting, Austin died unexpectedly, and his son Stephen Austin (1793–1836) took over as the settlers' leader. After renegotiating an agreement with the government of newly independent Mexico, whose leaders hoped these newcomers would bring prosperity to a remote and undeveloped region, Austin brought the first group of U.S. settlers to Texas. In order to live in the new land, these immigrants agreed to meet certain conditions, such as becoming Mexican citizens, obeying Mexican laws, and joining the state-sponsored Roman Catholic Church. It also was during this time that Austin and Navarro became friends, a relationship that would continue until Austin's death about fifteen years later.

Active in Mexican politics

In the wake of their revolution, and especially after the 1824 constitution established Mexico as a republic, most Mexicans hoped that they would enjoy the same rights and freedoms enjoyed by citizens of other democratic nations. This would not the case though, as Mexico would suffer over the next few decades from political instability and dictatorial leaders. Nevertheless, Navarro took an active role from the start, winning election to the Mexican legislature.

In 1825, the thirty-year-old Navarro married teenaged Margarita de la Garza, with whom he would have a happy, almost forty-year marriage that produced seven children. He soon began a second term in the legislature, while also becoming one of the area's largest landowners by buying about 50,000 acres (divided into a number of ranches) as well as the longhorn cattle that had been brought to the region by the Spanish.

Meanwhile, as the decade progressed, residents of the United States who had caught "Texas fever" poured over the border. Navarro approved of this, because he thought it was a good idea to develop this land in which Mexicans were not, by and large, settling. In fact, by the end of the decade, there would be about fifteen thousand former U.S. citizens living in Texas, compared to only three thousand Tejanos. As a law-

Texans Declare Their Independence

On March 2, 1836, four days before the disastrous clash between several thousand Mexican troops and less than two hundred Texans at the Alamo, in which all the Texan defenders were killed, representatives from all over Texas staged an important meeting in the town of Washington-on-Brazos. There they declared their independence from Mexico and signed the following document, thus establishing the Lone Star Republic.

The Unanimous Declaration of Independence made by the Delegates of the People of Texas in General Convention at the town of Washington on the 2nd day of March 1836.

When a government has ceased to protect the lives, liberty and property of the people, from whom its legitimate powers are derived, and for the advancement of whose happiness it was instituted, and so far from being a guarantee for the enjoyment of those inestimable and inalienable rights, becomes an instrument in the hands of evil rulers for their oppression.

When the Federal Republican Constitution of their country, which they have sworn to support, no longer has a substantial existence, and the whole nature of their government has been forcibly changed, without their consent, from a restricted federative republic, composed of sovereign states, to a consolidated central military despotism, in which every interest is disregarded but that of the army and the priesthood, both the eternal enemies of civil liberty, the everready minions of power, and the usual instruments of tyrants.

The Mexican government, by its colonization laws, invited and induced the Anglo-American population of Texas to colonize its wilderness under the pledged faith of a written constitution, that they should continue to enjoy that constitutional liberty and republican government to which they had been habituated in the land of their birth, the United States of America.

In this expectation they have been cruelly disappointed, inasmuch as the Mexican nation has acquiesced in the late changes made in the government by General Antonio Lopez de Santa Anna, who having overturned the constitution of his country, now offers us the cruel alternative, either to abandon our homes, acquired by so many privations, or submit to the most

maker, Navarro pushed legislation that would benefit the Texans, such as more lenient laws on slavery and religion. But gradually Navarro found that his fellow legislators considered him too close to the U.S. settlers, and they questioned his loyalty to Mexico.

Texans fight for independence

At the same time, there was growing fear that the Texans were becoming too independent. Much of this was intolerable of all tyranny, the combined despotism of the sword and the priesthood.

It incarcerated in a dungeon, for a long time, one of our citizens, for no other cause but a zealous endeavor to procure the acceptance of our constitution, and the establishment of a state government.

It has suffered the military commandants, stationed among us, to exercise arbitrary acts of oppression and tyranny, thus trampling upon the most sacred rights of the citizens, and rendering the military superior to the civil power.

It denies us the right of worshipping the Almighty according to the dictates of our own conscience, by the support of a national religion, calculated to promote the temporal interest of its human functionaries, rather than the glory of the true and living God.

It has demanded us to deliver up our arms, which are essential to our defence, the rightful property of freemen, and formidable only to tyrannical governments.

It [the Mexican government] hath been, during the whole time of our connection with it, the contemptible sport and victim of successive military revolutions, and hath continually exhibited every char-acteristic of a weak, corrupt, and tyrranical government.

These, and other grievances, were patiently borne by the people of Texas, until they reached that point at which forbearance ceases to be a virtue. We then took up arms in defence of the national constitution. We appealed to our Mexican brethren for assistance. Our appeal has been made in vain.

The necessity of self-preservation, therefore, now decrees our eternal political separation.

We, therefore, the delegates with plenary powers of the people of Texas, in solemn convention assembled, appealing to a candid world for the necessities of our condition, do hereby resolve and declare, that our political connection with the Mexican nation has forever ended, and that the people of Texas do now constitute a free, Sovereign, and independent republic.

Richard Ellis, President of the Convention and Delegate from Red River

Source: "The Texas Declaration of Independence (March 2, 1836)." Lone Star Junction. [Online] Available http://www.lsjunction.com/docs/tdoi.htm (accessed on January 31, 2003).

brought on by the Texans themselves, for, despite their promises, most of them openly disobeyed Mexican laws, especially those outlawing slavery and restricting gun ownership. The Texans also made no effort to practice Catholicism, learn Spanish, or blend in with the native-born community. They were, indeed, asking for more autonomy (self-rule), but the Mexican government was in no mood to listen. In 1835, a dynamic general named Antonio López de Santa Anna (1794–1876) had taken over as president and immediately overturned the 1824 constitution. Power was now concentrated in the central government, rather than the individual states, and Santa Anna ruled as a dictator.

In 1833, after having traveled to the nation's capital, Mexico City, to negotiate with the government, Austin was arrested and imprisoned. Two years later, Navarro was elected senator to the National Congress but, fearing that he also would be arrested because of his close ties to Austin, Navarro made excuses not to go to Mexico City. That same year, Austin was released from prison, but by this time Santa Anna had ordered Mexican troops into towns across Texas. He meant to show the Texans that the Mexican government would tolerate no nonsense. Now was the time for Tejanos to choose sides, and Navarro chose Texas.

In the early months of 1836, Texan leaders from across the region held a meeting in the town of Washington-on-Brazos. They were there to form an independent nation, which was to be called the Lone Star Republic. Navarro was one of only three Tejanos to participate in writing the constitution, which was closely modeled after that of the United States. The new republic's declaration of independence was signed on March 2, 1836, making the Lone Star Republic a reality.

Only four days later, Santa Anna's force surrounded and slaughtered a small group of Texans who had taken refuge in the Alamo, an old Spanish mission located at San Antonio. All of the Alamo's nearly two hundred defenders were killed, among them the legendary frontiersman Jim Bowie (1796–1836), the widowed husband of Navarro's niece. This incident, along with the later massacre of three hundred Texan prisoners at the town of Goliad, ignited Texans' rage. They rushed to join a rebellion that ended with the defeat of Santa Anna's troops at the Battle of San Jacinto by a Texan army under the command of Sam Houston (1793–1863), who would soon become the first elected president of the Lone Star Republic.

An uneasy truce and an ill-fated quest

Although the Mexican army withdrew, Mexico did not acknowledge Texas's independence. The two nations existed side by side in an uneasy kind of truce, as Texans began the work of running a country and Mexico bided its time. Navarro, too, had much to do, for his store needed rebuilding and his cattle stocks, depleted by the hunger of the Mexican army, needed replenishing.

Throughout the 1830s, Navarro served in the Texas Congress, working to help Tejanos gain legal ownership of their lands. Then, in June 1841, he made a decision that he would come to regret. The ambitious Mirabeau Lamar (1798–1859) was now the president of the Lone Star Republic. He believed that the residents of the Mexican territory of New Mexico, where the thriving trading center of Santa Fe was located, would gladly accept an offer to break away from Mexico and become part of Texas. Eager to pursue this goal, Lamar recruited more than three hundred individuals from a variety of backgrounds to take part in an expedition to Santa Fe. Navarro reluctantly agreed to become one of the leaders of the expedition, which set out with a long train of wagons loaded with trading goods.

The journey, however, was ill-fated from the start. Misled by an incompetent guide, the group became lost in the desert, soon discovering that its store of food and water was insufficient. They were attacked several times by hostile Native Americans, Comanches and Kiowas, who resented the Texans presence in the area, and many members of the expedition were plagued by illness and hunger.

But the worst was yet to come. Before reaching Santa Fe, the whole group was captured by the Mexican army and forced to make a long, difficult march to Mexico City that led to many of their deaths. Delighted with this chance to teach the Texans a lesson, Santa Anna ordered the group to be thrown into Acordada Prison. Because Santa Anna considered Navarro a traitor to Mexico, however, he was singled out for especially harsh treatment and was sentenced to be executed.

Imprisoned by Santa Anna

Much to Santa Anna's disappointment, Mexico's Supreme Court overturned Navarro's sentence, but Santa Anna retaliated as best he could. While the other expedition members were released in June 1842, Navarro was sent to the worst prison in Mexico, the notoriously dreary, damp San Juan de Ulloa, in the coastal city of Vera Cruz. He spent the next three years there, first in solitary confinement and then in a regular cell. When Santa Anna (whose grudge against Navarro, some said, dated back to the Navarro family's refusal of Santa Anna's proposal to marry Navarro's sister) came to visit him, Navarro would not say a word to the dictator, further enraging him.

By 1844, however, the Mexican people had had enough of Santa Anna. He was overthrown and exiled to Cuba, while the more moderate José Joaquin de Herrera (1792–1854) took over as president. With Herrera in power, Navarro now was finally allowed to leave the prison, and on February, 3, 1845 he returned to Texas. Receiving a hero's welcome in the port town of Galveston, he traveled immediately to his home to be reunited with his family and go back to work on his ranches.

The new state of Texas

Only a month after Navarro's return, Texas became part of the United States. The only Tejano elected to the convention to approve statehood and write a constitution, Navarro argued successfully against those who wanted only free white citizens of Texas to be able to vote. In the first elections held in the new state of Texas, Navarro was elected a state senator. The next year saw the beginning of the Mexican American War, when U.S. forces invaded Mexican territory, quickly taking control of New Mexico, California, and much of northeastern Mexico. The same year, a southern Texas county was named for Navarro, who requested that its county be called Corsicana, in honor of his father's birthplace.

The population of Texas had grown by leaps and bounds throughout the 1830s and early 1840s, bringing it to about two hundred thousand. The most recent immigrants, however, treated the Tejanos with prejudice and suspicion, especially during the years of the Mexican American War. This was surely disheartening for people like Navarro, who had lived in the region all their lives and who had worked, fought, and suffered for its independence. The fact was that many, if not most of the U.S. settlers, brought with them deeply racist ideas about Mexicans, whom they saw as ignorant, lazy, and incapable of self-government. The division between white Texans and Tejanos intensified even more after the war, expressed in occasional incidents of violence and in laws that prohibited the rights of Mexican Americans. These tensions and injustices were to continue well into the twentieth century.

Navarro's senate term ended in 1849 and he retired to private life, spending the next two decades working on his ranches. He did not give up politics altogether, however, for in 1853 he ran successfully for the office of San Antonio alderman (a position in city government). Navarro had been alarmed to witness the growing local influence of the strongly anti-Catholic and anti-immigration Know-Nothing Party, the name of which dated from its origins as a secret society, when members who were asked about the group's existence would respond that they did not know anything about it.

In the 1854 election, the Know-Nothings won the mayor's race as well as a majority on the city council. Navarro led a successful campaign to defeat the Know-Nothings in the next election. Voted out of office in 1855, they soon disappeared.

By 1861, rising tension over the issues of slavery and states' rights had brought the United States to the brink of civil war. Navarro supported the secession from the Union of the eleven southern states, including Texas, that made up the Confederacy. This action by the southerners resulted in a bloody four-year conflict between the North and the South, called the Civil War. All four of Navarro's sons fought for the Confederate Army. When Navarro died of cancer in 1871, he was recognized as a true Texas patriot and one of the key figures in its early history.

For More Information

Books

Dawson, Joseph Martin. *José Antonio Navarro: Creator of Texas*. Waco, TX: Baylor University Press, 1969.

Gurasich, Marj. *Benito and the White Dove: A Story of José Antonio Navarro, Hero of Early Texas*. Austin, TX: Eakin Press, 1989.

Meier, Matt S. *Mexican American Biographies: A Historical Dictionary, 1836–1987*. Westport, CT: Greenwood Press, 1988.

Montejano, David. *Anglos and Mexicans in the Making of Texas*. Austin, TX: University of Texas Press, 1986.

Navarro, José Antonio. *Defending Mexican Valor in Texas: José Antonio Navarro's Historical Writings, 1853–1857*. Austin, TX: State House Press, 1995.

Web Sites

"José Antonio Navarro: A Bicentennial Tribute 1795–1995." *Texas Parks and Wildlife*. [Online] Available http://www.tpwd.state.tx.us/park/jose/book.htm (accessed on January 29, 2003).

Jose Antonio Navarro, Biography & Index. [Online] Available http://www.rootsweb.com/~txnavarr/biographies/n/navarro_jose_antonio.htm (accessed on January 29, 2003).

"José Antonio Navarro, 1795–1871." *Sons of Dewitt Colony Texas*. [Online] Available http://www.tamu.edu/ccbn/dewitt/Navarro.htm (accessed on January 29, 2003).

Siegel, Stanley E. "Navarro, José Antonio (1795–1871)." *The Handbook of Texas Online*. [Online] Available http://www.tsha.utexas.edu/handbook/online/articles/view/NN/fna9.html (accessed on January 29, 2003).

James K. Polk

Born November 2, 1795
Pineville, North Carolina

Died June 15, 1849
Nashville, Tennessee

President of the United States

Although he maybe one of the least well-known of all U.S. presidents, James K. Polk is often rated as one of the most successful. He was a strong supporter of expansionism and "manifest destiny." This was the belief that citizens of the United States had both a right and a duty to push beyond the nation's borders and settle in as much of the North American continent as possible. Polk served as president throughout the Mexican American War, signing both the declaration by which the conflict officially began and the peace treaty that ended it. He took a very active role in directing the U.S. war effort, thus helping to shape the future role of U.S. presidents. During Polk's one term, the United States grew by more than 1,000,000 square miles, but some claimed that in the process it lost its status as a just and peace-loving country.

A young lawyer and politician

James K. Polk was a member of a family of Scotch-Irish descent that had arrived in the United States in the sev-

James K. Polk. *Photograph courtesy of The Library of Congress.*

Sarah Polk: The President's Partner

More sociable than her very reserved husband, Sarah Childress Polk played an important role in the White House and was much respected for her learning and social graces.

Sarah was born into a wealthy family that owned a plantation near Murfreesboro, Tennessee. Even though this was a frontier area, she grew up amidst culture and refinement. In an action that was unusual at a time when most people thought that education was wasted on girls, Sarah's father sent her and her sister to the Salem Academy in North Carolina. Considered one of the best schools in the South, it also was one of very few that admitted girls.

Thus, Sarah was not only refined but well educated when she met a young Tennessee legislator named James K. Polk (1795–1850), who had been her brother Anderson's classmate at the University of North Carolina. The two young people were married on New Year's Day in 1824. Polk served in the U.S. Congress for fourteen years, and Sarah usually accompanied her husband to Washington, D.C., for each year's legislative session.

The couple never had any children, but Sarah occupied herself with her very public role as the wife of a prominent lawmaker and, eventually, as the nation's First Lady. She was known as a woman of both intellect and social skills, who could talk politics and also converse easily with guests, making them feel comfortable. She also helped her husband with his speeches and correspondence, advised him on various issues, and tried to keep him from overworking.

A devout member of the Presbyterian Church, Sarah discouraged Polk from

enteenth century and eventually settled in Mecklenburg County, North Carolina (near the city of Charlotte). Polk was the oldest of ten children born to Samuel Polk, a prosperous farmer, and Sarah Jane Knox. When Polk was eleven years old, his family moved by covered wagon to Tennessee, then a part of the state of North Carolina, where his grandfather was already a successful land speculator (someone who buys land and sells it again for a profit). There the Polk family lived on a thriving farm with thousands of acres of land that was worked by more than fifty slaves.

Polk was tutored at home until he was eighteen. He went on to study classics and mathematics at the Universi-

Sarah Polk. *Photograph courtesy of The Library of Congress.*

augural ball (the ball traditionally held to celebrate a new president's taking office) she did not dance herself, as this went against her religious beliefs. Despite her somewhat strict views on such matters, Sarah was a popular First Lady.

Polk's term as president ended in March 1850. Worn out by his duties, he died only three months after leaving office. Sarah lived for another forty-three years, always dressed in the black clothing that marked her as a grieving widow. She adopted her orphaned grandniece, Sally Polk Jetton, who remained her beloved companion until the end of her life, which came just before her eighty-eighth birthday.

Sources: "Sarah Childress Polk." The White House. [Online] Available http://www.whitehouse.gov/history/firstladies/sp11.html (Accessed on January 31, 2003); Sarah Childress Polk, 1803–1891. [Online] Available http://www.jameskpolk.com/scpbio.htm (accessed on January 31, 2003).

receiving visitors on Sunday and banned the drinking of hard liquor at the White House (wine, however, was served at official dinners). Although she attended the in-

ty of North Carolina, graduating at the top of his class in 1818. Polk spent the next two years studying law with Felix Grundy, a successful lawyer who also had served as a member of the U.S. Congress. Polk became a lawyer himself in 1820 and established a law practice in Columbia. However, his intelligence and debating skill made him a natural politician, and he was elected to the Tennessee legislature in 1822, quickly developing a reputation as a promising young leader.

At this period in U.S. history, many citizens were becoming dissatisfied with the government, which seemed to have been run by the same group of leaders for its entire existence. A new system of political parties was evolving. These groups formed on the basis of common interests and beliefs. It was at this time that a new leader of the Democratic Party emerged. Often referred to by the nickname "Old Hickory" because of his toughness, Andrew Jackson (1767–1845)—a hero of the War of 1812 (1812–14) and Polk's cousin—proposed policies offering change and reform. As an avid Jackson supporter, Polk embraced Jackson's policies and even gained the nickname "Young Hickory."

Seven terms in the House of Representatives

Jackson was elected president in 1824. That same year, Polk married Sarah Childress, a well-educated woman whose refinement and social skills would make her an asset to the career of her more reserved husband. A somewhat short, slight person who usually had a sad expression on his face, Polk had very formal manners that made some people think he must be dull. Yet he was determined and firm in his beliefs, which included a strict interpretation of the U.S. constitution and an advocacy of states' rights. In other words, he believed that the federal government should not interfere too much in local affairs.

In 1825, Polk was elected to the U.S. House of Representatives for the first of seven two-year terms. During Jackson's time in the White House, Polk maintained close ties with the president and supported him on many issues. Elected Speaker of the House (the top leadership role in the House of Representatives) in 1835, Polk served for four years and worked so energetically that he permanently increased the power of this position.

Although Polk had not yet set his sights on the presidency, he had begun to think of himself as a possible candidate for the vice presidency. In pursuit of this goal, he ran successfully for the governorship of Tennessee. After serving a two-year term, he lost two successive re-election bids, in 1841 and 1843. As a result, Polk believed that his political career might be over, so he returned to farming. Nine months later, however, he was back in the spotlight when he came to the aid of the Democratic Party.

A Democratic campaign banner for James K. Polk and his running mate, George M. Dallas. Polk won the 1844 election by a very close margin over Whig candidate Henry Clay.
Photograph courtesy of The Library of Congress.

A "dark horse" candidate for president

As the 1844 presidential election approached, former president Martin Van Buren (1782–1862) was the leading contender for the Democratic nomination. But because he had antagonized many fellow party members with his stances against expansionism and slavery (two of the most controversial issues of the day), Van Buren was unable to get the majority of votes he needed to be nominated. At the last minute, the Democrats chose Polk as a compromise candidate who, everyone hoped, would be able to unite the many quarreling factions within the Democratic Party.

The Whigs (the other major U.S. political party) focused on Polk's status as a "dark horse," or unknown candidate, using the question "Who is James Polk?" as a taunt. Thus, Polk tried to inform voters about his positions, which included strong support for the two major expansionist issues of the period, involving Oregon and Texas. Since 1818, the United States and Great Britain had held joint control of Oregon, and now many people wanted the United States to take over the whole territory, which stretched north to the southern border of Russian-held Alaska. In fact, Polk's campaign slogan was "Fifty-four Forty or Fight!," which referred to that far northern parallel line.

Polk also agreed with those who wanted to annex (make a state) Texas, whose citizens had declared their independence from Mexico about ten years earlier and now wanted to become part of the United States. Mexico had threatened war if annexation did occur, but many expansionist-minded U.S. citizens actually welcomed this prospect as a chance to acquire not only Texas but the Mexican territories of California and New Mexico. Most members of the Whig Party opposed Texas's annexation, but at the last moment, the Whig candidate, Henry Clay (1777–1852), came out in favor of it. This caused a split in the Whig Party that allowed Polk to win the election by a very close margin.

The youngest president

The forty-nine-year-old Polk was the youngest president up to that time, and he took the helm of a nation that also was young and dominated by a mood of optimism, confidence, and ambition. Because he wanted to limit the friction within his own party and also prove that he would be a president to all U.S. citizens, not just Democrats, Polk promised to serve only one term and chose for his cabinet (the team of advisors that is made up of the heads of all the various government departments) men who claimed no presidential ambitions themselves.

Polk was to prove a very competent president with exceptionally strong administrative skills (he found many ways, for example, to tighten the government's budget and save a lot of money). And he was able to accomplish all of the major goals he set for his administration. One of these, of course, was the acquisition of the Oregon Territory. After the election, Polk softened his stance somewhat, offering a compromise to the British government by which the U.S. would take over the part of Oregon that was below the forty-ninth parallel, which already formed the border between the United States and British-held Canada east of the Rocky Mountains. After some haggling, the British eventually agreed to this arrangement, and the area that would become the states of Washington and Oregon became part of the United States in June 1846.

Meanwhile, the annexation of Texas had occurred just before Polk took office. As a result, Mexico had immediately broken off diplomatic relations with the United States, and war seemed likely. Polk was determined to assert the Rio Grande river as the boundary between Texas and Mexico, even though the traditional border had been the Nueces River, located about 100 hundred miles north of the Rio Grande. He also wanted to force Mexico to pay back debts owed to U.S. citizens, and, most ambitiously, to acquire California for the United States. He soon made it clear that although he would not rule out a peaceful means of achieving these results, neither would he shy away from an armed conflict.

War with Mexico on the horizon

Thus, in the summer of 1845, Polk ordered General Zachary Taylor (1784–1850; see biographical entry) to take several thousand U.S. troops to the Texas town of Corpus Christi, located on the Nueces River, where they were to protect Texas from Mexican aggression. In November, Polk sent former Louisiana congressman John Slidell (c. 1793–1871) to Mexico to try to negotiate with the Mexican government. Polk told Slidell to offer Mexico $25 million in exchange for California and New Mexico; Mexico must also recognize the Rio Grande as the border between the two countries, while the United States also would cancel all debts owed to U.S. citizens.

Mexico's president, José Joaquin Herrera (1792–1854), had more moderate views than some of the country's other leaders. He wanted very much to avoid war with the United States, but the other members of his government refused to even meet with Slidell, much less consider his offer. Slidell was forced to return to the United States, and Polk seethed with anger over this development. He immediately ordered Taylor to move his soldiers south to the Rio Grande and build a fort across the river from the Mexican town of Matamoros. During the remaining months of 1845, the U.S. force and a Mexican army under General Pedro de Ampudia (1805–1868) would watch each other warily from their different banks of the Rio Grande.

Polk was now waiting for a good reason to declare war on Mexico. In April, that opportunity arrived. More than one thousand of Ampudia's troops crossed the river, and when Taylor sent out sixty of his own soldiers to investigate, they were attacked and eleven were killed. As soon as Polk received this news, he sent a message to Congress asserting that the hostilities had now begun, and that Mexico had taken the first step. Now, he claimed, "Mexico has passed the boundary of the United States, has invaded our territory and shed American blood upon the American soil."

Leading the war effort

Despite a few dissenting voices, Congress agreed with Polk. The war declaration was signed on May 15, 1846, at which time Congress authorized $10 million to support the war effort. Congress also authorized the enlistment of fifty thousand volunteer troops. Attracting volunteers to fight in the war, especially at this early stage, before anyone knew what the fighting conditions would be like, was easy, since most U.S. citizens were in favor of the war, and many young men saw it as a romantic adventure that they assumed would be over soon.

The structure of the U.S. government makes the president the country's "commander-in-chief" during wartime, and Polk entered into this role with enthusiasm. Fighting this conflict meant raising, training, equipping, and moving large numbers of troops in a short period of time. Polk played a direct role in all of these details, as well as in appointing officers and making sure that the government was not wasting money. For instance, he discovered that wagons were being used in rough terrain that was much better suited to pack mules, and that horses were being transported across great distances, at great expense, when they could be purchased for much less in Mexico.

Polk also took responsibility for the U.S. war strategy. His initial plan was three-pronged: The United States would strike at Mexico through Santa Fe (in New Mexico), California, and the northern provinces located south of the Rio Grande. Choosing a commander to oversee this effort had been a problem for Polk, since most of the top-ranking officers of the U.S. Army seemed to sympathize with the Whig Party. Polk knew that any fame a Whig general gained during the war might propel this general into the White House, and Polk, as a loyal member of the Democratic Party, wanted to prevent this from happening.

A string of victories for the United States

At the time, the army's top officer was General Winfield Scott (1786–1866; see biographical entry), a much-respected veteran of the War of 1812 (1812–14). Polk disliked Scott, however, and as a result, chose Taylor, even though he was a Whig, to lead the invasion of northern Mexico while General Stephen W. Kearny (1794–1848; see biographical entry) would lead the Army of the West to California. Meanwhile, Polk continued to explore opportunities for peace, even agreeing in July 1846 to an ill-advised deal with Mexican general and former president Antonio López de Santa Anna (1794–1876). Claiming that he was the only leader who could control the situation in Mexico, Santa Anna convinced Polk that if the United States would allow him passage to Mexico from Cuba (where he had been exiled several years earlier) he would open peace negotiations with the United States. As soon as he reached Mexico, however, Santa Anna assumed the presidency and began gathering together an army with which he promised to crush the United States.

Santa Anna's grandiose promise was not to be realized, however. As the year 1847 began, the United States had taken control of New Mexico and California, and Taylor's forces had won important battles at Palo Alto, Resaca de la Palma, Monterrey, and Buena Vista against Santa Anna's much larger but poorly equipped army. It had become clear, though, that if the United States wanted to win the war, it would be necessary to capture Mexico's capital, Mexico City, located in the center of the country. In order to reach the city, an invasion would have to be launched from Mexico's eastern coast. Polk reluctantly turned to Scott to lead this invasion.

Despite Polk's negative opinion of him, Scott proved to be a skillful and dynamic commander. He launched his invasion in March 1847, bombarding the coastal city of Vera Cruz into submission, then marching southwest and winning the Battle of Cerro Gordo in mid-April, despite predictions that he would surely fail. The hard-fought conquest of Mexico City took place in September, ending with the Mexicans' surrender. Once the fighting was over, a lengthy and difficult process of peace negotiations could begin.

The Treaty of Guadalupe Hidalgo

Polk had sent Nicholas P. Trist (1800–1874; see biographical entry), a Spanish-speaking U.S. diplomat (official representative of the U.S. government), to Mexico soon after the fall of Vera Cruz. Relations between Trist and Scott were unfriendly at first, but the two men gradually became friends, a circumstance that very much annoyed Polk. With the end of the war and Santa Anna's departure from office, Mexico City was thrown into political chaos. As a result, the peace talks were stalled while the Mexican government scrambled to reorganize. Just when they were about to begin again, Polk, impatient with the delay, ordered Trist to return to the United States. Unwilling to abandon the negotiations at such a crucial time, Trist ignored Polk's order.

On February 2, 1848, the Mexican and U.S. representatives signed the Treaty of Guadalupe Hidalgo, by which Mexico gave the United States California and New Mexico (an area of 525,000 square miles and almost half of Mexico's total territory) and recognized the Rio Grande as the border in exchange for $15 million and the cancellation of debts owed to the United States. Although Polk was angry at Trist for ignoring his order to return to Washington, he was quite pleased with the terms of the agreement that Trist had secured. Because the treaty was quite favorable to the United States, it was soon approved by Congress and signed into law by Polk on March 16. On July 4, amidst a celebration marking the laying of the cornerstone of the Washington Monument, the news arrived that Mexico, too, had ratified (officially approved) the treaty.

The war's consequences

As a result of the Mexican American War, the United States had grown by more than 1,000,000 square miles, and its boundaries were established (except for another small piece that would be added in 1853) as they would remain for the next century. Many of those who had supported the war claimed it had done much to establish the United States as a major power in the region and in the world. Nevertheless, a few critics continued to assert that the war had been conducted out of pure greed and thus damaged the moral reputation of the United States. Still others warned that it had deepened the sectionalism (the practice of favoring one's own region or area over others), and especially the hostility between southern slaveholders and northern abolitionists, that could threaten the nation's survival.

Indeed, as Polk's administration drew to a close, a fierce debate had begun about whether the states that would be carved out of the new territories would or would not allow slavery. Even earlier, in August 1846, Congressional Democrats who opposed slavery had drawn up a bill called the Wilmot Proviso, which would prohibit slavery in any and all territories acquired during the war. The bill was passed twice by the House of Representatives but was never approved by the Senate. Although he did not believe that slavery should be extended into any new states, Polk opposed the Wilmot Proviso as too divisive. He was unable to propose any more workable solution, and the debate would continue to rage over the next several decades. Eventually, tension over the slavery issue and that of states' rights would result in the secession of southern states from the Union, followed by the bloody Civil War (1861–65).

A determined president

True to the promise he had made when he took office, Polk did not run for re-election, even though it is likely that he would have won. On the day that President Zachary Taylor, who had coasted into the presidency on the strength of his status as a war hero, was inaugurated—March 5, 1849—Polk and his wife left Washington, D.C., for a tour of the South. By this time, Polk was physically exhausted and in ill health; he had worked very long hours during his presidency, and taken few vacations. Soon after his return to Nashville, Tennessee, Polk contracted cholera. He died only three months after leaving office, at the age of fifty-four.

Polk has been faulted by some of his contemporaries as well as historians for waging a war of pure aggression against Mexico, a war motivated not by self-defense, as he claimed, but by greed. Others have called him a product of his time and of the spirit of manifest destiny. In any case, it is generally agreed that Polk was an energetic, determined president who strengthened that office and achieved both the goals he set for himself and the promises he made the nation.

For More Information

Books

Bergeron, Paul H. *The Presidency of James K. Polk.* Lawrence: University of Kansas Press, 1987.

Haynes, Sam W. *James K. Polk and the Expansionist Impulse.* New York: Longman, 1997.

Sellers, Charles Grier. *James K. Polk.* 2 vols. Princeton: Princeton University Press, 1957–66.

Web Sites

"James Polk." *The American President.* [Online] Available http://www.americanpresident.org/KoTrain/Courses/JP/JP_In_Brief.htm (accessed on January 29, 2003).

"James K. Polk." *The White House.* [Online] Available http://www.whitehouse.gov/history/presidents/jp11.html (accessed on January 29, 2003).

"James Knox Polk." *POTUS (Presidents of the United States).* The Internet Public Library. [Online] Available http://www.potus.com/jkpolk.html (accessed on January 29, 2003).

The San Patricio Battalion

At the time of the Mexican American War, about 40 percent of the U.S. Army was made up of recent immigrants to the United States, many of whom had chosen military service because other jobs were not available to them. Living and working conditions were harsh, and immigrants were often viewed unfavorably and treated unfairly. This was especially true for Irish Catholics, whose religion made them particular targets for prejudice in a society that was mostly Protestant. These and other factors led a group of U.S. soldiers, most of them Irish, to desert from the U.S. Army and fight on the Mexican side in a special military unit called the San Patricio Battalion. Considered traitors in the United States, these men were highly valued by the Mexican army and are still fondly remembered by the Mexican people. The story of the San Patricio Battalion helps to illustrate not only an interesting aspect of the war but social conditions in the United States in the nineteenth century.

"Criminal negligence...": Life in a U.S. Army Camp in Texas, 1846

Many U.S. soldiers who fought in the Mexican American War discovered that their worst enemies were to be found not among the Mexican troops but in their own camps. Ignorance or neglect of proper hygiene, sanitation, and nutrition led to widespread sickness and death. In fact, many more men died due to disease than to battle wounds. Those men who had come to Mexico in search of adventure faced more than they originally anticipated, as is illustrated in the following account by Lieutenant Daniel Harvey Hill of the Fourth Artillery.

> It becomes our painful task to allude to the sickness, suffering and death, from criminal negligence. Two-thirds of the tents furnished the army on taking the field were worn out and rotten. Transparent as gauze, they afforded little or no protection against the intense heat of summer, or the drenching rains and severe cold of winter. Even the dews penetrated the thin covering almost without obstruction. Such were the tents, provided for campaigning in a country almost deluged three months in the year, and more variable in its climate than any other region in the world, passing from the extreme of heat to the extreme of cold within a few hours. During the whole of November and December, either the rains were pouring down with violence, or the furious "northers" [winds] were shivering the frail tentpoles, and rending the rotten canvass [sic]. For days and weeks, every article in hundreds of tents was thoroughly soaked. During those terrible months, the sufferings of the sick in the crowded hospital tents were horrible beyond conception. The torrents drenched and the fierce blasts shook the miserable couches of the dying. Their last groans mingled in fearful concert with the howlings of the pitiless storm.

The hard lives of U.S. soldiers

In 1846, when the Mexican American War began, the regular U.S. Army was quite small. Military service was not viewed as a very promising, respectable profession and most young men considered it a last resort if they could not find other work. When Congress authorized funding for fifty thousand volunteer troops to help fight the war against Mexico, however, enlistment offices were crowded with men eager to sign up to travel to an exotic foreign country and fight an enemy they thought would be easy to beat. In time, however, these volunteers discovered the often unpleasant realities of a soldier's life, which included dirt, dust, nasty weather, disease, strict discipline and bad food, not to mention the risk of injury or death in battle.

All of these drawbacks led as many as nine thousand U.S. soldiers to desert, or leave, the army and head for home

*Every day added to the frightful-
ness of the mortality. The volley [crying]
over one grave would scarce have died on
the air when the ear would again be
pained by the same melancholy sound.
One procession would scarcely have been
lost to sight when the solemn tread of the
dead-march would announce another. At
one time, one-sixth of the entire encampment were on the sick report, unfit for
duty, and at least one-half were unwell.
Dysentery and catarrhal fevers raged like a
pestilence. The exposure of the troops in
flimsy tents, and their being without fires,
aggravated these diseases.*

*As the winter advanced, the en-
campment now resembled a marsh, the
water at times being three and four feet in
the tents of whole wings of regiments. All
military exercises were suspended, the black
gloomy days were passed in inactivity, dis-
gust, sullenness [sadness] and silence. The
troops, after being thoroughly drenched all*
*day, without camp fires to dry by, lay down
at night in wet blankets on the well soaked
ground. We have seen them bouyed up with
the hope of a fray, cheerful and hopeful,
when certain death seemed to impend over
them. But without occupation, without excitement, without the prospect of meeting
the foe; to sit, day after day, and week after
week, shivering in wet tents, and listening
to the low wail of the muffled drum, as fel-
low-soldiers, perhaps beloved companions,
were carried to their last resting place, was
not this enough, more than enough, to try
the discipline and fortitude of the best
troops in the world?*

Sources: Hill, D. H. "The Army in Texas," Southern
Quarterly Review, Volume 9, April 1846: 448–50;
The Mexican American War (1846–1848). [Online]
Available http://www.hillsdale/edu/dept/
History/Documents/War/America/Mexican/War/
19mex.htm (accessed on January 31, 2003).

when they decided they had fulfilled their duty to their country. Less than one hundred of these men were tried for the
crime of desertion, the punishment for which was usually
death. However, members of the San Patricio Battalion who
were still alive at the end of the war were captured after one
of its final battles, and most received the death penalty.
Among all the deserters of the Mexican American War, only
the San Patricios were sentenced to death by hanging; the
usual form of execution was by firing squad, which was considered more humane. Those who were not executed were severely punished with whipping and branding.

The low status of Irish immigrants

The reason that the men of the San Patricio Battalion
were signaled out for such harsh punishments was because of

the views of U.S. society during this period. In the 1830s and early 1840s, extremely poor economic conditions in Ireland brought a huge number of Irish immigrants into the United States. Unlike the Irish who had immigrated in the eighteenth and earlier nineteenth centuries, who tended to be skilled craftsmen and Protestants, most of these new Irish immigrants were poor farmers. They also were members of the Roman Catholic religion, to which only 1 percent of the total U.S. population belonged. The United States had been founded and long dominated by Protestants, and as a result, there was widespread prejudice against and fear of Catholicism. Many U.S. citizens thought that Catholics were superstitious, ignorant, and incapable of independent thought.

Although it is true that the U.S. Constitution guarantees freedom of religion, most Americans did not think their society had to accept or accommodate people who were racially or otherwise different from those who currently dominated it. Thus, even people who thought slavery was wrong did not think that white Americans would ever live side by side, in equality, with blacks; instead, they envisioned that African Americans would either return to Africa or form their own state in the Caribbean region. The racial prejudice that was used to justify the unfair treatment of blacks was extended to Mexicans, who were considered lazy, irresponsible, uncivilized, and too excitable. And it also was often applied to the Irish, who were assigned many of the same qualities as the Mexicans, and who also were predominantly Catholic.

Long discriminated against at home by the British, who had been in control of Ireland for many centuries, Irish immigrants discovered that they were subject to much of the same treatment in the United States. Many of the Irishmen, who were unable to find other jobs, joined the U.S. military. In fact, immigrants, including the Irish, made up almost half of the U.S. military. These immigrants were generally held in contempt by their officers and fellow soldiers. It was believed that since these newcomers were not yet U.S. citizens, they lacked the patriotism that motivated other soldiers. Critics cited that these new immigrants were fighting for money, not to defend the United States, and thus they were not "real" soldiers. As a result of this discrimination, Irish-born soldiers were usually given the lowliest and hardest jobs, received harsher punishments and fewer promotions, and were prevented from practicing their own religion. In fact, some historians have found it surprising that more of the five thousand plus Irish soldiers who did fight on the U.S. side in the Mexican American War did not desert.

The United States sends troops to Mexico

In March 1845, the nation of Texas, which had declared its independence from Mexico nine years earlier, became a U.S. state. Mexico had promised that this action would mean war, since Mexico never officially recognized Texas as an independent nation. Thus, the United States and Mexico were now on the brink of war. At this time, U.S. society was infused with the spirit of expansionism (the movement of U.S. settlers across the nation's current borders) and by the idea of "manifest destiny," the concept that it was not only the right, but the duty, of U.S. citizens to spread their way of life across, and in fact take control of the rest of the continent. President James K. Polk (1795–1849; see biographical entry) was an ardent expansionist, and he was only the most prominent among a large number of Americans who hoped Mexico would make the first move and start a war. If this occurred, it was believed that the United States could take over parts or even all of Mexico.

Soon after the annexation (granting of official statehood) of Texas, Polk sent several thousand troops under the command of General Zachary Taylor (1784–1850; see biographical entry) to Corpus Christi, a town on the Nueces River, the traditional border between Texas and Mexico. The following spring, Taylor was ordered to move his troops south to the Rio Grande, a river about 100 miles south of the Nueces that the United States was now declaring as its border. Across the narrow river was the pleasant Mexican town of Matamoros, whose citizens peered curiously across at the U.S. soldiers on the other side.

Deserters cross the Rio Grande

On Sunday mornings, the U.S. soldiers could hear the church bells calling the residents of Matamoros to mass, the

Pedro de Ampudia

Many historians claim that Pedro de Ampudia was one of several prominent Mexican military officers whose poor leadership actually weakened the Mexican war effort during the Mexican American War.

Pedro de Ampudia was born in Havana, Cuba, and entered the Spanish colonial army as a teenaged cadet (the lowest rank). He arrived in Mexico in 1821 as a lieutenant, and soon joined the army of Agustín Iturbide, who was leading an armed struggle against Spanish rule. After Mexico gained its independence from Spain, Ampudia served in the new Mexican army and quickly rose through the ranks.

During the early 1840s, the Mexican army clashed repeatedly with troops from Texas, which had previously been a part of Mexico. Although Texas had declared its independence from Mexico in 1836, Mexico never officially recognized Texas's action. Ampudia took part in the campaign against Texas. He was in command of Mexican troops at the town of Mier when it was attacked by the Texan army. Ampudia and his troops were able to capture the Texans by pretending to surrender to them. As a result, Ampudia executed a large number of the Texan soldiers on orders from General Antonio Lopéz de Santa Anna.

Ampudia's reputation as an especially cruel officer was reinforced in 1844, when he helped to put down a rebellion in the Mexican state of Yucatán. The rebels surrendered in good faith and expected mercy, but Ampudia had them executed and even displayed several of their severed heads on poles, as a warning to others about the perils of rebellion.

When the Mexican American War began, Ampudia was serving as general-in-chief of the Army of the North, headquartered at Matamoros. He was unpopular with the citizens of Matamoros, however, and they requested a replacement. President Manuel de Paredes y Arillaga thus sent Mariano Arista to replace Ampudia, who became second-in-command. Mutual resentment between the two officers led to quarreling that hindered their effectiveness as leaders.

Catholic church service. During the months between the arrival of the troops at the Rio Grande and the May 1846 start of the Mexican American War, about forty U.S. soldiers also answered that call, never to return to the United States. They deserted the army, swimming across the river to join the enemy on the other side, and fighting against their former officers and fellow U.S. soldiers. They did so for a variety of reasons—including the harsh discipline and treatment they had

In the first two battles of the war, which took place at Palo Alto and Resaca de la Palma (both very close to Matamoros) on May 8 and 9, 1846, the Mexican army was outgunned by the U.S. troops under the command of General Zachary Taylor. Mexico's leaders and citizens reacted to the losses with shock and dismay, but it was Arista who took most of the blame. He was replaced by General Francisco Mejía, who was soon replaced by Ampudia. Once again, Ampudia was in command of the Army of the North.

Following their early victories, Taylor's army headed west toward the city of Monterrey, where Ampudia commanded a defensive force. Santa Anna recommended that Ampudia evacuate the city, but Ampudia believed he should stay and fight the approaching U.S. troops. The battle that followed was bloody, as the U.S. force bombed the city (causing many civilian deaths and injuries) and finally stormed its walls. There was fierce hand-to-hand fighting along the city's streets. Finally Ampudia surrendered.

Even though Ampudia had managed to arrange a generous armistice (halt in fighting) with Taylor—by which the Mexican troops were allowed to leave, officers were allowed to keep their personal weapons, and an eight-week ceasefire was promised—Santa Anna relieved Ampudia of his command. Ampudia did lead troops again at the battles of Buena Vista and Cerro Gordo, but at a lower rank.

After the war, Ampudia served for a time as general-in-chief and governor of the state of Nuevo León. He fought on the side of the ruling liberals in the 1857 conflict known as the War of the Reform, a violent struggle between liberals and conservatives. Ampudia died on August 7, 1868, and is buried in the Panteón de San Fernando in Mexico City.

Sources: Frazier, Donald. The United States and Mexico at War. New York: Simon and Schuster, 1997. Crawford, Mark. Encyclopedia of the Mexican American War. Santa Barbara, CA: American Bibliographical Center-Clio Press, 1998; DePalo, William A., Jr. The Mexican National Army, 1822–1852. College Station, TX: Texas A&M University Press, 1997.

received from the U.S. Army, the lure of a friendly and welcoming people who shared their religion, and perhaps because of a feeling of sympathy for the Mexicans, whose homeland had been invaded.

At the head of this band of deserters was an Irish-born private (the army's lowest rank) named John Riley who may have earlier served in Great Britain's colonial army in Canada. Riley would later try to persuade more U.S. soldiers to desert, and he would become a leader of the San Patricio Battalion. Initially, though, this new unit was made up not only of the U.S. Army deserters, but of foreigners from Ireland, Germany, and other places who were already living in Mexico. It was called the Legión Extranjera (Foreign Legion) and, for the first year or so of the war, it was commanded by Mexican officers.

By August 1846, the unit had grown to include two hundred men who were known to the Mexicans as *colorados* (red heads; many people of Irish descent have red or reddish hair). It was then renamed the San Patricio Battalion (after Patrick, the patron saint of Ireland), and its men began to fly a distinctive flag of green silk with the traditional Irish images of Saint Patrick, a shamrock, and a harp sewn on it in silver thread. Even before this flag flew, however, and even before the official May 13 declaration of war, the men who would make up the core of the San Patricio Battalion had taken part in the first two battles of the war.

The battles of Palo Alto and Resaca de la Palma

The man in charge of the Mexican troops stationed in Matamoros was General Pedro Ampudia (1805–1868), a Cuban-born officer with a reputation for brutality. The residents of Matamoros had asked for a replacement and General Mariano Arista (1802–1855) had been sent to take over command from Ampudia, who now became second-in-command. Tension between the two men was to seriously undermine the Mexicans' war effort. On May 8 and 9, troops under these two officers fought the U.S. Army in the battles of Palo Alto and Resaca de la Palma. The men whose unit would soon be christened the San Patricio Battalion were probably present at both these battles, which turned out disastrously for the Mexicans. Outgunned by the U.S. troops, the Mexicans retreated.

Arista took most of the blame for these defeats, and as a result, Ampudia was again put in charge of the army. He halted his army of about nine thousand at the city of Monterrey. In September, the dynamic Mexican general and leader

Antonio López de Santa Anna (1794–1876; see biographical entry) tricked the United States into allowing him to return to Mexico from Cuba, where he had been exiled. Santa Anna now became Mexico's president and also took over control of its army, which would eventually number twenty thousand. Before this army was ready, however, Ampudia's smaller force met Taylor's army in a bloody battle at Monterrey.

The San Patricios help to defend Monterrey

The battle began on September 20, and lasted for three days, ending in brutal hand-to-hand fighting through the city streets. The San Patricio Battalion played a major role in the clash, proving their artillery (large guns such as cannons) skills as they mowed down many U.S. soldiers. After a high number of casualties on both sides (but more for the Mexicans, including many civilians), Ampudia surrendered. A ceasefire agreement that some, including Polk, felt was too generous allowed the Mexicans to walk out of Monterrey, with officers carrying their personal weapons. Among those who marched away were the San Patricios, their green flag held high.

Because of the high number of civilian casualties in the Battle of Monterrey, and the fact that U.S. soldiers had fired on people taking refuge in Catholic churches, led to even more desertions from the U.S. Army. Santa Anna decided to take advantage of this opportunity. He sent out notices that encouraged U.S. Catholic soldiers to turn their backs on an army and a nation that had no respect for their religion. According to Michael Hogan's book *The Irish Soldiers of Mexico,* Santa Anna told the soldiers: "Come over to us; you will be received under the laws of that truly Christian hospitality and good faith which Irish guests are entitled to expect from a Catholic nation."

An impressive performance

At the same time that Santa Anna was encouraging U.S. soldiers to desert the army, he also had been gathering his own country's soldiers. Ampudia joined his troops with

Santa Anna's and the huge force headed north on a grueling 150-mile march, during which they lost about five thousand soldiers to death or desertion. The Mexicans met Taylor's army again on February 22 and 23, 1847, at what is called the Battle of Buena Vista in the United States; the Mexicans call it the Battle of Angostura, after the mountain pass near which it took place. Realizing that their artillery was far inferior to that used by the United States, the Mexicans had to plan their strategy carefully. They assigned the well-trained San Patricio Battalion to the three biggest cannons, which were mounted on high ground above the battle field.

Although the United States won the Battle of Buena Vista due to their superior weapons and equipment and to the fact that their troops were in much better physical condition, the San Patricios performed well, even though they lost about a third of their men. Despite several costly attempts, the U.S. troops were unable to capture the San Patricios' cannons. In addition, the San Patricios captured two U.S. cannons. After the battle, they were recognized by the Mexicans for their bravery, and John Riley received a medal and a promotion to the rank of captain. By August 1847, the San Patricios had enough men for two companies, each made up of about one hundred soldiers.

The Mexican army now returned to the nation's capital, Mexico City, where Santa Anna bragged of their great victory at Angostura. In reality, of course, it had been a great loss. Mexican citizens were growing more and more alarmed, especially after troops under General Winfield Scott (1786–1866; see biographical entry), now in command of the U.S. war effort, invaded the coastal city of Vera Cruz in March 1848. Once again, many civilian lives were lost in the U.S. attack, causing a negative reaction even among the U.S. public. The U.S. Army was now on the march toward Mexico City, the conquest of which, it was believed, was necessary if the United States was to win this war.

Fierce fighting at Churubusco

In April, the two armies met again at the Battle of Cerro Gordo, where the U.S. troops forced the Mexicans to make a hasty retreat. The San Patricios were present, retreating afterwards with Santa Anna and his army to Mexico City. In early August, Scott's army arrived in the Valley of Mexico and began its difficult approach to Mexico City. They clashed with Santa Anna's troops at the village of Contreras on August 19, and at Churubusco the next day. From their position at a Churubusco convent, the San Patricios fought fiercely, and it is for this effort that they are most remembered in Mexico.

Fighting with both heavy artillery and rifles, the San Patricios held on to the convent valiantly, inflicting many casualties on the U.S. soldiers. At one point, the Mexicans ran out of ammunition. They made a plea for more, but received only supplies designed for U.S. guns, which would not work in the Mexicans' older weapons. However, since the San Patricios carried U.S.-made guns, they were able to use this ammunition, and they kept up their defense of the convent even to the point of hand-to-hand fighting. Three times the Mexican soldiers tried to raise a white flag of surrender, but each time the San Patricios tore it down, determined to fight on. Finally, knowing that they were defeated, a officer in the San Patricios put his own white handkerchief on the point of a bayonet and raised it in the air. The battle was over.

Thirty-five San Patricios had been killed in the battle, while about eighty had escaped. The remaining eighty-five members of the battalion were taken prisoner. Seventy-two of them were immediately charged with desertion from the U.S. Army. They were to be tried in two groups, on August 23, in the town of Tacubaya and on August 26, at San Angel. A panel of officers would hear the case, and the sentence would be sent to Scott for approval. Assigned to carry out the terms of the sentences was Colonel William Harney (1800–1889), an officer of Irish Catholic heritage who was known for his cruelty.

Found guilty of desertion

At the trials, the San Patricios were not represented by lawyers, but they were allowed to call witnesses who would testify that they were men of good character. Knowing that conviction meant the death penalty and unable to get formal legal advice, about half the men claimed that drunkenness had led them to desert from the army (this was a very common defense in military trials and sometimes led to lighter sentences). Others claimed that the Mexicans had forced them to join their army. None brought up the issues of religious or racial prejudice.

There was no question that the San Patricios had fought on the Mexican side, many U.S. soldiers and officers had seen them. In addition, they had refused to surrender when they had an opportunity. There was not much chance that many of them would be deemed innocent. Indeed, only two were found to be not guilty, since they had never actually joined the U.S. Army. Two others were found guilty but given the usual punishment for desertion, death by firing squad; one had deserted but had not actually joined the Mexican army, and the other had been forced to fight. Of the remaining San Patricios, fifty received the sentence of death by hanging, a less humane form of execution than death by firing squad. Because the other fifty, including John Riley, had deserted from the U.S. Army before war had been officially declared, they received a lesser sentence that included whipping with fifty lashes and being branded on the cheek with a "D" for deserter.

The punishments are carried out

The first executions took place at San Angel on September 10, where a small crowd of onlookers gathered at 6:00 A.M. The men were brought out and fourteen of them (one of whom was Riley) were whipped and branded. The rest were taken to the gallows on small wagons. Priests read them the last rites of the Catholic faith and nooses were placed around their necks. Then the mules were prodded to pull the wagons forward, so that the men were left hanging until they died. Riley and the others were forced to dig graves for the executed men.

The sentences of the San Patricios who had been tried at Tacubaya were carried out on September 13, the same day that U.S. forces overran Chapultepec Hill, a Mexico City landmark on top of which Mexico's National Military Academy was located. In charge of the punishments, Harney ordered the gallows to be built on high ground, in view of Chapultepec. At dawn the thirty San Patricios were brought out and told that they would have to stand on the wagons, the nooses around their necks, until the U.S. flag was raised over Chapultepec Hill, signaling that the battle was over.

These men stood in the hot sun, awaiting their deaths, until the U.S. flag appeared at 9:30 A.M. Harney signaled for the mules to be driven off, and the men were left hanging. Those who had been sentenced to whipping and branding now received their punishments. It is not known what happened to the bodies of those executed, though some say that they were left swinging from the gallows until, after several days, the townsfolk took them down and buried them.

After the war

In recounting what happened to the San Patricios, some historians have said that although their punishment seems extremely cruel to us, it was not uncommon in the middle of the nineteenth century. Others, however, assert that such practices as whipping and branding were already declining at the time of the Mexican American War, and receiving both punishments was very unusual. These historians suggest that the San Patricios may have been so harshly treated because of their low status as mostly Irish Catholic immigrants.

Soon after the fall of Chapultepec Hill, Scott rode in triumph into Mexico City, and the war was over. The Treaty of Guadalupe Hidalgo was signed on February 2, 1848, signaling its official end, and U.S. troops began withdrawing from Mexico in May. The members of the San Patricio Battalion still in U.S. custody were released in June. A number of them joined with Riley in forming a new battalion, which helped to put down rebellions against the government of Mexico's new president, José Joaquín Herrera (1792–1854). In the fall of 1848, this unit was dissolved.

Riley stayed on to serve in the Mexican army for two more years, but it is not known what happened to him after that. He may have returned to Ireland, or it may be that, like many other former San Patricios, he stayed in Mexico, started a family, and found a way to make a living there. In fact, even now, such Irish names as Murphy, Kelly, and MacDowell may be found in Mexican phone books.

In the United States, the memory of the San Patricio Battalion was a shameful one for many Irish Americans, who were eager to blend in with U.S. society and attain all the benefits and opportunities for which they had fled Ireland. Indeed, over the next century and a half they would largely realize this dream, as the prejudice and discrimination against them became less and less common. In Ireland, however, the San Patricios were remembered more fondly. According to Hogan, "despite their whippings, mutilations, and hangings, or perhaps because of them, [they] became a symbol in Mexico not of disgrace, but of honor in defeat, of glory in death."

In 1957, the residents of the town of San Angel put up a plaque that reads, "In Memory of the Heroic Battalion of Saint Patrick, Martyrs Who Gave Their Lives for the Mexican Cause During the Unjust North American Invasion of 1847." The plaque lists the names of seventy-one soldiers. Every year on March 17, St. Patrick's Day, the members of the San Patricio Battalion are remembered and honored with a special ceremony. Across the sea in Ireland, where many view the role of the San Patricios in helping Mexico as similar to that played by Irish people who resisted British oppression, commemorations have taken place at Riley's birthplace in County Galway.

For More Information

Books

Hogan, Michael. *The Irish Soldiers of Mexico.* Guadalajara, Mexico: Fondo Editorial Universitario, 1997.

Miller, Robert Ryal. *Shamrock and Sword: The St. Patrick's Battalion in the U.S.-Mexican War.* Norman: University of Oklahoma Press, 1989.

Miller, Robert Ryal and William J. Orr. *An Immigrant Soldier in the Mexican War.* College Station: Texas A & M University Press, 1995.

Stevens, Peter F. *The Rogue's March: John Riley and the St. Patrick's Battalion 1846–1848.* Dulles, VA: Brassey's, 2000.

Web Sites

McGinn, Brian. *The San Patricios: An Historical Perspective.* [Online] Available http://www.connemara.com/history/san-patricios/ (accessed on January 31, 2003).

Nordstram, Pat. "San Patricio Battalion." *Handbook of Texas Online.* [Online] Available http://www.tsha.utexas.edu/handbook/online/articles/view/SS/qis1.html (accessed on January 31, 2003)

Antonio López de Santa Anna

Born 1794
Jalapa, Mexico

Died June 21, 1876
Mexico City, Mexico

Mexican general and statesman

Antonio López de Santa Anna. *Photograph courtesy of The Library of Congress.*

One of the most important figures in nineteenth-century Mexico, Antonio López Santa Anna was a general who led his nation's forces against those of the United States during the Mexican American War. At the same time, he also was serving one of his numerous terms as Mexico's president. Santa Anna was a complex, flamboyant person with an impressive ability to persuade others, both soldiers and civilians, to follow him. Yet he also has been faulted for always pursuing his own glory rather than the good of Mexico. Some critics believe that Santa Anna deserves much of the blame for Mexico's defeat in the war, while others view this dynamic, self-centered general as just one of many contributing factors.

A young soldier gains experience

Antonio López Santa Anna was born in the town of Jalapa, but grew up in nearby Vera Cruz, an important port city on Mexico's eastern coast. His parents, Antonio Lafey de Santa Anna and Manuela Perez de Labron, were *criollos,* or descendents of the Spanish colonizers who had arrived in Mexico in the sixteenth century. At the time of Santa Anna's birth, Mexico was still under the control of Spain, and the criollos played a prominent role in its society and government.

Santa Anna's father was a prosperous minor official who did not approve of his son's desire to join the military. Instead, when the teenaged Santa Anna demonstrated a lack of interest in school, his father arranged for him to serve an apprenticeship (a period of work and training that was supposed to lead to a career in a particular trade) with a merchant. But this was not successful either, and finally Santa Anna's parents allowed him to become a soldier. In June 1810, when he was sixteen, Santa Anna joined the Vera Cruz infantry (foot soldier) regiment as a cadet, the lowest rank.

As a young soldier in the Spanish army, Santa Anna took part in crushing the uprisings that often occurred around Mexico, then called New Spain, as Native Americans and others rebelled against the harsh treatment they received from the Spanish. As a member of the infantry, and later of the cavalry (soldiers on horseback), Santa Anna was trained in a brutal kind of warfare that included the routine execution of prisoners. Later in his life, while leading troops in the Texas Revolution and the Mexican American War, Santa Anna would demonstrate the deadly influence of this training.

Mexico's struggle for independence

Santa Anna showed skill and courage as a soldier, but sometimes got into trouble because of gambling debts. A young man of average height and build with dark hair and eyes, pale skin, and very good manners, he was popular with women. He quickly rose through the ranks of New Spain's army and, in 1821, became a lieutenant colonel. About ten years earlier, with an uprising of about sixty thousand *mestizos* (those of Spanish and Native American heritage) and Native Americans led by a Catholic priest named Miguel Hidalgo y Costilla (1753–1811), Mexicans had begun rebelling against their Spanish rulers. Now the Spanish army was fighting another rebellion. This one was a joint effort by conservative Mexicans (criollos who did not want to lose any of their own privileges) under the leadership of Agustin de Iturbide (1783–1824) and liberals (rebels who sought a more democratic form of government for Mexico) under Vicente Guerrero (1783–1831).

When Santa Anna realized that the rebels were going to win, he switched sides and led the rebel army to victory. The Treaty of Cordoba, the agreement that gave Mexico its independence from Spain, was signed on August 24, 1821. After the rebellion, Santa Anna was recognized by all as a great hero of the revolution.

With Mexico gaining its independence from Spain, Iturbide soon declared himself emperor, but as he grew more dictatorial, he lost popularity. Despite Santa Anna's own lack of understanding or real concern about the meaning of the word "republic" (a democratic form of government in which power is held by the people, rather than an individual ruler), he joined with Guerrero and two other leaders, Guadalupe Victoria (1785–1843) and Nicolás Bravo (1787–1854), in overthrowing Iturbide and declaring Mexico a republic.

Called to duty again

Victoria was now elected president of Mexico, while Santa Anna retired to his country estate, Manga de Clavo. Over the next several decades, Santa Anna would often retreat in this way, for he was not much interested in the day-to-day work of government. He married fourteen-year-old Ines Garcia, who bore Santa Anna five children and would remain a devoted wife for the next nineteen years, despite Santa Anna's frequent affairs with other women.

In 1828, the Conservative Party's Manuel Gómez Pedraza (1789–1851) was elected president. Santa Anna came out of retirement and quickly raised an army to help put Guerrero, who had been the Liberal Party's candidate in the election, in power. The next year, Santa Anna again took up the role of military leader when Spain landed troops at Vera Cruz in a last attempt to reconquer Mexico. After fierce fighting, Santa Anna's army defeated the Spanish, who finally recognized Mexico's independence. Once again, Santa Anna was hailed as a hero, and he made every effort to promote this image. He even began to call himself "the Napoleon of the West" (Napoleon I [1769–1821] was a French emperor and a dynamic military leader who conquered much of Europe).

After his victory over Spain, Santa Anna again retreated to Manga Clavo, but returned to the spotlight in 1832. Two years earlier, the conservative statesman Anastasio Bustamente (1780–1853) had overthrown Guerrero and set up a dictatorship. Proclaiming himself a liberal, Santa Anna raised another army and forced Bustamente from office in 1832. Three months later, Santa Anna was himself elected president. He was not interested in governing, however, so he soon retired to his estate, leaving the government in the hands of his vice president, Valentin Gómez Farías (1781–1857).

A leader with absolute power

The very liberal Gómez Farías soon began to put a series of reforms in place to limit the privileges that the wealthy, the Roman Catholic Church, and the military had traditionally enjoyed. Members of these groups were horrified to see their power being reduced, and they complained to Santa Anna. So, in 1834, he renounced Gómez Farías and, calling himself "the liberator of Mexico," assumed absolute power. That meant that he dissolved the congress and reshaped the government to concentrate power in the national, or federal, government in Mexico City, while the individual states had little power. Furthermore, no dissent would be allowed.

Around the nation, this highly undemocratic system sparked a lot of complaints and even some violent resistance. Liberals in Zacatecas staged a revolt in May 1835, but they were soon crushed by Santa Anna's forces. An uprising in the northeastern region of Tejas y Coahuila, known to U.S. citizens as Texas, was more successful. For a little more than ten years there had existed a colony of settlers who, in search of opportunity, had crossed the U.S. border to settle in Mexico in the area known as Texas. In exchange for land grants from the Mexican government, these settlers had agreed to become Mexican citizens and Roman Catholics (Catholicism was the official religion of Mexico). But conflicts had been increasing as the settlers ignored Mexican laws, including those banning slavery and unregistered guns, and held themselves above and apart from the Mexican religion, culture, and people.

Trouble in Texas

The Mexican government's attempts to control the situation in Texas proved ineffective and even increased the tension. The issue came to a head after Santa Anna sent troops to Texas as a show of force. The Texans declared themselves independent from Mexico and chased the Mexican forces out of several towns. In the early months of 1836, determined to squelch this so-called Texas Revolution, Santa Anna himself led an army of 6,000 on the difficult journey to Texas. The Mexicans' siege of the Alamo, a former mission in the town of San Antonio that had been occupied by U.S. troops, on March 6, ended in the deaths of all of its 189 U.S. defenders.

Santa Anna's policy of no mercy for prisoners, who were all to be killed at the Alamo and at the town of Goliad, where about three hundred U.S. prisoners were executed, enraged Texans. As a result, the tiny army grew and, under the leadership of frontiersman Sam Houston (1793–1863; see biographical entry), launched a successful surprise attack on Santa Anna's troops at the Battle of San Jacinto (named for the river near which it took place) on April 21, 1836. Santa Anna had underestimated his enemy and his soldiers were unprepared. Santa Anna managed to escape but was later captured. Before he was taken prisoner he had changed into the uniform of a low-ranking soldier to avoid being recognized, however, as he was brought into camp his captured soldiers rose to salute him, addressing him as "El Presidente" (the president).

A president in disgrace

Even though many of the U.S. soldiers and officers thought Santa Anna should die for ordering the massacres at the Alamo and Goliad, Houston thought he would be more valuable alive. Santa Anna subsequently signed the Treaty of Velasco, which recognized Texas (called the Lone Star Republic) as an independent state and guaranteed the withdrawal of all Mexican troops. After being taken to the United States and meeting with President Andrew Jackson (1786–1845), Santa Anna was returned to Mexico in February 1837. The incidents in Texas had destroyed his reputation, and he resigned the presidency. Bustamente now became Mexico's chief executive, and he refused to recognize the treaty Santa Anna had signed as being valid. As a result, Santa Anna retired to his estate in disgrace.

In a pattern repeated throughout Santa Anna's career, Mexico soon turned to him in a time of need. In 1838, an armed conflict with France broke out over some unpaid debts that Mexico owed to the French. (This was called the "pastry war" because one of those owed money was a baker.) When other military commanders were unable to beat the French, Santa Anna answered the call to aid his country. He led the army to victory, but not before losing his left leg in battle. Santa Anna made the most of this injury by having the leg buried with full military honors, thus highlighting his status as a war hero.

Popular and powerful again

With his victory over the French, Santa Anna regained his popularity and replaced Bustamente as president in 1841. During this three-year term (his longest ever), he imposed order in the country but also concentrated power in himself, again dissolving the congress, putting his corrupt friends in political positions, and borrowing money to finance his favors and schemes. Convinced that all Mexico really needed was a strong leader, he built up his own image, placing statues of himself all around the country.

But once again, Mexicans grew disenchanted with Santa Anna. The people disapproved, for example, of their president's second marriage. Only a few months after the death of his wife Ines from pneumonia, the fifty-year-old Santa Anna married fourteen-year-old Maria Dolores de Tosta. In December 1844, General Mariano de Paredes y Arillaga (1797–1849) forced Santa Anna out of office. Santa Anna was imprisoned while Mexican officials discussed the possibility of trying him for treason. Instead, he was exiled to Cuba.

The following year was a bad one for Mexico. The country was in turmoil as four different governments took turns trying to rule, and war with the United States loomed on the horizon. Although Mexico had threatened to take up arms against its northern neighbor if the U.S. government annexed Texas (made it a state), Texas became a state on March 1, 1845. Several months later, General Zachary Taylor (1784–1850; see biographical entry) took four thousand troops to Corpus Christi, where they were ordered to guard Texas from Mexican aggression. It seemed that many U.S. leaders and citizens, including President James K. Polk (1795–1849; see biographical entry), would welcome a war with Mexico, which might bring even more territory to the United States. (Mexico would eventually give to the United States the area that would become the states of California, Arizona, and New Mexico.)

On the brink of war

In early 1846, Polk ordered Taylor to cross the Nueces River, which had been the traditional boundary between Texas and Mexico, and move about 100 miles south to the Rio Grande river, which the United States was now claiming as the boundary. Despite threats from Mexican general Mariana Arista (1802–1855), Taylor began building a fort directly across the Rio Grande from the Mexican town of Matamoros. In late April, Mexican troops crossed the river and attacked a small party of U.S. soldiers, killing a few of them. Taylor sent word of the clash to Polk, declaring that the war was already underway. Using this incident as its excuse, the United States officially declared war on Mexico.

However, in early May, even before the declaration of war was signed, Taylor's force defeated Arista's troops in the battles of Palo Alto and Resaca de las Palmas. Faced with this military emergency, Mexico again turned to Santa Anna, who managed to convince government officials that he could lead the nation to victory against the "Yanqui" (the Spanish version of Yankee, the popular nickname for U.S. citizens) invasion. He also managed to trick Polk into allowing him past the U.S. naval blockade (a barrier made with warships) of Mexico by promising to promote peace with the United States.

Santa Anna arrived in Mexico in September, took over as president and, instead of working for peace with the United States, quickly began assembling and equipping an army of twenty thousand that was based at San Luis Potosí. This task would take several months. Meanwhile, Taylor's army was on the move, heading west from the Rio Grande toward the town of Monterrey. There they met Mexican troops under Major General Pedro de Ampudia (1805–1868) in a tough,

The Angels of Buena Vista

The following poem titled "The Angels of Buena Vista" was written by John Greenleaf Whittier. It pays tribute to the *soldaderas*, made up of Mexican soldiers' wives, sisters, and girlfriends, who fed and nursed the men and kept their clothing and quarters clean. These women also took part in battles, and the U.S. troops were shocked to find their bodies among the dead.

A letter-writer from Mexico during the Mexican war, when detailing some of the incidents at the terrible fight of Buena Vista, mentioned that Mexican women were seen hovering near the field of death, for the purpose of giving aid and succor to the wounded. One poor woman was found surrounded by the maimed and suffering of both armies, ministering to the wants of Americans as well as Mexicans with impartial tenderness.

SPEAK and tell us our Ximena, looking northward far away, O'er the camp of the invaders, o'er the Mexican array, Who is losing? who is winning? are they far or come they near? Look abroad, and tell us, sister, whither rolls the storm we hear.

"Down the hills of Angostura still the storm of battle rolls; Blood is flowing, men are dying; God have mercy on their souls!" Who is losing? who us winning? "Over hill and over plain, I see but smoke of cannon clouding through the mountain rain."

Nearer came the storm and nearer, rolling fast and frightful on! Speak, Ximena, speak and tell us, who has lost, and who has won?

"Alas! alas! I know not; friend and foe together fall, O'er the dying rush the living: pray, my sisters, for them all!

"Lo! the wind the smoke is lifting. Blessed Mother, save my brain! I can see the wounded crawling slowly out from heaps of slain. Now they stagger, blind and bleeding; now they fall, and strive to rise; Hasten, sisters, haste and save them lest they die before our eyes!

"O my heart's love! O my dear one! lay thy poor head on my knee; Dost thou know the lips that kiss thee? Canst

bloody battle that featured hand-to-hand fighting through the city streets. When it ended, the United States was in control not only of Monterrey, but of all of northern Mexico.

The Battle of Buena Vista

Through an intercepted letter, Santa Anna learned that in January 1847, Polk had ordered about half of Taylor's army to be transferred to the command of General Winfield Scott (1786–1866; see biographical entry), who would soon thou hear me? canst thou see? O my husband, brave and gentle! O my Bernal, look once more On the blessed cross before thee! Mercy! mercy! all is o'er!"

Dry thy tears, my poor Ximena; lay thy dear one down to rest; Let his hands be meekly folded, lay the cross upon his breast; Let his dirge be sung hereafter, and his funeral masses said; To-day, thou poor bereaved one, the living ask thy aid.

Close beside her, faintly moaning, fair and young a soldier lay, Torn with shot and pierced with lances, bleeding slow his life away; But, as tenderly before him the lorn Ximena knelt, She saw the Northern eagle shining on his pistol-belt.

With a stifled cry of horror straight she turned away her head; With a sad and bitter feeling looked she back upon her dead; But she heard the youth's low moaning, and his struggling breath of pain, And she raised the cooling water to his parching lips again.

Whispered low the dying soldier, pressed her hand and faintly smiled; Was that pitying face his mother's? did she watch beside her child? All his stranger words with meaning her woman's heart supplied; With her kiss upon his forehead, "Mother!" murmured he, and died!

"A bitter curse upon them, poor boy, who led thee forth, From some gentle, sad-eyed mother, weeping, lonely, in the North!" Spake the mournful Mexie woman, as she laid him with her dead, And turned to soothe the living, and bind the wounds which bled.

But the noble Mexie women still their holy task pursued, Through that long, dark night of sorrow, worn and faint and lacking food. Over weak and suffering brothers, with a tender care they hung, And the dying foeman blessed them in a strange and Northern tongue.

Not wholly lost, O Father! is this evil world of ours; Upward, through its blood and ashes, spring afresh the Eden flowers; From its smoking hell of battle, Love and Pity send their prayer, And still thy white-winged angels hover dimly in our air!

Source: Whittier, John Greenleaf. The Complete Poetical Works of John Greenleaf Whittier. New York: Houghton, Mifflin, and Company, 1894.

be launching an invasion of Mexico from coastal Vera Cruz. Convinced that this was the time to strike Taylor's diminished force, and eager for a victory in the north before focusing on Scott's invasion, Santa Anna marched his huge but still ill-prepared army toward Saltillo. The almost 300-mile journey was grueling, and Santa Anna lost about five thousand men along the way to both disease and desertion. Meanwhile, Taylor was pushing his own troops south from Monterrey.

The two armies met about 150 miles south of Monterrey, in an area of very rugged terrain. On February 23, Taylor's troops halted at Angostura Pass, located near a ranch called

Buena Vista that would give its name to the battle fought here. On one side of the pass were mountains, on the other a network of perilous gullies, or ditches. Waiting on the other end of the pass with his army, Santa Anna sent a message to Taylor demanding that the U.S. forces surrender. Taylor refused. After some minor skirmishes, the two armies prepared themselves for battle on the morning of February 24. The U.S. troops noted that the very fancy uniforms of the Mexican soldiers and the colorful banners they flew made their army a beautiful sight.

This bright spectacle did not last long, however, for soon the bullets and cannonballs began to fly. The U.S. troops were far outnumbered, but the higher quality of their weapons and ammunition and the effectiveness of their artillery (very large guns, such as cannons), as well as the protection afforded by the trenches they fired from, gave them the upper hand. When night fell, a temporary ceasefire was called. The U.S. troops awoke the next morning expecting that the battle would continue, but they were surprised to see that the enemy had retreated. No doubt dismayed by the estimated three thousand casualties (soldiers killed, wounded, or missing), while the United States had about eight hundred, Santa Anna had fled during the night, retreating southward.

The U.S. Army captures Mexico City

Ignoring the loss of so many men, Santa Anna declared the Battle of Buena Vista a glorious victory for Mexico (of course, the United States also claimed a victory at Buena Vista). However, it was hard for Mexicans to ignore the evidence. Their army had been repeatedly defeated. Now Scott was set to lead his Army of Invasion from Vera Cruz to Mexico City, the nation's capital. The Mexicans were hesitant to believe that Santa Anna, who was clearly more skilled at persuasion and pomp than military tactics, could protect them from the godless and brutal Yanquis.

Battles at Vera Cruz and Cerro Gordo

In March, Scott landed an amphibious assault force (involving both the army and the navy) on the Mexican coast and bombarded Vera Cruz into submission. On April 8, he headed west with a force of eighty-five hundred, traveling along the impressive National Highway toward Mexico City. Scott's army met Santa Anna's on April 17 at a narrow mountain pass near the village of Cerro Gordo, only 12 miles west of Vera Cruz. This is where Santa Anna hoped to stop the U.S. advance since the area was surrounded with many extremely steep hills. Santa Anna underestimated his enemy and only ordered one of the hills, called El Telégrafo, fortified. The U.S. troops, however, were able to move equipment and men up the steep hills without detection through a quickly devised conveyer system. The next day, the U.S. forces attacked the Mexicans from three sides, causing huge losses among Santa Anna's troops.

Once again, Santa Anna had to either retreat in a hurry or face even more devastating casualties. Santa Anna himself was forced to leave many belongings behind, including a spare wooden leg that made a treasured souvenir for the U.S. soldier who found it. The Mexicans had an estimated one thousand casualties in this short battle, compared to only about four hundred for the U.S. side. In addition, three thousand Mexican soldiers were captured, although they were released after their guns were taken and they had promised not to fight again. The U.S. forces also took possession of forty-three Mexican cannons and four thousand smaller weapons, as well as ammunition and other supplies.

Scott's army invades the capital

By August, Scott's army had been boosted by reinforcements, and he was again ready to continue the march toward Mexico City. On August 11, they entered the valley (actually a volcanic crater) in which the capital lies. Santa Anna had put in place a complex system of fortifications all around the city, but Scott's army found safe passage along a muddy, difficult route that circled around south of the city. After crossing a treacherous 15-mile-wide expanse of jagged rocks called the pedragal, they met the Mexican army in battles at the villages of Contreras on August 19 and Churubusco on August 20. Once again, casualties were lopsided, with the Mexicans suffering about four thousand and the United States, less than a thousand.

Through Mexican Eyes: The Battle of Chapultepec Hill

To the Mexican people, Chapultepec Hill, the site of the National Military Academy, was an important symbol of a proud heritage. Thus, the Mexicans' defeat in the brief but bloody battle that raged there on September 13, 1847, was an especially bitter loss. For the U.S. forces under General Winfield Scott, it was a first and important step in the conquest of Mexico City. The following narrative provides a Mexican perspective on the battle. It was written by Ramon Alcaraz, one of several Mexican participants in the war who, soon after it ended, chronicled his experiences as a way of recording and analyzing how and why Mexico had lost the war.

After the event of the Molino del Rey, the necessity was felt for a great number of troops and sufficient artillery to defend so extensive a city as Mexico.

The aspect of the city, saving the frequent passing movement of troops through the streets, was truly sad and frightful. The emigration of many families from the beginning of hostilities by the enemy in the valley of Mexico, had deprived this city of the bustle and life which are observed ordinarily, a circumstance which was increased by the seclusion to which others had resorted either from excessive selfishness or pusillanimity.

The troops on the 12th were some 200 men at the foot of the hill, distributed in groups, assisted by the students of the military college, and some more forces, who in all did not amount to 800 men.

At dawn on the 12th, the enemy's batteries began to fire upon Chapultepec. At first they caused no destruction. But rectifying their aim, the walls of the building commenced to be pierced by balls in all directions, experiencing great ravages also in the roofs, caused by the bombs which the mortar threw. The artillery of Chapultepec answered with much precision and accuracy. The engineers worked incessantly [nonstop] to repair the damage done by the enemy's projectiles, and the troops quite behind the parapets suffered from this storm of balls. The most intelligent in the military art judge that the troops could have been placed at the foot of the hill, to avoid the useless loss, leaving in the building only the artillerymen and the requisite engineers. This was not done, and the carcasses of the bombs and hollow balls killed and wounded many soldiers, who had not even the pleasure of discharging their muskets.

The next day, Scott sent Santa Anna a message suggesting that the two nations begin peace talks, and a truce (temporary halt in fighting) went into effect. Santa Anna enlisted the help of former president José Joaquín de Herrera (1792–1854), whom Santa Anna had earlier forced from office, in negotiating with the United States. But not even the influence of this more moderate voice could temper Santa Anna's demands, and the truce ended on September 7. Now

Lic. Lazo Estrada and other officers who accompanied General Bravo, gave also to the troops the most beautiful example of valor, despising the danger to which they were exposed; General Saldaña being especially distinguished, who remained serene in the midst of the shower of stones, which a bomb had thrown down on his head. In the evening, General Santa Anna in person, entered the woods with a battalion to reinforce the work which looked to the east from the side of the cattle pond, and where the enemy were directing their fire to dislodge the troops guarding it. As soon as his presence was noticed, the firing was redoubled, and a bomb cut to pieces the commandante of battalion, Mendez, a valiant officer who had served in the North, and killed or wounded thirty soldiers. General Santa Anna ordered the troops to withdraw, and he himself retired with his staff to the gate, where he ordered a work to be thrown up to defend that side of the garden and the foot of the entrance. At nine, after concluding, he returned with his reserves to the Palace.

The bombardment had been horrible. It commenced a little after five in the morning, and did not cease until seven in the evening. In these fourteen hours the American batteries, perfectly served, had maintained a projectile in the air, and the greater part of their discharges taking effect. In the corridor, converted into a surgical hospital, were found mixed up the putrid bodies, the wounded breathing mournful groans and the young boys of the college; and, singular fact! the assistance and requisite medicines were wanting.

In the balance of the night General Monterde labored with assiduity to repair the damage caused by the bombs, and to replace the blinds and strengthen the fortifications. But the time was very limited and peremptory. Nevertheless all hope was not lost.

On the 13th at daybreak the enemy's batteries returned to open their fire upon Chapultepec much more vividly than on the day before.

Our defenders, astounded by the bombardment, fatigued, wanting sleep, and hungry, were hurled over the rocks by the bayonet or taken prisoners. A company of the New York regiment ascended to the top of the building, where some of the students still fired, and who were the last defenders of that Mexican flag which was quickly replaced by the American.

Source: The Mexican American War (1846–1848). [Online] Available http://www.hillsdale.edu/dept/History/Documents/War/America/Mexican/War/19mex.htm (accessed on January 31, 2003).

Scott's troops continued their relentless push toward Mexico City, defeating Mexican troops at Molino del Rey and Casa Mata on September 8. The only obstacle remaining between them and the city gates was Chapultepec Hill, a large slab of rock on top of which perched the majestic National Military Academy, an important symbol of Mexico's proud heritage.

After a bloody assault on Chapultepec on September 13, in which all of its defenders, including fifty cadets from the academy who earned the title "Los ninoes heroes" (the boy heroes) for their bravery, were killed, the U.S. troops poured through the gates of Mexico City. Scott himself rode into the city early the next morning and accepted the Mexican surrender. Santa Anna, meanwhile, had already fled to the nearby town of Guadalupe Hidalgo. On September 16, he resigned the presidency, issuing a statement, as quoted in John Weems's *To Conquer a Peace,* in which he highlighted his own heroism and blamed others for Mexico's defeat: "With the most profound and poignant grief do I announce to you that it is after repeated and extraordinary efforts I saw myself under the necessity of abandoning the capital. You have been witnesses that I labored day and night. The insubordination of one general subverted my entire plan of operation. I announce to you that I have spontaneously resigned the Presidency of the Republic because I feel it incumbent on me ever to place myself in that quarter in which there is the most peril."

A treaty is signed

Santa Anna did not yet resign as commander of the army, however, and even made one last, unsuccessful assault on the U.S. forces who had remained at the northern town of Puebla when Scott's army moved on to Mexico City. Now increasingly seen by the Mexican people as a traitor who had done a poor job of planning and preparing Mexico's army for war, Santa Anna was not involved in the treaty negotiations that took place over the next several months. Finally signed by both sides on February 2, 1848, the Treaty of Guadalupe Hidalgo gave the territories of California and New Mexico (an area of more than 500,000 square miles) to the United States, in exchange for $15 million and the cancellation of some old debts owed to the United States by Mexico.

Mexicans were reeling from the loss of nearly half of their total territory as well as from the shame and resentment they felt after having been invaded by another country. Many blamed Santa Anna for Mexico's defeat, and the country's new government, headed by Pedro María Anaya (1795–1854), launched an official investigation into his behavior during the war. Although Santa Anna received no jail term as a result of the investigation, he again was ordered exiled from the country. He spent the next two years in Jamaica, then moved to Cartagena, Columbia, where he lived a quiet life on a country estate.

One last presidency

Santa Anna's role in Mexico's public life was not finished, however. In the years immediately following the war, the country remained chaotic, with five different liberal presidents holding power for short periods. Gradually people seemed to lose their distrust of Santa Anna, remembering only his success in rallying followers. The conservatives took power in 1853, and one of their leaders, Lucas Alamán, devised a plan to take advantage of Santa Anna's revised popularity. Santa Anna would serve as interim (temporary) president for one year, after which the country would become a monarchy (ruled by a king or queen). Alamán also planned to keep a close watch on Santa Anna and correct him if he became too dictatorial.

Santa Anna became president on April 20, 1853, and immediately began strengthening the national government, just as he had during his previous presidencies. When Alamán died unexpectedly in June, Santa Anna was free to create a dictatorship along the same lines as he had before; this time, he even took the title "His Most Serene Highness." Between extravagant spending and pay-offs to corrupt officials, Santa Anna soon found himself in need of cash. Thus he arranged the Gadsden Purchase, by which he sold the Mesilla Valley in what was to become southern Arizona, to the United States for $10 million.

For the Mexican people, the Gadsden Purchase seemed to be the final straw. They had finally had enough of Santa Anna, and the liberals were able to push him from office and again into exile. He spent the next two decades living in Central and South America and the Caribbean, while back in Mexico the political turmoil continued. The liberals defeated the conservatives in the War of the Reform (1857–69). Santa Anna made an unsuccessful attempt to intervene in this situation, and also tried in vain to oppose the liberal administration of U.S.-backed Benito Juarez (1806–1872), which followed it.

A lonely, unnoticed death

In the meantime, Santa Anna worked on his memoirs, in which he painted himself as an ardent patriot concerned only with Mexico's welfare. When Juarez died in 1874, Santa Anna was allowed to return to Mexico. By this time he was eighty years old and in poor health. Two years after returning to Mexico, Santa Anna died. Although once Mexico's leading political and military figure, his death went mostly unnoticed by most Mexicans.

Since then, historians have pondered Santa Anna's great appeal to the Mexican people, who always seemed ready to forgive his past transgressions and return him to office. Most have concluded that his dynamic personality and driving ambition helped propel him to the forefront of a society that, due to a combination of social and economic factors, lacked other, better leaders and clung to the hope inspired by his grandiose promises.

For More Information

Books

Callcott, Wilfrid Hardy. *Santa Anna: The Story of an Enigma Who Once Was Mexico.* New Haven, CT: Archon, 1964.

Crawford, Ann Fears, ed. *Autobiography of Santa Anna.* Austin, TX: State House Press, 1988.

Jones, Oakah, Jr. *Santa Anna.* Boston: Twayne, 1968.

Miller, Robert Ryal. *Mexico: A History.* Norman: University of Oklahoma Press, 1985.

O'Brien, Steven. *Antonio López de Santa Anna.* New York: Chelsea, 1992.

Tolliver, Ruby. *Santa Anna: Patriot or Scoundrel?* Dallas, TX: Hendrick-Long, 1993.

Web Sites

Callcott, Wilfrid H. "Santa Anna, Antonio Lopez de." *The Handbook of Texas Online.* [Online] Available http://www.tsha.utexas.edu/handbook/ on-line/articles/view/SS/fsa29.html (accessed January 31, 2003).

Winfield Scott

Born June 13, 1786
Petersburg, Virginia

Died May 29, 1866
West Point, New York

American military leader

Considered one of the greatest military leaders in U.S. history, Winfield Scott played an important role in the Mexican American War. Assigned the task of capturing the Mexican capital, Mexico City, Scott led a successful invasion that began with an amphibious (involving both army and naval forces) attack on the coastal city of Vera Cruz. In September 1848, after a series of bloody clashes that demonstrated Scott's skill both in planning battles and motivating soldiers, he marched triumphantly into Mexico City. This was, perhaps, the high point of a long career that spanned most of the major events and conflicts of nineteenth-century America.

Beginning a military career

Winfield Scott was born on his family's estate, Laurel Branch, located near the town of Petersburg, Virginia. He was one of four children born to Ann Mason Scott and William Scott, a successful farmer and veteran of the American Revolution (1775–83) who died when Scott was six. Educated at home until he was twelve, Scott attended several boarding

Winfield Scott. *Photograph reproduced by permission of Getty Images.*

schools as a teenager, growing into a strapping young man who stood 6 feet, 5 inches tall and weighed 230 pounds. Due to a legal technicality, he did not inherit any of his family's estate or considerable fortune and had to borrow money to pay for his tuition at William and Mary College in Williamsburg, Virginia, which he entered in 1805.

Disappointed by his fellow students' lack of religious faith, Scott left William and Mary after less than a year. He studied law with a Petersburg attorney and passed the bar examination (the test that qualifies lawyers), but practiced law for only one year. In 1807—angered, like many young U.S. men of the period, by what he saw as Great Britain's crimes against U.S. ships, sailors, and trade rights on the high seas—he joined a Virginia militia unit (a private, volunteer army that could be called to assist the federal government in emergencies). The next year, Scott went to Washington, D.C., and met with President Thomas Jefferson (1743–1826) and Congressional leaders, lobbying successfully to be commissioned a captain in the U.S. Army.

Scott was ordered to report to the staff of General James Wilkinson (1757–1825), stationed in New Orleans, Louisiana. He was widely admired as a promising young officer, but his sharp tongue soon got him into trouble when he called Wilkinson a "liar and a scoundrel." Although almost everybody agreed with Scott's judgment, insulting a superior officer in this way was a clear violation of army rules. A court-martial, or military trial, found Scott guilty and sentenced him to a one-year suspension from the army. Thus Scott spent 1810 as a civilian, during which period he made a great effort to educate himself about military practices.

The War of 1812 erupts

In 1811, Scott returned to military service, reporting to General Wade Hampton (1751–1835), who had replaced Wilkinson in New Orleans. Tensions between the United States and Great Britain had by now reached a head, and war was declared in June 1812. Promoted to the rank of lieutenant colonel, Scott was sent to Philadelphia, Pennsylvania, to recruit an artillery unit (a group of soldiers trained in the use of large guns, such as cannons). Scott then took his unit

north to the Niagara region (located on the border between New York State and what was then the British colony of Canada), one of several parts of the country in which fighting was to take place.

At the Battle of Queenston on October 13, 1812, in which the United States was defeated by British troops after U.S. volunteers refused to participate, Scott was captured by the enemy. After several months, he was released in exchange for a captured British officer. Soon promoted to colonel, Scott led a successful attack on British-occupied Fort George in May 1813, receiving serious wounds in the process.

An illustration of the Battle of Queenston during the War of 1812. It was during this battle that Scott was taken prisoner by the British. *Photograph reproduced by permission of the Corbis Corporation.*

Training soldiers to fight well

In this period of U.S. history, most U.S. citizens looked down on the military as a profession, and little attention was paid to improving soldiers' skills. Scott's experiences in the generally disastrous first year of the war, however, had convinced him that the U.S. troops would need much more training and discipline if their performance was to improve. Thus, he took charge of a training camp established at Buffalo, New York. There he worked hard to prepare troops for the fighting that would begin in the spring of 1814. Scott not only drilled his soldiers for many hours to sharpen their military skills, but also taught them about sanitation, the best way to prevent the diseases that often killed more soldiers than did enemy troops, as well as proper military dress and behavior.

Scott's troops lived up to his high expectations, performing well in the Battle of Chippewa on July 3, a victory for the United States, and the Battle of Lundy's Lane on July 5, which ended in a draw. For the first time, U.S. regulars (professional soldiers in the U.S. Army) had held their own against British regulars, and Scott was given much of the credit. Although his role in this war was now finished, Scott was heralded across the United States as a hero and made the rank of major-general.

A busy mediator

One of only six generals chosen to remain on active duty after the war, Scott went to work writing the army's first training manual. In 1835, this manual would be revised and published as *Infantry Tactics*, establishing standards that remained in use for most of the nineteenth century. Scott also traveled to Europe and studied French military methods. In 1817, he married Maria D. Mayo of Richmond, Virginia. Around this time, he also became a leader of the temperance movement, whose members warned against the dangers of drinking alcohol. Scott was famous for the punishment he gave to soldiers arrested for drunkenness; they had to dig a grave, so that they could see where they would end up if they kept drinking.

Scott returned to battle in 1832 when he led 950 troops in the Black Hawk War, the government's action against an uprising of Sac and Fox Indians, who lived in what are now the states of Wisconsin and Illinois. Three years later he undertook a similar task, though with less success. Sent to subdue members of the Seminole and Creek tribes in Florida and Georgia, Scott found his efforts limited by a lack of supplies and support from the government.

Perhaps even more than his accomplishments as a soldier, Scott earned praise for his skill as a mediator (someone who helps to work out disagreements between individuals or groups). In the decade before the Mexican American War, Scott played a key role in resolving disputes in South Carolina (where citizens had threatened to secede, or separate, themselves from the United States over a tax issue) and along the Canadian border. In 1838, he met with the Cherokee Indians and convinced them to move peacefully from their traditional home in Georgia to Indian Territory (now the state of Oklahoma), which the U.S. government had designated for them. The next year, the Whig Party considered Scott as a possible presidential candidate for the 1840 election, but instead they nominated General William Henry Harrison (1773–1841), another hero from the War of 1812.

The army's top commander

In 1841, President John Tyler (1790–1862) named Scott commander-in-chief of the U.S. Army, which made him the army's highest-ranking member. In this position, Scott introduced many reforms, such as making punishments for misbehavior less cruel, and discipline less harsh. At the same time, he lived up to his nickname "Old Fuss and Feathers," which referred to his preference for formal dress and polished manners. Although Scott was sometimes faulted for being egotistical and pompous, he also was known for his kindness and humane approach to leadership.

As the decade of the 1840s progressed, tensions between the United States and Mexico, its southern neighbor, increased. In 1836, U.S. citizens living in the Mexican state of Texas had declared their independence, forming the Lone Star Republic. Mexico had not accepted this action, and vowed to go to war against the United States if it annexed, or made Texas a state, as seemed likely. In 1845, the annexation of Texas did occur, and war loomed large on the horizon. President James K. Polk (1795–1849; see biographical entry) and others who supported expansionism (the movement of U.S. settlers into as much as of the north American continent as possible) actually welcomed war with Mexico, for they saw it as a means of acquiring more land for the United States. Polk had his eyes not only on Texas but on the Mexican territories of California and New Mexico.

The war with Mexico begins

Since Scott was in charge of the U.S. Army, he seemed the obvious choice to lead the coming struggle against Mexico. But Polk was eager for action, and he disagreed with Scott's more cautious approach to war preparation and planning. Furthermore, Polk was a member of the Democratic political party while Scott favored the rival Whigs. Polk knew very well that any fame and glory that Scott, who had already demonstrated his interest in attaining political office, might earn in a war with Mexico could land him in the White House. Thus Polk turned to another officer, General Zachary Taylor (1784–1850; see biographical entry), even though he too was thought to be a Whig sympathizer, to lead the war effort.

In the summer of 1845, Taylor took several thousand troops to Corpus Christi, Texas, located on the Nueces River, the traditional border between Texas and Mexico. In early 1846, Polk ordered Taylor to move about 100 miles south to the Rio Grande river, which the United States was now claiming as its border with Mexico. When Mexican troops crossed the river and attacked and killed some of Taylor's troops, Polk asked Congress to approve a declaration of war against Mexico based on the claim that American blood had been shed upon American soil. As a result of Polk' request, war was officially declared on March 15, 1846.

Though inferior in number to the Mexican army, Taylor's force had superior in weapons and leadership, and the United States won an impressive series of battles as the U.S. troops marched across northeastern Mexico. By the end of 1846, however, it had become clear that in order to win the war, the United States would have to strike directly at the heart of Mexico, its capital, Mexico City, located in the center of the country. To accomplish this goal, Scott proposed an amphibious attack on the eastern coastal city of Vera Cruz, followed by a 200-mile march along the well-constructed National Highway to Mexico City. Despite his reluctance to give Scott such a prominent role,

Polk put him in charge of the attack and ordered half of Taylor's troops to be transferred to Scott's command.

The attack on Vera Cruz

By the beginning of 1847, Scott was in Tampico, Mexico, at the mouth of the Rio Grande. Tampico had come under U.S. control in October the previous year. Scott's army now numbered fourteen thousand, although several thousand of those soldiers were suffering from various diseases. In March, Scott launched what would become the largest amphibious assault the United States would undertake until World War II (1939–45). Using a specially designed, flat-bottomed "surf boat," Scott landed about ten thousand troops at a point about 3 miles south of the well-protected city of Vera Cruz.

Scott's advisors recommended an infantry assault, with armed soldiers advancing on foot to attack the town. But Scott's policy had always been to avoid unnecessary casualties, and he believed that such an attack would cost too many lives. Instead, he ordered the combined army and navy forces to bombard Vera Cruz. The bombing began on March 22, and resulted in the Mexican army surrendering the town six days later. While only nineteen U.S. lives had been lost in the attack on Vera Cruz, almost two hundred Mexicans, including many civilians, had been killed.

Having accomplished his first goal by capturing Vera Cruz, Scott was eager to move his troops inland. The month of April marked the beginning of the season when yellow fever (called "el vomito Negro," or Black Vomit by the Mexicans, in reference to one of its symptoms) would invade the coastal region, and Scott knew that his soldiers would soon be at great risk of contracting the deadly disease. Both reinforcements and supplies were slow to arrive, but Scott decided to push ahead, regardless. On April 8, he headed west on the National Highway with about eighty-five hundred troops.

Scott's force advances toward Mexico City

Meanwhile, the dynamic Mexican general Antonio López de Santa Anna (1794–1876; see biographical entry) had regrouped after being defeated by Taylor's force at the Battle of Buena Vista in February. On April 17, backed by an army of nearly twenty thousand, Santa Anna met Scott's troops at a narrow mountain pass near the village of Cerro Gordo, which would give its name to this battle. Thanks to a clever system for moving troops and supplies that was devised by future Civil War general, Lieutenant Robert E. Lee (1807–1870), the U.S. force was able to overcome the area's difficult, mountainous terrain and move into an advantageous position. As a result, the United States won a lopsided victory here, suffering only four hundred casualties to the Mexicans' one thousand. In addition, about three thousand Mexican soldiers as well as a large number of cannons, other weapons, and supplies were captured.

Continuing to move west, Scott's troops reached Jalapa on April 19, and captured the town with no bloodshed. They occupied Puebla in a similar manner on May 15. By now, Scott's force had dwindled by seven regiments, or about three thousand troops, as soldiers' enlistments expired and they returned to the United States. Thus, Scott and his men spent the next three months at Puebla, waiting for newly enlisted troops to arrive. Meanwhile, with Mexico City still 75 miles away, other problems plagued the force. Many soldiers were too ill to fight, and the route by which supplies were carried from Vera Cruz was constantly being attacked by guerilla soldiers (armed men operating apart from the regular Mexican army).

Because of these obstacles, many observers predicted that Scott would not be able to pull off the feat of capturing Mexico City. In fact, as quoted in David Nevin's *The Mexican American War*, the great British general, the Duke of Wellington (1769–1852), who had defeated French dictator Napoleon I (1769–1821) several decades earlier, declared that "Scott is lost!" Scott, however, would not give up, and decided that the time had come to attack the Mexican capital. With his army now at almost eleven thousand men, he set out for Mexico City on August 5. On August 11, his forces reached the Valley of Mexico, the volcanic crater (46 miles long and 32 miles wide) within which the capital nestled. Home to about two hundred thousand people, Mexico City was now defended by nearly thirty thousand troops under the command of Santa Anna, who had made sure

that approaches to the city were well protected from the U.S. invaders.

The conquest of the Mexican capital

There was, however, one route that had been left unguarded, perhaps because the terrain it crossed was so rough that it seemed an unlikely choice by the U.S. troops. This was the route that Scott's forces took, circling around south of the city. When they came to a particularly difficult area of broken rocks and crevasses known as the pedragal, Scott again relied on Lieutenant Robert E. Lee to scout a passage. Lee met the challenge, and as a result, the U.S. troops met Santa Anna's forces at the village of Contreras on August 19. The two armies met again the next day at Churubusco, where the Mexicans were using a convent (a residence for Roman Catholic nuns) as a weapons storehouse. The fighting was

General Winfield Scott leading the American troops during the Battle of Contreras. *Photograph courtesy of The Library of Congress.*

fierce and deadly for both sides, but the Mexicans were the losers, suffering about 4000 casualties to 950 on the U.S. side.

A brief armistice

On August 21, Scott sent Santa Anna a message in which he proposed that the two armies stop fighting and try to negotiate peace. The Mexicans agreed, and an armistice (a halt in the fighting) went into effect. After several weeks, however, it became clear that the Mexicans were only stalling for time in order to regroup, and the armistice was called off on September 7. The next day, Scott's forces fought an extremely bloody and costly battle at Molino del Rey, where the Mexicans were rumored to have a cannon factory. It turned out that no such factory existed, and the casualties from the battle were very high. In fact, 23 percent of those taking part in the battle were killed, wounded, or missing, the highest casualty rate of any battle of the war.

The Mexicans surrender

On September 12, Scott ordered a bombardment of Chapultepec, the steep hill that was now all that lay between the U.S. troops and Mexico City. Scott understood the importance of this site for the Mexicans, for it housed their beloved National Military Academy and had been a proud symbol of their nation since the days of the great Mexican ruler Montezuma (c. 1480–1520). It was now defended by about eight hundred soldiers, including a small group of young cadets from the academy who had refused to leave. After the bombardment came an infantry attack that ended with hand-to-hand fighting and the deaths of all Chapultepec's defenders, including los Ninoes Heroes (the boy heroes), as the cadets would be remembered.

After capturing Chapultepec, the U.S. troops poured into Mexico City, and the brutal fighting continued throughout the day on September 13, with casualties mounting to 850 for the U.S. side and 3,000 for the Mexicans. That night, knowing that defeat was inevitable, Santa Anna fled the capital for the small, nearby town of Guadalupe Hidalgo. Scott rode into Mexico City at dawn on September 14 to accept the Mexican surrender.

The work of peacetime

Now that the war was over, the difficult task of governing this chaotic nation began. As leader of the occupying army, Scott had to cope not only with the disorder within the city walls, but with such problems as the snipers who continued to shoot at his troops and the guerillas who continued to attack his supply line. But Scott's belief in protecting the rights of civilians in occupied territory won him many admirers among the Mexican people. In fact, a small group of them asked Scott to become the nation's leader. He turned down this offer, however, and after several months the Mexicans were finally able to elect a new president and begin peace talks.

Meanwhile, some of the top U.S. officers who had taken part in Scott's campaign, including generals William Worth and Gideon Pillow and Colonel James Duncan, argued amongst themselves about who deserved credit for the U.S. victory. They sent reports to Polk that were critical of Scott. Thus, when Scott returned to the United States in February 1848, he was ordered to face a court of inquiry to face charges of misconduct. Before this could take place, however, he enjoyed a hero's welcome from the public and from Congress, and the charges were soon withdrawn.

Scott had long harbored a wish to become president of the United States, and in 1852 he had a chance to pursue this dream when he received the nomination of the Whig Party. He was, however, badly defeated by the Democratic candidate, Franklin Pierce (1804–1869), who had served under Scott during the Mexican American War. In 1855, Scott was given the highly honored title of lieutenant general, which had previously been held only by the first president of the United States, George Washington (1732–1799).

A long career comes to a close

Once again at the helm of the U.S. Army, Scott set up his headquarters in New York City. In 1859, he returned to the role of mediator when he helped to resolve a dispute with Great Britain over ownership of the San Juan Islands in Puget Sound (in what is now the state of Washington). In 1861, with the American Civil War about to begin, Scott moved the army's headquarters back to Washington, D.C., and went to work preparing the wartime defenses of the nation's capital. Now seventy-five years old, Scott was eclipsed by the military's younger leaders. Nevertheless, his plan for the war, which involved an "anaconda" (referring to the snake that squeezes its prey to death) approach that would isolate and thus weaken the Confederate states, was eventually the one used by the federal government.

In October 1861, after fifty-three years of public service, Scott retired from the army, receiving praise from President Abraham Lincoln (1809–1865) as someone to whom the nation owed a great debt. Scott spent the remaining five years of his life traveling to Europe and writing his memoirs. Upon his death, he was buried at West Point, the site of the National Military Academy whose values and practices he had helped to shape.

Scott's military career spanned the administrations of all the U.S. presidents from Jefferson to Lincoln. As a young soldier, he had joined an army that lacked efficiency and that was not much respected by the U.S. public. By the time he died, however, he had done much to bring professionalism and dignity to military service, helping to make it a career that young men (and eventually young women) could choose with pride. Scott's actions during the Mexican American War highlighted the leadership qualities that made "Old Fuss and Feathers" an influential and memorable figure.

For More Information

Books

Eisenhower, John S. D. *Agent of Destiny: The Life and Times of General Winfield Scott.* Norman: University of Oklahoma Press, 1999.

Elliott, Charles W. *Winfield Scott.* New York: Macmillan, 1937.

Nevin, David. *The Mexican War.* Alexandria, VA: Time-Life Books, 1978.

Periodicals

Schwarz, Frederic D. "Great Scott." *American Heritage,* 48, No. 2 (April 1997): 99.

Schwarz, Frederic D. "The Halls of Montezuma." *American Heritage,* 48, No. 5 (September 1997): 105.

Web Sites
"General Winfield Scott and the Mexican-American War (1846–1848)." *About North Georgia.* [Online] Available http://www.ngeorgia.com/ other/scottinmexico.html (accessed on January 31, 2003).

Zachary Taylor

Born November 24, 1784
Montebello, Virginia

Died July 9, 1850
Washington, D.C.

American military leader and president of the United States

One of two commanding U.S. generals in the Mexican American War, Zachary Taylor led troops to victory in several battles in northeastern Mexico. A career army officer, he was known both for his courage and aggression on the battlefield and his plainspoken, easygoing manner and casual style of dress. Well-liked by his soldiers, who called him "Old Rough and Ready," Taylor also became very popular with the U.S. public through his success in the war. Despite his lack of political experience, he was elected president soon after the war's conclusion. Although he died only a little more than a year after taking office, Taylor was forced to deal with an issue that would have lasting consequences on the country: whether the institution of slavery would be allowed in the nation's new states.

Growing up in Kentucky

The third of nine children of Richard Taylor and Sarah Dabney Strother, Zachary Taylor was a member of a family that had settled in Virginia in 1640. As a reward for serving as an officer in the Revolutionary War (1775–83), Richard Taylor received 6,000 acres of land in Kentucky, which was then a new state on the nation's western frontier. Soon after Zachary's birth, the family settled on Beargrass Creek near present-day Louisville. Richard Taylor was active in state politics and served as a customs official for the port of Louisville.

Even though his family was fairly prosperous, Zachary Taylor received only a little education from private tutors, and he would never become a confident reader or writer. He spent most of his time working on the family plantation (a large farm), but when he grew up he did not choose to become a farmer. He was drawn to the military instead, and in 1808, with the help of his second cousin, secretary of state and future president James Madison (1751–1836), Taylor was made a lieutenant in the U.S. Army's Seventh Infantry. Thus began Taylor's forty-year career in the army.

A frontier army officer

In 1810, Taylor also began a career as a devoted husband and father when he married Margaret Mackall Smith of Maryland. The couple had five daughters (two of whom died in infancy) and one son. Taylor's eldest daughter, Sarah, went against her father's wishes and married Jefferson Davis (1808–1889), who was then a soldier serving under Taylor, but who would one day play a major role in the American Civil War (1861–65) as president of the Confederacy. After several years, however, Taylor overcame his dislike of Davis. Taylor's son Richard was a Confederate general in the Civil War. His daughter Mary Elizabeth, who married Taylor's devoted aide, Colonel William "Perfect" Bliss (1815–1853), served as White House hostess during her father's presidency, when Taylor's wife was too ill to fulfill that role.

Serving at various posts throughout the western frontier of the United States, Taylor gradually rose through the ranks of the army. During the War of 1812 (1812–14), a conflict with Great Britain that erupted over trade and territorial issues, Taylor gained fame for his successful defense of Fort Harrison in Indiana Territory. Taylor's force of only fifty men fought off an attack by four hundred Native American warriors led by the great Shawnee chief Tecumseh (c. 1768–1813).

After the war and until 1831, Taylor's assignments included service in Wisconsin, Louisiana, and Minnesota.

Promoted to the rank of colonel in 1832, Taylor was sent to Fort Crawford (now Prairie du Chien, Wisconsin) to command four hundred troops in the Black Hawk War, in which a Native American alliance of the Sauk and Fox tribes fought the United States over territorial rights. From 1837 to 1840, Taylor took a leading role in the effort to bring Florida's Seminole Indians under U.S. control. With a force of eleven hundred soldiers, Taylor defeated the Seminoles in a battle at Lake Okeechobee on December 25, 1837. It was during this period that Taylor earned the nickname "Old Rough and Ready" from his men, who admired his determination and his indifference to physical hardship.

In 1840, the sixty-year-old Taylor was assigned to command the army's Southwest Department, based at Baton Rouge, Louisiana. Taylor bought a house in Baton Rouge and also purchased a 2,000-acre cotton plantation, Cypress Grove, located on the Mississippi River near Natchez, Mississippi. Taylor now became the owner of one hundred slaves; despite his status as a slaveholder, Taylor would later oppose the extension of slavery to the new western territories.

Called to action in Texas

Beginning in the 1820s, settlers from the United States had been pouring into the Mexican region of Tejas y Coahuila (which U.S. citizens called Texas). Under an agreement with Mexico, these settlers were to become Mexican citizens in exchange for land. This arrangement had not worked well, though, and Texans had established an independent nation, the Lone Star Republic, in 1836. Nine years later, Texas became part of the United States, despite Mexico's threat to wage war if this occurred, since that country never officially recognized Texas as an independent nation.

At this point, many expansionists (those who believed the United States should expand beyond its current borders), including President James K. Polk (1795–1849; see biographical entry), were looking towards the Mexican territories of California and New Mexico. They wanted not only this land, but the area that lay between the traditional border of the Nueces River and the Rio Grande river about 100 miles south.

In August 1845, Polk decided to provoke Mexico into making good on its threat. He ordered Taylor to proceed with four thousand troops from Fort Jesup, Louisiana, to Corpus Christi, Texas, on the Nueces River. These soldiers would spend the next five months here, suffering from the harsh weather and from the diseases that soon ran rampant through the camp. Their leader, however, was a popular figure who inspired confidence and loyalty by putting up with the same hardships as his men.

Now in his mid-sixties, Taylor was a stocky man with graying hair and a deeply lined face. He dressed casually in a wide-brimmed straw hat and mismatched pants and shirt, just like a southern farmer. In fact, a story is often told about one young officer who did not recognize Taylor when he saw him. Passing by the general's tent, the officer saw an old man sitting on a chair, polishing a sword. He offered the old man a dollar to clean his sword as well, to which the man readily agreed. Later in the day, the young officer was introduced to Taylor and realized his mistake.

War with Mexico begins

In early 1846, Taylor was ordered to move his troops across the disputed territory between the Nueces River and the Rio Grande. They halted on the banks of the Rio Grande, at a spot directly across from the Mexican town of Matamoros. Mexican general Pedro de Ampudia (1805–1868), stationed with his troops in Matamoros, sent Taylor a strongly worded message demanding that he retreat. Instead, Taylor ordered his men to set to work immediately to build a fort, which would be called Fort Texas (and later Fort Brown).

For a few uneasy months, the two armies watched each other from their opposite sides of the Rio Grande. In late April, suspecting that General Mariano Arista (1802–1855), who had by now taken over for Ampudia, may have begun moving his troops across the river, Taylor sent about sixty soldiers on a scouting mission. These troops were surrounded and attacked by a Mexican force of about sixteen hundred men. Eleven U.S.

troops were killed and the rest taken prisoner. Taylor immediately sent a report of the incident to Polk, declaring that hostilities between the two nations had now begun.

On May 11, two days after receiving Taylor's report, Polk sent a declaration of war to Congress, stating that Mexico had "invaded our territory and shed American blood upon the American soil." Despite some opposition, Congress approved the declaration on May 13. Mexico and the United States were now officially at war.

The battles of Palo Alto and Resaca de la Palma

Even before the declaration of war had been signed, however, several battles had been fought. On May 1, in desperate need of supplies, Taylor had taken most of his force to the army's arsenal (a place where weapons and other equipment are stored) at Point Isabel, about 30 miles from Fort Texas. Arista moved his soldiers into position in order to intercept Taylor's much smaller force on their return trip; at the same time, he began a bombardment of Fort Texas.

The armies met in two battles, one the flat plain of Palo Alto on May 8, and another at nearby Resaca de la Palma the next day. At Palo Alto, Taylor used his artillery (large guns, such as cannons) effectively against the Mexican troops, and the U.S. infantry and cavalry both performed well at Resaca de la Palma. When both battles were over, the Mexicans had suffered three times as many casualties (dead, wounded, and missing soldiers) as the U.S. troops. As recorded in the writings of a young lieutenant named George Meade (1815–1872), who would one day command Union Army troops in the Civil War, Taylor expressed pride in his "gallant little band" of soldiers. Many of the men fighting were inexperienced, but they had been inspired by the personal courage shown by Taylor himself during the heat and chaos of the battles.

A victory at Monterrey

News of these victories made Taylor an instant hero in the United States, where people were waiting anxiously to

hear how the war was going. He received a promotion to major general and two gold medals from a grateful Congress. Not pausing long to receive these honors, Taylor soon set out with his army of six thousand for the city of Monterrey, where Ampudia was waiting with about seven thousand defending troops. Between September 21 and September 23, Taylor's force attacked the city in a bloody battle that ended with hand-to-hand combat in the streets.

After heavy casualties had been suffered by both sides (120 killed and 368 wounded on the U.S. side; 700 killed and an unknown number wounded on the Mexican side), the Mexicans surrendered on September 24. Assuming that Polk would now try to arrange peace negotiations with Mexico, Taylor arranged a very generous eight-week armistice (end of fighting) that allowed Arista's troops to leave the city. But Polk had never intended to be so lenient with the Mexicans, and he was very angry at Taylor for letting the Mexicans leave. The U.S. public, on the other hand, was happy to hear of another victory.

General Zachary Taylor leading American troops into battle at Palo Alto.
Photograph reproduced by permission of Getty Images.

Polk had mixed feelings about Taylor's success in Mexico. Although he wanted the United States to win the war, he did not want Taylor to become too popular. Polk's reason behind this was because leaders of the Whig political party were talking about Taylor as a possible presidential candidate. If Taylor became too popular, it would be possible that Taylor would easily defeat the Democratic candidate, of which Polk was a member, during the next presidential election. Thus, when military leaders determined that winning the war would require an invasion of Mexico City, Polk chose a different general to lead that invasion.

Defeating Santa Anna's troops at Buena Vista

Polk's choice was Winfield Scott (1786–1866; see biographical entry), a well-respected veteran of the War of 1812 and a very different soldier than Taylor. While Taylor was informal, plainspoken, and often dressed in a casual manner, Scott believed in strict discipline, formal manners, and perfectly starched and pressed uniforms. Not surprisingly, the two generals disliked each other. Taylor's resentment increased when, in early 1847, Polk transferred half of his troops—including most of his regular soldiers, leaving him with less experienced, less professional volunteers—to Scott's command.

The two armies move into place

Meanwhile, Mexico's dynamic general, as well as its president, Antonio López de Santa Anna (1794–1876; see biographical entry) had spent the previous fall gathering and equipping an army of twenty thousand that was based at San Luis Potosí (about halfway between Mexico City and Monterrey). From an intercepted letter, Santa Anna learned that Taylor's army had been reduced in order to support Scott's planned invasion. Determined to defeat Taylor in the north before dealing with Scott, Santa Anna relentlessly pushed his army north, losing about a quarter of them along the way to disease and desertion.

Taylor was moving his own forces, which numbered about five thousand, including five hundred regulars, at this time. The two armies would meet in a rugged area about 150 miles south of Monterrey, at a narrow pass near a ranch called Buena Vista. On one side of the pass were mountains, on the other were a number of treacherous gullies, or ditches. Arriving on the scene on February 22, Taylor's force set up a series of defensive trenches in the pass, beyond which the Mexican troops waited. The next day, Santa Anna sent Taylor a formal demand for a U.S. surrender. As recorded in Don Nardo's *The Mexican American War,* Taylor's immediate response, "Tell Santa Anna to go to hell!" was edited by his more refined aide William Bliss to read, "I decline acceding [agreeing] to your request."

The Mexicans retreat

After some minor clashes that afternoon, the two armies spent a rainy night preparing for what would be the main battle the next day. Before it began, the U.S. troops admired the sight of the Mexicans' fancy uniforms and colorful banners. But pageantry fell by the wayside as the fighting began. The Mexicans, who outnumbered the U.S. troops four to one, made repeated assaults, but Taylor shifted his forces around so effectively that Santa Anna's troops could make no progress.

As the sun set, the fighting came to what was supposed to be a temporary end. But when the U.S. troops awoke the next morning, expecting to resume the battle, they were surprised to find that the Mexicans had disappeared. Having suffered an estimated two thousand casualties (while the U.S. side had seven hundred), Santa Anna had no doubt thought it best to retreat. Santa Anna called Buena Vista a victory for the Mexicans, but in the United States it was considered ringing proof of how well an outnumbered, mostly volunteer U.S. force could perform.

A war hero runs for president

Scott would go on to lead a successful invasion that began in the coastal city of Vera Cruz and ended inside the gates of Mexico City, but Taylor's role in the war was essentially over. He had already accomplished enough to fix himself in the public eye as a hero and great leader. Soon after his

November 1847 return to the United States, people were begging him to run for president in the 1848 election. Reluctant at first, for he had no political experience and had never even voted in an election, Taylor was finally persuaded to run as the candidate of the Whig Party. New York public official Millard Fillmore (1800–1874) was his vice presidential candidate.

The most divisive issue of the election was slavery. Southerners defended the practice vehemently, claiming that their agricultural economy depended on it. But many northerners had come to see slavery as wrong, and they sought not only to limit its spread but to outlaw it altogether. So far, the number of states in which slavery was allowed and those in which it was illegal was equal, but with victory in the Mexican American War came more than 500,000 square miles of new territory that would be divided into several states.

Interestingly, Taylor's greatest advantage in the election was the fact his views on this and other issues were not known. "Old Rough and Ready" was not only a war hero but a plainspoken, unassuming figure who believed the president should represent all the people and not just a particular party or region of the country. His being a slaveholder, however, helped gain him southern votes. Taylor's opponents were Michigan senator Lewis Cass (1782–1866), who ran on the Democratic ticket, and former president and strong abolitionist (someone who believes slavery should be illegal) Martin Van Buren (1782–1862), who had formed the new Free Soil Party. Because some Democrats voted for Van Buren instead of Cass, Taylor was able to win a narrow victory.

Slavery issue is hotly debated

Taylor's short presidency was dominated by the slavery debate, which caused such strong feelings on both sides that some members of Congress got into fistfights, while others came to the House and Senate armed with guns. The central question was whether the new states of California and New Mexico would become free or slave states. Taylor saw this as a problem with a simple solution: admit them both immediately and allow each to decide for itself. Taylor owned slaves himself and recognized slaveholders' rights, but he did not believe that slavery could or would be expanded into the new territories.

Meanwhile, other leaders thought the issue was more complicated. Led by Senator John C. Calhoun (1782–1850) of South Carolina, southerners threatened to secede (leave) the union if the Missouri Compromise (an 1820 agreement that allowed slavery below the 49th parallel line) was not honored. Even though he was himself a southerner, Taylor vowed to use the U.S. Army to preserve the union if any states tried to secede. The issue was only resolved after Taylor's death, and even then, only temporarily, with the Compromise of 1850. Among other measures, this agreement allowed for the admittance of California as a free state and New Mexico with no reference to slavery; abolished slavery in the District of Columbia; and strengthened the Fugitive Slave Law, which aided slaveholders seeking to recapture runaway slaves.

In foreign affairs, Taylor's main achievement was the Clayton-Bulwer Treaty, through which the United States and Great Britain agreed to cooperate to promote the building of a canal through Central America, which would ease trade between the Atlantic and Pacific Oceans.

A short presidency ends unexpectedly

By the time Taylor became president, he had spent forty hard years as an army officer, serving mostly on the western frontier. He had been president for only eighteen months when the demands of the job seemed to take a heavy toll on his health. On July 4, 1850, Taylor spent a long day on his feet, presiding at a ceremony at the Washington Monument. It was a very hot day, and he drank a lot of cold water and ate some cherries and iced milk to cool off. Suddenly, Taylor became extremely ill with what was probably gastroenteritis (a stomach ailment) and fever. He died on July 9. More than a century later, suspicions that Taylor may have died from intentional arsenic poisoning were ruled out when an exhumation of his body revealed no presence of arsenic.

Taylor may not have been the most brilliant military strategist, but he is remembered as a strong leader whose soldiers admired him for his courage and willingness to share their hardships. Indeed, those qualities influenced such future leaders as Jefferson Davis, Andrew "Stonewall" Jackson (1767–1845), and Ulysses S. Grant (1822–1885), all of whom served under Taylor before going on to win fame in the American Civil War.

For More Information

Books

Bauer, K. Jack. *Zachary Taylor: Soldier, Planter, Statesman of the Old Southwest.* Baton Rouge: Louisiana State University Press, 1985.

Downey, Fairfax. *Texas and the War with Mexico.* New York: American Heritage Publishing, 1961.

Eisenhower, John S. D. *So Far from God: The U.S. War with Mexico, 1846–1848.* New York: Random House, 1989.

Frazier, Donald, ed. *The United States and Mexico at War.* New York: Simon and Schuster, 1997.

George, Isaac. *Heroes and Incidents of the Mexican War.* San Bernardino, CA: Borgo Press, 1982.

Hamilton, Holman.*Zachary Taylor, Soldier in the White House.* Indianapolis: Bobbs-Merrill, 1951.

Nardo, Don. *The Mexican-American War.* San Diego, CA: Lucent Books, 1991.

Smith, Elbert B. *The Presidencies of Zachary Taylor and Millard Fillmore.* Lawrence: University Press of Kansas, 1988.

Web Sites

"Zachary Taylor." *The White House.* [Online] Available http://www.whitehouse.gov/history/presidents/zt12.html (accessed on January 31, 2003).

Nicholas Trist

Born June 2, 1800
Charlottesville, Virginia

Died February 11, 1874
Alexandria, Virginia

American diplomat and lawyer

A skilled diplomat who spoke Spanish fluently and was very familiar with the situation in Mexico, Nicholas Trist was serving as chief clerk of the State Department (the part of the government that handles relations with foreign countries) when he was chosen for an important task. Trist was to accompany the army of General Winfield Scott (1786–1866; see biographical entry), then on the move toward Mexico City, and be prepared to negotiate if a chance for peace should arise. The chance did not come until the end of 1847, after the U.S. Army had captured Mexico's capital. In a controversial action, Trist defied an order from President James K. Polk (1795–1849; see biographical entry) to return to Washington, D.C. Instead, Trist stayed in Mexico to work out the Treaty of Guadalupe Hidalgo, the agreement that finally ended the Mexican American War.

Growing up in Louisiana

Born in Charlottesville, Virginia, Nicholas Trist was one of two sons of Hore Browse Trist, a lawyer, and Mary

Nicholas Trist. *Photograph reproduced by permission of the Corbis Corporation.*

227

Louisa Brown Trist. His grandmother, Elizabeth Trist, was a friend of fellow Virginian Thomas Jefferson (1743–1826), who served as president of the United States from 1801 to 1809. When Trist was a small child his father moved to the frontier town of Natchez (in what is now the state of Mississippi) to become the territory's tax collector. After he moved to the even newer territory of Louisiana, his wife and sons joined him.

The family lived a happy, prosperous life in New Orleans until the death of Trist's father in 1804. Only a month later, Trist's mother married another lawyer, Philip Livingston Jones. Attending the local school, Trist demonstrated a gift for learning foreign languages as well as beautiful penmanship (handwriting). When Jones died in 1810, Trist's mother quickly married again, this time to St. Julien Tournillon, the wealthy owner of a plantation (large farm). At this time, Trist and his brother were enrolled in a school called Orleans College, where they received a good education in language, history, and government.

From Monticello to West Point

Leaving school in 1817, Trist was unsure what to do next. He accepted an invitation to visit Monticello, the Charlottesville, Virginia, home of the now retired Thomas Jefferson. Six feet tall and slim with dark, curly hair and dark eyes, Trist was handsome and had a charming, pleasant personality that made him a popular figure among Jefferson's extensive family. He soon fell in love with Jefferson's granddaughter, Virginia Jefferson Randolph, although it would be several years before he would declare his feelings publicly.

In 1818, Jefferson arranged for Trist to receive an appointment to the National Military Academy, which had recently been established at West Point, New York. He adapted well to the program of rigorous academics, drilling in all kinds of weather, and stiff discipline. His ability to speak French fluently allowed him to become a special assistant and translator for a French-speaking professor. Nevertheless, Trist found that he was not interested in a military career, and he left the academy after three years.

Returning to Monticello, Trist became engaged to Virginia Randolph. The prospect of having to support a family spurred him to pursue a career as a lawyer. Leaving his fiancée behind, Trist returned to Louisiana in 1821 to study law with Edward Livingston, the father of an old school friend. The next few years passed frustratingly slowly, as Livingston was often too busy to work with Trist, and as Trist became involved, after the unexpected death of his mother, in legal struggles with his stepfather. In the summer of 1824, Trist returned to Monticello to study law with Jefferson and also to serve as his part-time secretary. It was at this time that he and Virginia were married.

A job at the State Department

Jefferson died in the summer of 1826, and three months later, Trist passed the Virginia bar (the test that qualifies attorneys to practice law). He served as executor of Jefferson's will (the person who makes sure it is carried out properly) and for a brief period was a half-owner of a newspaper. Unenthusiastic about practicing law, Trist was in search of a new career. Through the help of a relative, he was offered a clerk's job at the State Department by Kentucky statesman Henry Clay (1777–1852), who was then serving as secretary of state.

The job did not pay much, but Trist accepted it and moved to Washington, D.C., in November 1828. He lived alone in a boarding house and his work, which was mostly copying letters and documents that others had produced, was boring, but he soon began making friends and developing a reputation as an intelligent man and a hard worker. Trist even met the new president, Andrew Jackson (1767–1845), through a West Point classmate who was Jackson's nephew. In 1829, Trist's family, which now included two children, joined him in Washington.

Representing the United States in Cuba

In early 1830, Trist began serving as a kind of unofficial secretary for Jackson, a position that brought him very close to the president but left him less time for his State Department duties. Three years later, as a reward for his dedication, Jackson appointed Trist to the post of U.S. Consul (the official representative of the U.S. government) in Havana, Cuba. In this position he was to promote the interests of U.S. citizens who were living and working in and around the Caribbean nation. Trist arrived in Cuba in March 1834. For the first two years, he stayed there without his family, but in November 1836, his wife and three children joined him in Havana.

Trist's tenure as U.S. Consul was somewhat marred when a group of sea captains charged him with neglecting their interests. As a result of the accusations, he had to return to Washington to answer the charges, but he was able to defend himself successfully. With the election of a new president (William Henry Harrison; 1773–1841) in 1840, Trist had to leave his position as U.S. Consul, but he decided to remain in Cuba to farm and perhaps write political articles. Neither of these pursuits proved profitable, however, and the family became so strapped for cash that they had to rent out rooms in their house.

In August 1845, Trist returned to Washington to take up a prestigious new job as deputy, or chief clerk, to the new secretary of state, James Buchanan (1791–1868). The next few years would prove especially challenging ones for those involved in U.S. foreign affairs, for war with Mexico was now looming on the horizon. Ten years earlier, Texas had declared its independence from Mexico, although Mexico never officially recognized this independence. At the same time, there was a strong movement to make Texas part of the United States. In addition, expansionists (those who sought more land for U.S. citizens to settle in) had their eyes on the Mexican territories of California and New Mexico.

The Mexican American War begins

The March 1845, annexation of Texas resulted in the cutting off of diplomatic ties between the United States and Mexico. By the time Trist began his new job, President James Polk had sent troops to the border between the two nations. Following an attack by Mexican troops on a small unit of U.S. soldiers, the United States declared war on May 13, 1846. General Zachary Taylor (1784–1850; see biographical entry) soon had the Mexican army on the run as the U.S. Army won several important battles in northeastern Mexico, while General Stephen W. Kearny (1794–1848; see biographical entry) led the Army of the West in successful conquests of California and Santa Fe, New Mexico.

In April 1847, when it became clear that the United States would have to take Mexico City (the nation's capital) to win the war, General Winfield Scott launched an invasion from the coastal city of Vera Cruz and begun the long march westward. By now this war that many had assumed would be over quickly and easily was in its second year. There had been some major victories, but many U.S. soldiers had died to secure those victories, and it appeared that many more might have to perish before Mexico would surrender. Polk and Buchanan preferred to seek a peaceful resolution. Thus they began to look around for a diplomat they could send south, someone who could travel with Scott's army and be on hand whenever and wherever an opportunity to negotiate with the Mexicans should arise.

A challenging new assignment

Buchanan soon suggested his able, intelligent deputy, the Spanish-speaking, calm-mannered Trist, who knew both State Department protocol (official rules and standards) and Mexican politics well and who was, like Polk and Buchanan, a member of the Democratic Party. Historians have since debated whether Trist was really qualified for this important job. Some have seen him as naïve and unrealistic, while others have called him conceited and self-important; still others claim he was chosen because he was conscientious and hardworking. In any case, Polk accepted Buchanan's advice and sent Trist to Mexico.

Meeting with Trist, Polk told him that he must not bother Scott with the details of his mission, advice that would result in a lot of hard feelings between Scott (whom Polk detested) and Trist. Polk authorized Trist to offer Mexico $20 million to $25 million in exchange for Texas, California, and New Mexico. In addition, Mexico would have to recognize the Rio Grande river as the border between Texas and Mexico, and not the Nueces River, which was located farther north and had previously been the border.

An exchange of nasty notes

Although he was not particularly happy about leaving his family for the unknown dangers and difficulties of war-torn Mexico, Trist accepted the assignment and headed south. He arrived on May 6, after Scott's army had won the battles of Vera Cruz and Cerro Gordo and was now resting at the town of Jalapa. Trist sent a brief note to Scott, instructing him to send a copy of the peace proposal to the Mexican authorities. Scott was enraged to be receiving orders from a civilian (and one who had only just arrived on the scene), and deeply insulted that Polk had over-ridden his own role as general in charge of military operations. Thus, Scott sent Trist a sarcastic, scornful response, making it clear that no mere clerk was going to order him around.

Trist, too, was outraged, for he felt that he was only following orders from the president. He wrote Scott an eighteen-page letter defending himself. On May 14, Trist joined the army in Jalapa, and soon sent Scott another note in which he warned the general not to interfere with Trist's mission. Scott responded with another insulting letter to Trist. This nasty exchange was getting out of hand, and finally both Trist and Scott, who had not yet met in person, were told by their superiors to stop quarreling. They both began to cool off, and a real reconciliation occurred when Scott, hearing that Trist had become sick, sent him a gift of guava marmalade. This had been one of Trist's favorite treats when he lived in Cuba, and it helped him to think much more favorably of Scott.

Meanwhile, Trist had managed to get a British diplomat to deliver his peace proposal to the Mexicans. On this diplomat's suggestion, Trist now gave an unknown Mexican official $10,000 to help push the peace process forward. This action, which was really a bribe, produced no results, however, and the U.S. Army continued to move toward Mexico City, which they reached in early August. On August 20, the United States won the battles of Contreras and Churubusco, and the Mexicans requested that peace negotiations be opened. So Scott called an armistice (halt in the fighting) and Trist prepared to negotiate.

The war comes to an end

During the thirty years that had passed since Mexico had, gained independence from Spain in 1821, Mexico had suffered from a weak and unstable government, with the country's leadership changing fifty times. The current head of the government, General Antonio López de Santa Anna (1794–1876; see biographical entry), was also its top military leader. A dynamic figure who could rally thousands of Mexicans to follow him, Santa Anna did not always do what was best for his country. And now he directed his peace negotiators to make demands that the United States considered unreasonable. Finally, both nations began to accuse the other of stalling, and the armistice was called off on September 6.

A week later, Scott's army invaded Mexico City and the Mexicans were forced to surrender. Santa Anna fled, leaving his government shattered. After a few days, Scott had gotten the chaotic situation in the city under control, but a strong mood of instability still prevailed. No Mexican leaders authorized to undertake peace talks were emerging. Meanwhile, across the border, members of the All-Mexico Movement called for the United States to take control of all of Mexico. Like many other U.S. citizens, however, Trist believed that such an action would be morally wrong, racially distasteful (racist beliefs held that the "pure blood of white Americans would be tainted through contact with Mexicans' mixed racial heritage), and disastrous in practical terms.

A controversial decision

Faced with the monumental task of rebuilding their government, the Mexicans finally managed to form a congress. They elected Manuel de la Pena y Pena (1789–1850), who was known to have moderate political views and who was on good terms with Trist, as interim (temporary) president. Both he and Trist were feeling optimistic about the possibility of peace talks beginning soon when, on November 16, Trist received an order from Polk, who demanded that Trist return to Washington immediately. Worried over the unexpected length of the war and its cost in both money and lives, Polk wanted it to end quickly, and he blamed both his longtime enemy Scott, and now Trist, for what he saw as an unreasonable delay in getting the Mexicans to negotiate. However, because of the delay in communications at the time, Polk was unaware that the peace talks were very close to beginning.

Even though Trist had been longing to return to his own country and family, he was dismayed by Polk's order. Nevertheless, he started to make preparations for his departure, which was delayed while he waited for an escort to take him across the dangerous territory between Mexico City and Vera Cruz. Meanwhile, Mexico had appointed its three peace commissioners. Pena and his fellow moderates were shocked to hear that Trist was leaving, and they predicted that Mexico would soon collapse into chaos.

Gradually, encouraged by several associates, including Scott, who was indirect about it, and journalist James Freaner of the New Orleans *Delta* newspaper, who was not, Trist began to change his mind about leaving. In a letter to his wife, as quoted in Wallace Ohrt's *Defiant Peacemaker: Nicholas Trist in the Mexican War,* Trist wrote that "Knowing it to be the very last chance, and impressed with the dreadful consequences to our country which cannot fail to attend the loss of that chance," he was going to ignore Polk's order.

Trist sent a sixty-one-page letter to Buchanan explaining in great detail the reasons for his actions. On January 2, 1848, in the nearby town of Guadalupe Hidalgo, Trist went into secret negotiations with Mexico's three peace commissioners. Thirteen days later, Polk received the news of Trist's defiance and was enraged. As quoted in Ohrt's book, Polk wrote in his diary that this proved "that [Trist] is destitute of honor or principle and that he has proved himself to be a very base man." Polk immediately cut off Trist's pay from November 16, 1847 (the day the recall order had arrived). At the same time, he relieved Scott of his command, replacing him with General William O. Butler.

Trist may or may not have been aware that his career in government service was now over. In any case, he continued with the difficult task of forging peace with Mexico. As the sole U.S. representative, he had to do all of the work himself, performing the jobs of secretary, lawyer, file clerk, and negotiator simultaneously. He worked straight through the month of January with hardly a break, emerging on February 2, with a signed peace agreement.

The Treaty of Guadalupe Hidalgo

Trist may have been working in defiance of Polk's orders, but he carried out his original assignment faithfully, achieving a peace treaty that benefited the United States. Under the treaty's terms, the Mexicans recognized the Rio Grande as the border between Texas and Mexico. (In addition, Trist managed to establish a point several miles south of the important port city of San Diego as the border between California and Mexico.) Mexico agreed to cede (give up) the territories of California and New Mexico to the United States, in exchange for $15 million (much less than the higher figure originally discussed by Polk and Trist) and the cancellation of debts owed to the United States. Mexicans who were living in the affected territories could choose either to become U.S. citizens or to return to Mexico; if they had not chosen after one year, they would automatically become U.S. citizens.

The Mexican representatives emerged from the peace talks in shock at the loss of so much land (more than 500,000 square miles, or about two-fifths of Mexico's total territory) and, as one of them told Trist, with a deep sense of shame that the war had ended this way. Upon hearing about the treaty, many people in the United States, especially those who had opposed the war from the start, would also feel ashamed, for the United States had crossed the border of another nation, killed many of its citizens, destroyed much of its property, and taken its land by force. According to Ohrt, even Trist would later comment that "my feeling of shame as an American was far stronger than [the Mexicans'] could be."

Having taken this bold step, Trist was anxious to bring the peace process to a speedy conclusion. His journalist friend James Freaner agreed to deliver the document to Washington, D.C., and made the trip in a near-record seventeen days. When he received the treaty, Polk felt so angry at Trist that he wanted to tear it up, but when he looked it over he saw that it had been faithfully and well executed, he changed his mind. On February 23, he sent the treaty on to Congress. After a certain amount of debate between those who wanted the United States to claim even more Mexican territory and those who were eager to get the whole affair over and done with, the Treaty of Guadalupe Hidalgo was ratified (officially approved by both houses) on March 10.

A forgotten public servant

Trist had long been relieved of his official duties, but he stayed on for several months in Mexico. Finally, he was forced either to leave or face arrest by a U.S. military officer, so he returned to the United States. His diplomatic career now over, he had to find another way to make a living. The next years were hard ones for him and his family. They moved to Pennsylvania, where Trist's wife opened a boarding school. The family then moved to New York, where Trist briefly practiced law. After moving back to Philadelphia, Trist got a job as a clerk with a railroad company. He remained there for the next twenty years, eventually working his way up to the position of paymaster.

Trist was horrified by the outbreak of the Civil War (1861–65) but, despite his southern background, remained a staunch supporter of the Union. Although it seemed that he had been forgotten, there were in fact a few people who remembered his contribution to U.S. history. One of these was Massachusetts senator Charles Sumner, who made a speech to the senate in which he said that it was wrong that Trist had never been paid for his work on the treaty. Thus the Senate voted to pay Trist the $14,500 (plus interest) that they believed he was still owed. In addition, he was offered the job of postmaster of Alexandria, Virginia. He was serving in this position when, following a stroke, he died at the age of seventy-three.

Since Trist's death, scholars and diplomats have pondered his role in the Mexican American War. It is unclear whether he overstepped his bounds, or whether he was justified in defying a direct order of the president of the United States. Some scholars believe that Trist acted in the best interest of his country, based on his own knowledge of the situation—knowledge that the president and others in Washington could not have had, given the difficulties of communication of that period. In any case, Trist's actions did succeed in bringing to a timely end a bloody conflict that had damaged, in ways both physical and psychological, both Mexico and the United States.

For More Information

Books

Drexler, Robert W. *Guilty of Making Peace: A Biography of Nicholas P. Trist.* Lanham: University Press of American, 1991.

Ohrt, Wallace. *Defiant Peacemaker: Nicholas Trist in the Mexican War.* College Station: Texas A & M Press, 1997.

Periodicals

Farnham, Thomas J. "Nicholas Trist and James Freaner and the Mission to Mexico." *Arizona and the West* 11, No. 3 (Autumn 1969): 247–60.

Nortrup, Jack. "Nicholas Trist's Mission to Mexico: A Reinterpretation." *Southwestern Historical Quarterly* 71, No. 3 (1968): 921–46.

Sears, Louis M. "Nicholas Trist: A Diplomat with Ideals." *Mississippi Valley Historical Review* 11 (1924): 85–98.

Web Sites

Landeros, David. "The Treaty of Guadalupe Hidalgo, and the American Gain." *Mexican American War.* [Online] Available http://www.acusd.edu/~landeros/mexican/mexican.html (accessed on January 31, 2003).

"The Treaty of Guadalupe Hidalgo." *Our Documents.* [Online] Available http://www.ourdocuments.gov/content.php?page=document&doc=26 (accessed on January 31, 2003).

Where to Learn More

Books

Bauer, Karl J. *The Mexican War*. New York: Macmillan, 1974.

Bredeson, Carmen. *The Battle of the Alamo*. Brookfield, CT: Millbrook Press, 1996.

Butler, Stephen R. *A Documentary History of the War with Mexico 1846–1848*. Richardson, TX: Descendents of Mexican War Veterans, 1994.

Callcott, Wilfrid Hardy. *Santa Anna: The Story of an Enigma Who Once Was Mexico*. North Haven, CT: Archon, 1964.

Chance, Joseph E., ed. *The Mexican War Journal of Captain Franklin Smith*. Jackson: University Press of Mississippi, 1991.

Chance, Joseph E., ed. *Mexico Under Fire*. Ft. Worth: Texas Christian University Press, 1994.

Chance, Joseph E., and Lawrence R. Clayton, eds. *The March to Monterrey: The Diary of Lt. Rankin Dilworth*. El Paso: The University of Texas at El Paso, 1996.

Chidsey, Donald Barr. *The War with Mexico*. New York: Crown, 1968.

Conner, Seymour V., and Odie B. Faulk. *North America Divided: The Mexican War 1846–1848*. New York: Oxford University Press, 1971.

Crawford, Ann Fears, ed. *Autobiography of Santa Anna*. Austin, TX: State House Press, 1988.

Del Castillo, Richard. *The Treaty of Guadalupe Hidalgo: A Legacy of Conflict.* Norman: University of Oklahoma Press, 1990.

Downey, Fairfax. *Texas and the War with Mexico.* New York: American Heritage Publishing, 1961.

Eisenhower, John S. D. *So Far from God: The U.S. War with Mexico, 1846–1848.* New York: Random House, 1989.

Ferrell, Robert H., ed. *Monterrey is Ours! The Mexican War Letters of Lieutenant Dana, 1845–1847.* Lexington: University Press of Kentucky, 1990.

Francaviglia, Richard V., and Douglas Richmond, eds. *Duel Eagles: A Reinterpreting Mexican-American War 1846–1848.* Ft. Worth: Texas Christian University Press, 2000.

Frazier, Donald, ed. *The United States and Mexico at War.* New York: Simon and Schuster, 1997.

George, Isaac. *Heroes and Incidents of the Mexican War.* San Bernardino, CA: Borgo Press, 1982.

Goetzmann, William H. *Sam Chamberlain's Mexican War: The San Jacinto Museum of History Paintings.* Austin, TX: Texas State Historical Association, 1993.

Hogan, Michael. *The Irish Soldiers of Mexico.* Guadalajara, Mexico: Fondo Editorial Universitario, 1997.

Johannsen, Robert W. *To the Halls of the Montezumas: The Mexican War in the American Imagination.* New York: Oxford University Press, 1985.

Jones, Oakah, Jr. *Santa Anna.* Boston: Twayne, 1968.

Katcher, Philip R. *The Mexican American War, 1846–1848.* New York: Osprey Publishing, 1989.

McCaffrey, James M. *Army of Manifest Destiny: The American Soldier in the Mexican-American War, 1846–1848.* New York: New York University Press, 1994.

McCaffrey, James, ed. *"Surrounded by Dangers of All Kinds": The Mexican War Diaries of Lieutenant Theodore Laidley.* Texas A & M University Press, 1995.

Meyer, Michael C., and William L. Sherman. *The Course of Mexican History.* New York: Oxford University Press, 1982.

Miller, Robert Ryal. *Mexico: A History.* Norman: University of Oklahoma Press, 1985.

Miller, Robert Ryal. *Shamrock and Sword: The St. Patrick's Battalion in the U.S.-Mexican War.* Norman: University of Oklahoma Press, 1989.

Miller, Robert Ryal, and William J. Orr. *An Immigrant Soldier in the Mexican War.* College Station: Texas A & M University Press, 1995.

Nevin, David. *The Mexican War.* Alexandria, VA: Time-Life Books, 1978.

Nardo, Don. *The Mexican-American War.* San Diego, CA: Lucent Books, 1991.

O'Brien, Steven. *Antonio López de Santa Anna.* New York: Chelsea, 1992.

Roberts, David. *A Newer World: Kit Carson, John C. Fremont, and the Claiming of the American West.* New York: Touchstone, 2000.

Robinson, Cecil, ed. and trans. *The View from Chapultepec: Mexican Writers on the Mexican-American War.* Tucson: University of Arizona Press, 1989.

Sanford, Charles L., ed. *Manifest Destiny and the Imperialism Question.* New York: John Wiley and Sons, 1974.

Schroeder, John H. *Mr. Polk's War.* Madison: University of Wisconsin Press, 1973.

Stephenson, Nathaniel W. *Texas and the Mexican War.* New Haven, CT: Yale University Press, 1921.

Stevens, Peter F. *The Rogue's March: John Riley and the St. Patrick's Battalion 1846–1848.* Dulles, VA: Brassey's, 2000.

Tinkle, Lon. *The Alamo.* New York: New American Library, 1958.

Tolliver, Ruby. *Santa Anna: Patriot or Scoundrel?* Dallas, TX: Hendrick-Long, 1993.

Werstein, Irving. *The War with Mexico.* New York: W. W. Norton & Co., 1965.

Winders, Richard Bruce. *Mr. Polk's Army.* College Station: Texas A & M University Press, 1997.

Zinn, Howard. *A People's History of the United States.* New York: Harper and Row, 1980.

Collections

Special Collections Library. University of Texas at Arlington.

Web Sites

Descendents of Mexican War Veterans. *The U.S.-Mexican War: 1846–1848.* [Online] Available http://www.dmwv.org/ (accessed on February 25, 2003).

Documents on the Mexican-American War. [Online] Available http://www.hillsdale.edu/dept/History/War/19Mex.htm (accessed on February 25, 2003).

The Mexican-American War Memorial Homepage. [Online] Available http://sunsite.unam.mx/revistas/1847/Summa.html (accessed on February 25, 2003).

"Mexican-American War Timeline." *America at War.* [Online] Available http://www.semo.net/suburb/dlswoff/mexwar.html (accessed on February 25, 2003).

Sanchez, Mario. "A Shared Experience's Historical Survey: The Mexican-American War: 1846–1848." *Texas Historical Commission.* [Online] Available http://www.rice.edu/armadillo/Past/Book/Part2/1846-48/html (accessed on February 25, 2003).

"U.S.-Mexican War: 1846–1848." *PBS Online.* [Online] Available http://www.pbs.org/kera/usmexicanwar/ (accessed on February 25, 2003).

Index

Bold type indicates main entries and their page numbers. Illustrations are marked (ill.)

B